D A N E
SWAN

MY STORY

WITH MARTIN BLAKE

hardie grant books

Published in 2016 by Hardie Grant Books

Hardie Grant Books (Australia)
Ground Floor, Building 1
658 Church Street
Richmond, Victoria 3121
www.hardiegrant.com.au

Hardie Grant Books (UK)
5th & 6th Floors
52–54 Southwark Street
London SE1 1UN
www.hardiegrant.co.uk

A Cataloguing-in-Publication entry is available from the catalogue of the National
Library of Australia at www.nla.gov.au

Dane Swan: My story

ISBN 978 1 74379 261 2

Publisher: Pam Brewster
Cover design by Luke Causby/Blue Cork
Cover photograph by James Braund
Editorial services by Andrea McNamara
Typeset in ITC New Baskerville by Kirby Jones
Printed by McPherson's Printing Group, Maryborough, Victoria

FSC
www.fsc.org
MIX
Paper from
responsible sources
FSC® C001695

The paper this book is printed on is certified against the Forest
Stewardship Council® Standards. FSC promotes environmentally
responsible, socially beneficial and economically viable management of
the world's forests.

To everyone who has believed in me ...
Mum, Dad, Bonnie, my partner Taylor, all my family,
Collingwood Football Club, Ed, my coaches,
my team-mates and my mates

CONTENTS

1

OVER AND OUT

'I'll prob retire at 30 coz I don't want footy
to get in the way of my social life.'

—@swandane 23 February 2012

This is how quickly the end can come for a footballer.

It's 26 March 2016, the Sydney Cricket Ground, the start of a new season. Collingwood is chock-full of the optimism and new hope that comes around just about every March as we confront Sydney in the season-opener on the road, having won all three of our pre-season games.

It's funny, but you start every season with the same doubts, wondering whether you still have whatever it is that makes you the player you are. As you get older, that feeling only grows. I have had a good 2015 season, being nominated for All Australian status and finishing runner-up in the club's best and fairest behind Scott Pendlebury, and yet I have the same feeling of nervous anticipation in the dressing rooms and as I make my way to the bench at the start of the game.

I am beginning my fifteenth season in black and white, and as for Collingwood, we have missed the finals in the previous two seasons under Nathan Buckley's coaching, but undergone a significant rebuild of the list that has left me as the oldest player at 32. Potentially, it's my last season. I just don't know.

Many of the so-called experts who make their living out of spruiking the game, but who probably know less than 95 per cent of the fans do, have picked the Magpies to play finals in 2016. There's a strong feeling that we're emerging again with our youth, exemplified by the four players in the team for round 1 who have played ten games or fewer. It's a Saturday night and a big game, a chance for us to launch our season and, needless to say, a test against one of the best teams of the modern era, the Sydney Swans.

For a few more tense moments I have to temper the anxiety. When the ball is bounced to start our season I am watching from the bench, not unusual since Collingwood likes to use this as a method of disrupting the taggers that come my way. Sydney is all over us, with Lance Franklin extracting the first goal for the home team and sending most of the 33,000 spectators into raptures. Then just a little more than seven minutes in, I get the call and make my way to a position up forward. I am needed, but the grim reaper comes knocking, arriving in the form of Zak Jones, the young Sydney defender.

I am on the wing, near the sponsor's logo, when my teammate Adam Treloar's scrambled kick forward comes my way. I've been on the ground just 45 seconds. At the eight-minute mark, I edge my opponent, Dane Rampe, under the fall of the ball with what is probably a blatant push in the back so that I can mark, a simple manoeuvre that I have completed hundreds of times in the past 15 years. Really, I should mark it.

But back with the flight comes Jones, hitting me as I try to wrap my mitts around the Sherrin. His body and mine hit like a thunderclap, tipping his body horizontal and sending me to the deck. My feet have been spread out for balance, my right foot splayed to the side, so that when I go down, my right leg twists under my body just in time for Zak Jones to land on top of me. The ball spills from my hands and is swept away, and I feel a sharp pain and grab the base of my right foot. Immediately, I know something is wrong. I've played enough footy to know that this doesn't feel right, the way I landed with my leg folded up beneath me.

My pain threshold is okay – I've missed only a handful of games since becoming a regular in the team – but this is something else. My first thought is that I have badly sprained my ankle. The physio who has run out to me says, 'Are you right, can you get up?' I say, 'Hang on, I'm hurting here, give me a second!' The medicos help me back to the bench, then after a few minutes to gather my breath, I hobble down to the dressing rooms.

At this point, I figure that with a bit of tape, I might be able to come back on the ground and play. But on my way down the race, I stop suddenly because I can feel a shifting in the top part of my lower right leg, just below the knee. I only manage about five steps and when I touch my leg, I can feel a hole, so I say to our doctor, Chris Bradshaw, 'Doc, man, something's really wrong up here.'

A few minutes later in the rooms at the SCG, Bradshaw has poked and prodded and confirmed the news for me: 'You've broken your leg.' My first thought is that my season has gone, just like that, but he reassures me, 'No, maybe four to six weeks for that.' Then Bradshaw gets to my foot, performs some testing to see what range of movement I have. Initially, it's okay, but then we can see a golf-ball sized growth emerging on the outside of my right foot.

It is throbbing now, and after originally waving off painkillers, I am begging for them; I feel like I can see my pulse pounding up and down in my foot. Chris says, 'You'd better get this X-rayed. You could have a broken bone in your foot.' Then he adds the rider. 'What we *don't* want, is for it to be the Lisfranc.'

Never in 15 years of footy have I heard anyone mention the Lisfranc ligament, but I now know it to be the tissue that holds your mid-foot together. It is named after Jacques Lisfranc, a French surgeon famous for his work in the Napoleonic wars, and when it fractures or ruptures, the five metatarsals become displaced. Bearing in mind that the human foot has 26 bones, one-quarter of all the bones in your body, it is basically a jigsaw puzzle and the Lisfranc is one of the keys to holding it together.

Lisfranc rupture is not a common injury in football; it's more likely to be the result of a car accident, where a driver's foot is pushed back too far the wrong way on a brake pedal. On this night, I can see from Chris Bradshaw's expression that he's worried, although only a proper scan will tell us for sure. One thing's for sure. I am done for the night as Sydney proceed to smash us.

First stop is the X-ray facility at the Sydney Football Stadium, out the back of the SCG, while the game goes on. It has been a dreadful start to our season and even worse for me, personally. By night's end the Swans will have humiliated us by 80 points, but I am largely oblivious to the result. As I wait for my X-ray, I chat to a Manly player who has just suffered a bad hand injury in the NRL game being played at this stadium, both of us sitting up there in our gear waiting to face the music.

While the X-ray confirms a broken fibula in the right leg and some foot trauma for me, it will be a couple of days before I'll know the full extent of my troubles in the foot area. *How serious can a broken foot be?* I remember thinking. *That should be okay.* I've played footy with a broken hand before, but I am naive about this; I keep thinking that bone damage has to be worse than ligament trouble. But when a broken leg is the least of your worries, that's not what a footballer wants to hear.

• • •

I take some painkillers and try to sleep that night in Sydney, but I'm restless. At the airport, the club has organised for me to speak to the press about the injury, saying that the media will hound me otherwise. *Not for the first time in my career*, I think to myself! But there's not much I can say. I am on crutches, wearing a moon boot, cannot put any weight on my foot, and whatever the future holds for me as a player can't be told until I'm scanned back in Melbourne, after the injury settles a little.

Right now, my foot has blown up to almost twice its normal size and turned black. Sometimes you just have to laugh, and I do my best to keep the game in proper perspective. On Twitter, I post a reference to my zero possessions for the night: 'And to make matters worse it's the first time in my career I've had donuts (on the field, I eat real ones all the time).'

Monday lunchtime comes and I'm at Olympic Park in Melbourne, next to Collingwood's headquarters, for an

MRI scan. I still don't know much detail, but the experts tell me that the Lisfranc is ruptured and all five metatarsals – the bones connected to my toes – are displaced. Three metatarsals are broken: the bone pulled away when the ligament came away from them. All of which means that I will require surgery and around six months off football, if I can get back at all. I take the pragmatic view, saying, 'Just get it sorted, just get the surgery done.'

But nothing is so simple. It's a wait of ten days before there is any point in visiting the orthopaedic surgeon, Andrew Oppy, because my foot has grown so fat and bruised. I'm stuck at home on crutches with two sets of stairs to negotiate, and I need to keep my foot elevated, otherwise it throbs. My partner, Taylor Wilson, makes up a little bed for me on the couch, and I live on painkillers and the NBA on television and Netflix to keep me vaguely sane. Barney, our cavoodle, is the only one rapt with the situation. He keeps me company.

I can't drive a car, and I have no proper sleeping pattern; I might wake at three in the morning and watch a movie, then sleep all day. I can barely shower, and on the rare occasions that I try, I'm like a dog dragging its backside on the ground, crabbing around the shower base to clean myself.

Eventually after a few days the surgery takes place, and my foot is filled with plates and wires to stabilise it. More waiting at home, unable to drive, reliant on Taylor for just about everything. Then much later, around the end of May, after another surgery to remove the wires, I return to the footy club to start my rehabilitation program. I do it gladly, first for the change of scenery but also because I don't want to be crippled for life.

For five months I live in the faint hope that I might be able to play footy again. But by August, I still can't run without pain and the season has basically slid by without my input. Worse, I know that my heart is no longer in playing. I am done.

It is not often that you know when the curtain will fall, or receive a triumphal march out of the game. Hawthorn champion Shane Crawford was an exception I remember, climbing the goalpost at the MCG after playing in a premiership in the last of his 305 games, when the Hawks surprised Geelong in 2008. But really, the romance is rare and the reality more brutal. Think of Chris Judd's career finishing on the back of a motorised cart at the MCG, after rupturing the anterior cruciate ligament in his left knee in a round 10 game against Adelaide in 2015. For me, my football mortality was realised at the SCG that night when I hit the deck under Zak Jones.

I have turned the page, having prepared myself for this for several years, and I am ready. Looking back, I can't find any regrets. I was so lucky. Footy has set me up for the rest of my life, and my job now is to grab the opportunity. Maybe five times in my career, Collingwood could have sacked me for off-field behaviour that didn't fit the criteria of the modern sporting organisation. As you will read in these pages, I worked hard, but I could have worked harder. I did what I could within the constraints of my own personality, and in the end, I worked out that I had to do it in a certain way, *my way*.

I would never last in AFL football if I was starting now, not with all the restrictions and rules and orders that are put in place. Footy clubs, the AFL and the media turn the players into robots these days – they suck all the personality out of them before they have a chance to express themselves. At the start of my career I tried to fit that mould as best I could, falling out of line from time to time until ultimately, I realised it was just not me. I realised that I had to be *myself* or I would never succeed.

Now there's a theme for a book …

2

CONSTANT AND FAITHFUL

'Some players look like racehorses; this bloke
looked like a bloody Clydesdale, you know,
until he started finding the footy all the time,
and you realised that he could play.'

—Robert Hyde, Calder Cannons coach 1996–2006

My habit of creating a little controversy might have started at birth, I reckon, because I was not supposed to be called Dane. Virtually all the males in my family were called Bill, including my father and my grandfather William, who had emigrated from the Scottish city of Glasgow in the 1940s. Not only that, there was also a bunch of Bills on the Ramsay side of the family, my dad's mother's lot, also of Scottish heritage.

It was my mother, Deirdre, who insisted that the sequence be halted right there and then with a Dane, the name coming from a character in one of her favourite books, *The Thorn Birds* by Colleen McCullough, a bestseller that was also made into a TV series. In the book, Dane is the son of Meggie and Ralph, and he ends up drowning in Greece (so maybe I should remove that country from my list of future holiday destinations!). The carefully constructed compromise was sealed with William being nominated as my middle name.

I grew up in Westmeadows, the older end of Broadmeadows in the outer north-west of Melbourne. Westmeadows, population around 5000, is not far from the Tullamarine airport, and we lived in Hillcrest Drive, tucked in behind the Tullamarine Freeway. Our area was originally part of Broadmeadows, with the commercial centre and a hotel, but later on when a railway line and station were opened 2 kilometres to the west, our part was renamed Broadmeadows West, and in 1963 it became Westmeadows.

Grandad and a bunch of his brothers and sisters had all chosen to leave Scotland; roughly half came to Australia, and half went to Canada. My grandparents lived in a Housing Commission flat in Port Melbourne, in Melbourne's inner bayside area, then shifted camp to Broadmeadows later. The move to Broady was initiated by my nan, Betty, who thought there were too many pubs in Port Melbourne for Grandad's best interests, and he was a wharfie. But I am not sure what she was thinking, because there are hotels in Broady too!

Mum and Dad met when she was 14 and Deirdre Hale. They went on to get married a few years later and when she was pregnant with me, they had the option of taking a new house either out in Sunbury, 20 minutes to the north-west, or in Port Melbourne, so they took the new home, but they did not last too long. Mum hated being out of the city and that was when they settled on Westmeadows and bought in Hillcrest Drive, where they lived for years until recently moving closer in, to Ascot Vale. Most of my family is still in the Broadmeadows and Westmeadows area.

I had a happy childhood there with Mum and Dad and my sister, Bonnie, who is a couple of years younger than me. We lived a normal family life, and pretty much every year we went to Merimbula in New South Wales in a group, and we also went overseas for holidays, to Bali, Phuket and to Disneyland. We were middle class, whatever that means, and we did not want for much, with both parents always bringing in a wage, Dad at the docks and Mum as an executive assistant.

Westmeadows might not have been Toorak or Brighton but it was fine for me. As a boy, I attended the School of the Good Shepherd in the adjoining suburb of Gladstone Park without breaking any records for academic achievement, and then St Bernard's College in Essendon, a secondary school renowned for producing great footballers. The list is impressive: Matthew Lloyd, Scott Lucas, Justin Madden, Simon Madden, Garry Foulds and Jude Bolton all came out of that school to play premiership football at AFL level, and there are many others, although that was not the reason that I went to the school. Really, my parents just chose it because it was local and had a decent reputation, and I hardly ever played footy for the school when I was there.

Like his own father, Dad has worked at the docks for decades, but he is not a wharfie as such; he does maintenance, working on the cranes, and he has been the union representative for years. It is probably the same place that I would have ended up working, although I am terrible with my hands, so it was fortunate for me that the footy came along.

Dad's style was to go in to bat for his mates, and that is probably where I get my loyalty to friends and family from. The Swan family motto is 'Constant and Faithful'. I am pretty sure that I got my refusal to take any crap, a certain defiance, from Dad, the union rep, and I have been like that forever. I reach a certain point where I go, *I don't think I have to do that.* And the more I am goaded and asked to do something I don't want to do, the less chance there is that I actually will do it.

If I played up, Mum would chase me with the wooden spoon, but I was always too quick for her, and she would get

Dad involved. I'd hear, *'Bill!'* and that would be the signal for me to hightail it up the stairs. Dad was gentle on me, and he never carried it for too long. I would cop my whack, I might have a nervous wait for him to come home from work with the punishment, but by the next day it would all be fine.

We have a great relationship, my parents and I, and while I am sure both would say that I had my moments, I was a pretty normal teenager. Yes, I sneaked out to parties, might have lied about where I was going, and I even faked running away from home a couple of times. We would have a fight or two but on the whole, we were fine. It was my sister they had to worry about!

• • •

Dad was an excellent footballer in the VFA – the Victorian Football Association, now known as the VFL – and he played for a long time, so it followed that I would get interested in the game. The old VFA was the second-best competition in Victoria and a pretty good standard, and Dad played for Port Melbourne and for Williamstown. I was old enough to be there, and I remember hanging around at the Port ground, probably out the back causing trouble.

Originally he played for Port, having come through the local juniors, and he is a hall-of-famer at that famous old club. He played 219 games, three years as captain, won two best and fairest awards and two Liston Trophies for the best and fairest in the league. He was part of the 1976, 1980, 1981 and 1982 premiership teams in one of Port's great eras.

But Dad's biggest football moment was still to come. In 1989 he crossed over to the arch rival, Williamstown, after a disagreement about money, and in 1990 Willy won the VFL flag in a famous grand final against Springvale at Princes Park in Carlton. Willy had trailed by 34 points early in the final quarter, and after a huge comeback Dad kicked the winning goal from just outside 50 metres in the last minute of the game, a drop punt that wobbled and ducked and dived and eventually soared over the line.

That goal gets longer and longer as the years pass – he claims it's from the wing – and it has been shown on television so many times that I have it memorised, the ugliest kick he ever launched, but straight! Kicking was not necessarily his strong point, but he managed to get the job done when it counted that day.

As for my memories of the day, they are vague. I was six years old and definitely there at Princes Park, but too young to absorb it all. Dad certainly dines out on it, calling it 'something to hang your hat on', as he should do, and he is always asked about it when discussion comes to his footy. In the history of that competition, which dates back to 1877, it is regarded as one of the greatest single moments, the comeback and the goal itself.

Dad ended up playing five years at Willy, winning two more best and fairest awards. By the time he retired in 1993 his tally was five premierships, 301 VFA games (a league record, overtaking Fred Cook) and two Listons. He played in the centre and won a lot of the football, overcoming a conspicuous lack of height (he is 173 centimetres) and speed with competitive spirit and will to win.

He did have a chance to play with Carlton in what was then the VFL (now AFL), and it is the greatest regret of his career that he did not nail it. Carlton played him in the reserves, and Dad reckoned the Blues were playing all the country boys ahead of him, so he took it up with the coach, they disagreed, and he walked. I am okay with this, because I could have been a *Carlton* father–son player! That would have been a disaster.

We used to kick the footy at the park across the road in Westmeadows, and I developed a low tolerance for being told what to do that would prove to be significant for my footy career as an adult. Dad tried his best to coach me; he would make me kick on the non-preferred left foot as much as possible and in the end, I would go home in a huff. It is probably the reason that I am not a great left-foot kick today.

I remember when I first went down to the oval at Gladstone Park to what they called VicKick at that time, nowadays known as Auskick, the phenomenally successful participation program for kids. I had been haranguing my parents to let me play for a couple of years, from the time I was seven, but I recall Dad saying, 'You're too little. You can go down there when you're ten.'

He taught me the basics but he was never one to come in at quarter time and stand over the coach or yell instructions to me from the fence, and if he had, I probably would not have listened anyway. He has told me that on one rare occasion when he offered up some feedback for me during a game, I sat down on the ground and put a finger in each of my ears, just to send him a little message of my own. I was only a little kid at the time, but it was already obvious that I didn't like being told what to do. So we sorted it out quickly, and if I ever asked him for advice, he would say something simple like, 'Get yourself fitter' or, 'Don't waste your time.'

I have actually seen parents going end-to-end at football grounds abusing their kids and others on the field at junior games, and I guess that kind of behaviour was more accepted a few years ago, but Dad was not like that at all. He never pushed me to be a great player, he was never a parent living his dream through me because he'd missed out on it. He never said, 'Right, we're getting you out, we're going to run you, we're going to get you to do weights, we're going to make you skilful.'

Dad figured out my rebellious ways, and I think he knew that the more I was pushed to do something, the more I'd just say, 'No, I'm not doing it.' He was supportive of me in whatever I chose to do. He never actually coached me in footy; at Westmeadows, my first club, he applied for the coaching job when I was in Under 16s but was rejected, and that was the last time he was directly involved in footy, even though he loves the game.

Dad and I often went to the footy and watched AFL games, and I barracked for Hawthorn. I loved Shane Crawford, Darren Jarman and John 'The Rat' Platten in the 1990s but I can't recall thinking that I could emulate them and play at that level. I followed the game more out of interest – playing footy was not my dream.

My earliest junior footy was played at Westmeadows Tigers in the Essendon District Football League (EDFL), in Richmond colours, but I was not an overnight sensation by any stretch of the imagination. To be truthful, I was more interested in basketball at the time, playing that sport locally and at representative level for Broadmeadows Broncos in the state league juniors, so much so that Dad had to drive me all over Melbourne to play.

I played as a guard in state league basketball on Friday nights, local basketball on Saturday and then squeezed footy into my life on Sundays. We had a hoop and backboard in the backyard at Westmeadows to shoot around, and while I was okay, I was not exactly NBA standard. Most AFL players who dabbled in basketball have an inflated opinion of their abilities in that code, and I was not much different.

Like most sportspeople, I loved everything and tried most sports. I played cricket on Saturday mornings over the summer, even though I was never going to be a world-beater, bowling left arm and batting left-handed without being particularly good. But in the end it became too much, and cricket was the first to go. At 16, I had to make a big decision because footy changed to Saturdays, and then the basketball was cut, too. By then, sport was interfering with my social life!

I played footy at Westmeadows from Under 10s to Under 16s and I made my way, never the best or the worst in our team, happy to plod along in the middle most of the time. I played in an EDFL Under 14 premiership in 1997 at Coburg City Oval with the Tigers, but I was very slightly built at that stage, and my output would dip and rise, depending whether I was a top-age or bottom-age player, and my interest level was not especially high. I kicked a few goals, 11 in a game one day, and about 90 in a season, but if you had asked people back then, there is no way they would have picked me to go on and play at AFL level. I would have been ninth or tenth in the team, and I was never a star, although I do remember people at the Tigers saying one thing about my game, which was that I made good decisions with the football.

I was also involved with the Calder Cannons, who had a team in the TAC Cup, the top-level Under 18 competition that produced a lot of players for the AFL national draft each year. Initially this was only as an under-age player when I was around 15, a top-up player. I had a few games in their Under 16 team but with no amazing results. Then as I was approaching 17, Calder put me on its primary list for the 2001 season, my last year of school.

I was finishing my VCE studies in Year 12 at St Bernard's, doing enough to get by although I had no intention of studying beyond that year, no desire to follow through to university. When the careers people came to school to evaluate us all on prospects of future employment, they thought me so unemotional that my ideal occupation would be working in a funeral parlour! Mum and Dad were pretty amused by that, and I had no feelings either way. Bonnie ended up being the family academic. She undertook a Masters degree in Politics at Melbourne University, worked for the Victorian Responsible Gambling Foundation and is now a senior policy and programs adviser in a state government department.

The Cannons had a great history of producing league footballers, from Sydney's Ryan O'Keefe and Jude Bolton to Geelong's James Kelly, Darren Milburn and Paul Chapman, Adelaide's Daniel Talia and Eddie Betts to Essendon's Jason Johnson to name but a few. They were one of the strongest clubs in the best junior competition in the country, and I played against Luke Ball, who was at Sandringham Dragons and dominating, and I can remember him kicking it to teammates, running forward, then they would wait for him and kick it to him again. Andrew Welsh, the future Essendon defender was in the team, and so was David Rodan, who ended up playing a lot of AFL footy with Richmond and Port Adelaide later, as well as James Kelly, who later came to fame at Geelong, and Brent Reilly, who played some great footy later with Adelaide. I was not as good as any of those blokes at that point. I had won just the one best and fairest award, for instance, and that was in the Westmeadows Under 10 B team.

I was shocked that the Cannons put me on their main list, but they must have seen something in me. I had been in and out of their system and in reality I'd been cut from the squad in the Under 15s and Under 16s. It didn't interest me all that much – as far as I was concerned I was only there to muck around with my mates, and they treated me with the respect that I deserved, calling me 'Dwayne' all the time. I recall that, and I remember calling them out: 'It's *Dane*!'

This was footy at a level I was not familiar with. Robert Hyde, who had played for Collingwood in the 1970s, was the coach of Calder and we used to train on Wednesday nights at Coburg Oval or at the Essendon Keilor College ground. I was not a fan of hard training and it annoyed me that I had to play with a bunch of new guys, some of whom I had played against in juniors and did not especially like. Often it would be hosing down rain, too. One of the good parts of joining the Cannons was that my cousin Aaron Ramsay was playing there, as well as Kade Carey, nephew of the great Wayne Carey, and we became friends. Brendon Hollow was another mate from the Cannons, and I hung around with them as much as possible.

It was a rude shock, I must admit. Hyde was intimidating, he was flint-hard, and the training went to a new level of intensity that I was unprepared for as a teenage boy, including weights programs that we were required to do away from the club. I sometimes did the programs, sometimes did not, filling out the paperwork as though I had done it all, and so began a lifelong hatred of lifting weights that continued right through my AFL career. Obviously I put in some work, or I would not have stayed on the list, but it was only enough to keep myself there.

Halfway through the TAC Cup season Hyde dropped me from the main team for 'poor attitude', and for not getting a kick, and I guess that could have been it for me. I had the shits, and the club did not want me going back to Westmeadows, so I played a couple of games for St Bernard's before they allowed me to resume with the Cannons in the TAC Cup. At that point, I never thought that I was going any further than Under 18s, and in any case, I had another year of eligibility – I wouldn't turn 18 till the next February. But they just wanted to send me a message; Dad told me later that Hyde told him that I would probably only be a couple of weeks out of the team.

A month out from the end of that 2001 season I would have been a million miles from being drafted, but the breakthrough for me came with about three games to go. Calder was playing against the Tassie Mariners in Hobart, and one of our kids who had been playing in the midfield got hurt. Prior to that, I had been playing down in the forward line, mainly half-forward, but on this day I went up to the wing, had about 15 possessions in the second half and kicked a goal, and they left me in the midfield after that.

On the eve of the finals, by a piece of good fortune that would leave a mark on me forever, the Collingwood coach, Mick Malthouse, came down to the Cannons to speak to us after training. I was not fussed about this, because as a Hawthorn barracker I hated Collingwood. Unless you barrack for Collingwood, you hate them, which is the way it goes. Later, as a player, I loved that fact like all my teammates did!

Hyde had used his Collingwood connections to lure Malthouse out to our club for our weekly Thursday night pancake feast after training. Mick was at the end of his second year of coaching the Magpies after winning two premierships with West Coast Eagles. Frankly, I was more interested in the pancakes to start with, and Mick was keeping me from the feast. I can remember saying to teammates, 'Couldn't give a shit. He's not talking to me.'

Most of his words were going in one ear and out the other (a little like the next ten years, I guess!), until he hit the subject of how he judged players. 'Boys, this is how we recruit kids,' he said. 'We judge them on big games, and there's nothing bigger than finals. Don't worry about what you've done, we'll judge you on how you go in finals.'

Truthfully, those words stuck with me for the rest of my playing days. I played three decent games that season with Calder Cannons, and they were all finals, immediately after

Mick Malthouse's visit to my club. In those games, I averaged more than 30 touches, kicked about ten goals, and won an award for being Calder's best player of the finals, which completely went against everything that had happened in the first half of the year when I had averaged around 12 touches.

The Cannons went on to win the premiership. We had a great side that year, and we hurdled over the top of a brilliant Geelong Falcons team (featuring Luke Hodge, Gary Ablett, Jimmy Bartel, Matt McGuire, Tom Davidson and Nick Maxwell) in the preliminary final, then stepped out in the Under 18 grand final against Bendigo Pioneers (including future St Kilda and North Melbourne player Nick Dal Santo).

I had been to the MCG plenty of times to watch the footy with Dad, but it was an awesome feeling to run out and play, and in a grand final no less. Again, I gathered 30-plus possessions and I knew that I was close to winning the medal for best afield, but I was denied that honour by Jordan Barham, who kicked six goals. Jordan stitched me up! He kicked a few late goals and won the medal; he ended up being rookie-listed by a couple of clubs, although he never played an AFL game, which was a shame.

The Cannons had a few players who were in line to be drafted in that year, but personally, I had very few of those thoughts and no nerves, and I think that it helped me to relax for the grand final. It was a great day for us; we did a lap of honour after winning the flag, and because I had not been invited to the AFL's draft camp the following week, I was allowed to celebrate with a few mates, guys like Kade Carey and Aaron Ramsay.

It was my first experience of the traditional footy booze-up-after-grand-final, like a mini-Mad Monday; we sneaked into a few bars and went to Kade's house, and none of us had to concern ourselves with keeping in some sort of shape for the 3-kilometre time trial that the draft camp boys were preparing for that week. The draft camp was big for the boys who were hoping to be picked by an AFL club; most of the coaches would be there and it was the place where all the physical testing was done. All of the top players would be there, but not us, and I was very thankful to the clubs for failing to invite me. I really enjoyed that week!

It was November 2001, and I was not expecting to be drafted. I still had a year of eligibility with the Cannons, and I had not been picked to play for Vic Metro in the Under 18 championships, and not been invited to the draft camp, which were the main indicators. I was off the radar, I thought, although Noel Judkins, the Collingwood recruiter, did pay a visit to our home in Westmeadows, and so did Liam Pickering, who became my manager. 'Pickers' was a good friend of Leigh Tudor, who back then was an assistant coach at the Cannons, that pair having played together at North Melbourne, and Tudor must have mentioned me to Liam, the only manager who thought me worthy of a visit in the lead-up to the national draft.

But that was the only little indication of any interest from AFL people. I thought that if I was ever to be picked up it would be the following year, and Dad also thought it was a year too early, because I was still quite small. Plus I had bigger priorities, and number one on the list was going to schoolies week on the Gold Coast.

Although I skipped one or two of my VCE exams, I had passed Year 12. Maybe if I'd tried, I might have got into the sixtieth percentile with my marks, but in the end, I was happy with something in the 50s. I remember my parents asking me how the exams went, and I'd say, 'Yeah, it went great.' Little did they know that I was a non-attendee at a couple, although I did confess to my crime much later.

I am not sure what I thought I was doing with my future; the wharf was an option, although Dad was not keen for me to do that, and for the whole year all I had really concerned myself with was schoolies, which I was organising with my schoolmates. I had booked early, a fair way out, and I reckon I had been planning that week since Year 8! I just wanted to get up to the Gold Coast and do it, and I was already in Queensland having a lot of fun on the day of the 2001 AFL national draft.

I got to the Gold Coast with my mates on the Saturday, and the draft was the following day, Sunday 25 November. Back in 2001 there was no television coverage or radio broadcast like there is now, and no smart phones to keep track of the latest recruiting moves by the AFL clubs, and little information on the new band of juniors coming through the ranks. Personally, I had a little Nokia 3210 and all that I had on it was the game, Snake, so the draft was the last thing that I was thinking about as I necked beers in a bar, carrying on.

The first word I had that Collingwood had drafted me came with a text from Kade Carey, who was back in Melbourne: 'You've been drafted to the Pies!' And I actually thought he was winding me up. My reply was succinct: 'Fuck off mate.'

But then the Cannons' regional manager, Ross Monaghan, got through on my phone, and it started to run hot. Back at home in Westmeadows, Eddie McGuire, the Collingwood president, rang to congratulate me and copped Mum on the telephone. It is part of the folklore that Mum hung up on Eddie, thinking it was some kind of joke. That's how much faith they had in me!

Meanwhile I rang Ross and thanked him, and I remember getting a text from Tarkyn Lockyer, the Collingwood player, welcoming me to the Magpies, one of those things that current players do to make the draftees feel welcome.

We were into day two of a full week of schoolies, and my world had been turned upside down. I had been drafted by Collingwood with pick 58, the fourth player selected by the club that year behind Richie Cole (pick 11 from Eastern Ranges), Tom Davidson (pick 27 from Geelong Falcons) and Mark McGough (pick 43 from Murray Bushrangers) and just ahead of Tristen Walker (pick 72 from Claremont). My Calder teammates Brent Reilly (to Adelaide), James Kelly (to Geelong), Andrew Welsh (to Essendon) and David Rodan (to Richmond) had all been picked up, too, in what became known later as 'the super draft'.

Hawthorn had traded Trent Croad to Fremantle in exchange for the first selection, and took a great young player by the name of Luke Hodge from Geelong Falcons, while Luke Ball, who was a superstar junior, went from Sandringham Dragons to St Kilda with pick 2 and Eastern Ranges' Chris Judd, another gun junior, went to West Coast Eagles with pick 3. Looking back at that draft now, it had some serious quality: Jimmy Bartel was pick 8, Nick Dal

Santo pick 13, Steve Johnson pick 24, Sam Mitchell pick 36 and Leigh Montagna pick 37, while Jarrad Waite and Gary Ablett Jr were both taken as father–son selections.

Then there was D Swan down in the fourth round, one of the surprise picks of the draft, sending all the footy journos scrambling around for information because I had come from nowhere. And when Collingwood rang later that afternoon, they told me that they had booked a flight for me to come home the following day, so that I could begin pre-season training with my new teammates.

Right then and there, I made my first big decision in football.

BILL SWAN

Father

The rebellious side probably means he's a little bit like me. But he was a good kid, we never had any real trouble with him. He had the odd issue, but he was never disrespectful to us, or to other family members. He's a very loyal person with his family.

I'm glad he didn't go to work on the wharves, Dane, because he has no idea. Can't change a light bulb, but that's probably my fault for doing too many things for him. We should have made him do it himself. Anyway, it would've been interesting to see what he did had footy not come along.

How has he done it? He's a *footballer.* There are athletes now, but they don't know how to play footy. Dane knows how to play football, and he's taller than people think. He's six foot one (185 centimetres) and he was always a good mark, always good one on one, hard to beat in the contest. Even as a kid, no one could beat him one on one, he had such good hands.

We used to have a kick over at the park when he was a boy, and I tried to tell him to kick with his left foot, which didn't work too well! He was actually keener on basketball early; he was handy at that, and he played a bit of cricket, too.

He says he was no good as a junior but that is not strictly true. He was always one of the better kids in the team, but when you are bottom-age it's harder, and at 11 or 12 he was skinny and little. He just improved every year as he got older and in his last year of Under 16s he had a good year for Westmeadows. He kicked 90-odd goals, playing centre half-forward a bit, and on the ball too.

The next year he went down to the Cannons but he was not one of the first picked. I didn't know if he would make it as a bottom-ager, but he could always get the footy, he just had that knack. He was probably best on the ground in the grand final that year in the TAC Cup, and he got drafted, which was too early, in my view. He was only 17, and he didn't handle it well. He was still knocking around with the kids he grew up with, he didn't work hard enough at training, obviously, and he moved out of home.

In the end the club said he had to get out of that house and set a few rules for him. That's when we bought the house in Yarraville for him, and then it turned around a bit. The board wanted to sack him in 2003 over the fight, but Dane's involvement was minimal, certainly less than the others. There were heaps of charges, although most of them were dropped. We had a meeting with the club and looked at the CCTV footage, and you could see Dane get involved fleetingly, and then take off. Even the judge said that his involvement was small, but it cost him a lot of money.

After that, the Rat Pack got hold of him, and they were really good for him.

3

SIDE BY SIDE

'Dane is a very good crumber, with a smart football brain and is a very good mark overhead. Although not exceptionally quick, he is a real footballer.'

—Noel Judkins, Collingwood recruiter, draft day 2001

I managed to give Collingwood its first taste of my mentality before I even set foot in the place, because I refused to come home from the Gold Coast when I was supposed to. I had put too much time and effort into the preparations for schoolies week, and I was having way too much fun to throw that all away.

Sure, I was happy that I had been drafted; it gave me some sort of future. But Collingwood had said, 'Enjoy tonight, and we've booked the flight for tomorrow.' And I just said, 'No. Schoolies is a good time.' I found my stocks had soared with the young women who were hanging around the bars and night clubs of Surfer's Paradise with the news that I was going to be an AFL player, and deep down, while I knew that I was at risk of upsetting my new employer, I was thinking, *Collingwood have already got me for two years. Another five days' wait is not gonna hurt them. I'm staying up here.*

So I politely declined the club's first request and it is true, I was drunk at the time, although not so bad that I didn't know what I was doing. I knew exactly what it was about, and I guess it was one of the first moments of defiance that would characterise my career. In truth, I did compromise slightly. Instead of staying the full week on the Gold Coast,

I rearranged my flight and came back one day earlier than I had planned, on the Friday.

The family had launched a big party at home. All our friends and family and half the neighbourhood were there to greet me, everyone was happy, and to be honest, I probably drank just as much as I would have if I'd stayed up in Queensland. Technically, I was a professional athlete, but in reality I was still acting like a teenager.

Dad drove me to the Collingwood headquarters in town. I remember it was a Saturday morning session out at Olympic Park, in the middle of the running track that was there at the time but has since been demolished, and I recall that I was fearsomely hungover for my arrival at the biggest football club in the country, the result of not only one big night but a full week's hard drinking. When you have been playing at Westmeadows Under 16s, so long as you arrive by the time they are doing the group stretch and warm-up lap, that's fine. At AFL level, this does not fly, which I quickly learned. In AFL footy, the way it works is if you are not early, then you are considered to be late. If you are training at 8 am then get there by 7 am, that is the rule of thumb. I had no idea about that at the time, and therefore I was late to my first training session.

I was the last of the draftees to arrive, even though we had only needed to drive for 20 minutes or so from the suburbs, by comparison with Tristen Walker from Perth, Tom Davidson from Geelong, Mark McGough from up-country, and Richie Cole from the Northern Territory. They did the introductions, and Dean 'Tunnel' Laidley, Collingwood's assistant coach began the wind-up straight away: 'This is our fourth pick. He's been on schoolies getting pissed all week with his mates!'

I am not sure what the hardened professionals of Collingwood Football Club would have thought about their new teammate at that moment, perhaps something along the lines of: 'Why have we drafted *this* bloke?' What I do know is that the group that would later become known as the Rat Pack, guys like Chris Tarrant, Alan Didak and Ben Johnson, were quick to get around me. I guess that they identified with a young guy who preferred to spend the week socialising rather than coming back early for pre-season training.

Collingwood was in a building phase as a club, having brought Mick Malthouse back to Melbourne from Perth after his successful period as coach of the West Coast Eagles, in which he had won the 1992 and 1994 flags, the first in that club's history. Under Malthouse, who replaced a club legend in Tony Shaw, Collingwood had finished fifteenth in 2000 with a 7–15 record and then risen to ninth, with an 11–11 record in 2001.

Eddie McGuire was flying as club president, the ultimate Collingwood supporter who had taken over the job at the end of 1998 when the club was in difficulties and struggling on the field, and one of his first appointments was Greg Swann, the former Carlton chief executive. Nathan Buckley was captain of the club and the Magpies had a few other good players like Chris Tarrant, Anthony Rocca and James Clement.

In 2002 Collingwood ended up playing in a grand final, soaring under Malthouse, and this was the environment into which I walked. Mind you, I only had a small role at that point, and it took me at least two years to make any impact whatsoever. It has been said that I failed to set the world on fire in my early years; actually, I was more likely to literally set Collingwood on fire!

Collingwood had a VFL affiliation with Williamstown Football Club, which had a nice ring to it since Dad had played his last few years for the Seagulls. My first game in 2002 was for Willy's reserves team, down at Geelong on the ground outside the main Kardinia Park stadium, and I started on the bench. That is about how I was regarded at the time, basically on the *third* level of Collingwood's list, behind the AFL team and the main VFL team. Not exactly the Big Show.

I don't think I had ever been to Geelong in my life, and we had to be there by around 8 am, which of course I was not, meaning that the coach, Anthony 'Ace' Eames, chose to start me on the pine. It was an ordinary start to my football career.

Dad has always said that I was drafted too early, that I was too immature both physically and emotionally. I had turned 18 in February 2002, and only a few weeks later was expected to act like a professional footballer. I found it extremely difficult and my answer to the issues was to find the shortest route to doing it. I was the champion of finding shortcuts. I skipped weights, massages and the extra training that the senior guys were doing – I preferred to do the minimum, then go home.

I moved out of the family home and into a house with Kade Carey in Essendon, and every bit of spare time that

I had was spent catching up with mates. Dad was getting angry with the way I was carrying on, and he'd say, 'What the hell are you doing?' I'd say, 'Nothing at all!' Drinking was now legal because I had turned 18, and I probably did myself no favours in terms of making new friends at Collingwood. I spent more time with my old friends from outside the club, and the Magpies players did not offer up that much in return.

I made no real attempt to win their respect and I did not deserve their respect, either. They did not give a shit about me, and all I wanted to do was hang out with my mates, which is exactly what occurred. I did not play a single senior game in that first season, 2002, and I was not even close, although I did win a promotion from the VFL reserves to the seniors, kicking a few goals on debut in a game that was televised by the ABC. In moments like these, the media tended to focus on the fact that I was Bill Swan's son, as indicated by the *AFL Season Guide*'s little bio of me in 2002:

> The son of former 300-game VFA player for Port Melbourne and Williamstown, Bill Swan. A half-forward or half-back with poise and awareness. Likened to former Essendon premiership star of the 1980s, Leon Baker. A smart footballer who is expected to improve enormously in his first season with the Pies.

But I did not improve enormously at all. I broke a hand, which scarcely helped, and I was struggling to fit in at Collingwood. Most of my time was spent with the Willy boys and coach Brad Gotch, because back then the groups trained separately for the majority of the week, and I had not yet made my full connection with Johnno (Johnson), Taz (Tarrant) and Dids (Didak).

Footy clubs were much different then. Arriving at a club now, you would be surrounded by a leadership group who would make a point of ensuring you felt welcome, they'd take you out for dinner and help you to find some comfort in the new environment. Back then there was no welfare officer or development officer to help you through any issues, but nowadays you'd be educated at TAC Cup level about lifestyle and professionalism. The downside is that you might be turned into a robot. For me in 2002, it was sink or swim, just try your best. And I was sinking, pretty much.

Football was running a very poor second to my lifestyle back then. I was earning $36,000 as a first-year player, which seemed like a small fortune to me in my first year out of school, and drink cards were available at certain bars and night clubs for AFL-listed players. I had not been a big drinker before, at least not regularly; now I ramped it up.

Getting out and having fun was exactly what my mates were doing, and it was all I ever wanted to do, too. Playing AFL footy, or at least being on a list, gave me the platform to do it. I would be out Thursday nights, Friday nights, play footy in the VFL on Saturdays and then out again on Saturday night and all day Sunday. And I was far from the only one who pursued that lifestyle from the comfort of an AFL playing list.

We trained most of the week down at Williamstown's ground, and we were not required there until 5 pm on any day, so I could sleep all day after a big night. We were supposed to do weights at Collingwood's facility near the MCG during the day, but as I discovered, if you were not there, how would they know? I might poke my head in at the club, walk around the weight room for half an hour, and then head down to Willy for training.

None of us had great cars, but we would literally race over the Westgate Bridge, and there was a chicken shop in Williamstown that we haunted. I tended to scoff down a huge thigh of chicken with chips and gravy half an hour before training under Gotchy, then hit the track. A lot of us operated like that, guys like Rhyce Shaw, Heath Scotland, Tom Davidson, Guy Richards. If you behaved like that in a modern AFL environment, you would be cut before you knew what hit you.

I spent every cent that I had, week after week. Collingwood gave us a monthly advance of our pay, about $3000 a month, and it would disappear in the first two or three weeks after it arrived. Then I would ring the footy club and ask for next month's pay to be forwarded, which, initially, they went along with. Not surprisingly, Collingwood put a stop to that after a while.

I am not too sure how much Collingwood knew about my behaviour in the first three years, because I was rarely caught out, and I did not have the public profile that I have today. There was no real social media back then, no Twitter or Facebook or Instagram where the public could post photos of a player if he was out having a beer or two. I found that I was invisible to the public and could pretty much do what I liked.

Even the senior guys had a certain amount of protection in the era before the 24-hour news cycle, and while AFL footy was big, it was not quite the monolith that it is today. It's not that I am trying to glorify it; far from it. But that was the culture of footy in the early 2000s, and if the best player in the game could get away with it, then I figured anyone could have a crack. I knew Wayne Carey would go out a lot, drink hard, but by Monday morning he would be ready and he would be the hardest trainer and, of course, the best player. There were players like that at every club back in the early 2000s.

Wayne Carey had won two premierships at North Melbourne (in 1996 and 1999) despite heavy drinking on weekends, a fact that he went public about in a TV interview with Andrew Denton on ABC's *Enough Rope* in 2008:

> Yeah I was the captain of the club and you could probably say I was captain of the social scene as well and it was, after every game I'd make sure that the players got together and we'd go and have you know 20 or 30 beers and I know that sounds like a lot and if a player now had 20 or 30 beers on a Saturday night after a game you'd, well one you'd probably think how do they play the next week or how do you train the next day, but you do, you become accustomed to it and yeah and I was always the first one there making sure everyone else was there and I was always the last one to leave.

When Denton asked how big a part alcohol played in his life generally at that time, Carey answered:

> Well look I'd have to say that I would drink after every game, I haven't told anyone, oh well probably friends, good friends

know and a few team-mates but even right up to preliminary finals when you know most players say that you know if you make the finals for instance you stop drinking at the end of the home-and-away season. I thought that what worked for you in the home-and-away season you continue through to the grand final. So I drank every single weekend, I don't think there was a weekend that I didn't drink during my football career.

It has changed now, but to an 18-year-old lad from Westmeadows, that sounded like the way to go. I just did not know any different. I had money, I did not have to work nine-to-five, and I thought I was a rockstar living a glamorous lifestyle. I was carried away with myself, no doubt, when in actual fact I was a shitty, low-level AFL footballer, lucky to be on the list and lucky to *stay* on the list at Collingwood. That's what I was.

Mick Malthouse was a scary individual, I quickly discovered. When I trained at Victoria Park with the senior group, if you messed up a kick he would throw you off the track and you would not return. 'That'll do. See ya, mate,' he'd say, and you would walk off the ground with your tail between your legs, a kind of walk of shame. 'Don't come back until you've had ten kicks with Gotchy on the sidelines!' This happened to me plenty of times, but I was known to stuff up a kick on purpose just so I could go inside, and I am not sure what Mick thought of me. Probably not much at all.

Having said that, the 2003 season, my second at Collingwood, was ever so slightly better. I played some decent football for Williamstown and we won the VFL premiership, a nice bit of symmetry since Dad had done

LEFT This is how Mum likes to remember me: no tattoos.

RIGHT Dad was a VFA footy legend and had a big influence on me as a player.

BELOW: My Under 10 coach is the only person to predict that I'd actually make it.

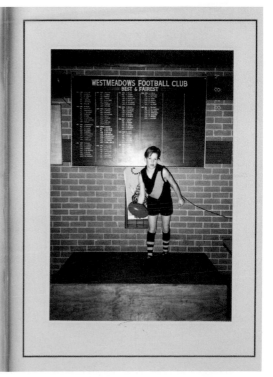

NAME: Dane Swan

HEIGHT: 145 cm

WEIGHT: 37 kg

JUMPER No: 13

COACH'S COMMENTS

An excellent year. Club Best & Fairest and runner-up in the Competition. An excellent player, able to bring his teamates into play. I'm sure he can go on to play A.F.L. A pleasure to coach. Good luck in the future.

BROADMEADOWS BASKETBALL ASSOCIATION

BROADMEADOWS
BRONCOS
UNDER 16 B
1998

I was more interested in basketball and played in the state league juniors but in the end I chose footy because it fitted in better with my social life.

Calder Cannons Football Club 2001 TAC Cup Premiers

Row 7: Kade Carey (SECOND FROM LEFT).

Row 6: Bo Nixon (SECOND FROM LEFT) Ryan Crowley (FOURTH FROM LEFT), Andrew Welsh (SIXTH FROM LEFT), Dane Swan (FOURTH FROM RIGHT).

Row 5: Brendon Hollow (SECOND FROM LEFT), Brent Reilly (FOURTH FROM LEFT), James Kelly (SECOND FROM RIGHT).

Row 2: David Rodan (FIRST FROM LEFT), Aaron Ramsay (THIRD FROM LEFT).

Row 1: Coach Robert Hyde (CENTRE).

ABOVE My first senior game, round 13, 2003. You can see our captain, Nathan Buckley, in the background.

LEFT Mick used to tell me to pull my socks up. He was deadly serious: 'If you can't play like a footballer, at least look like one.' In 2004, I did what he said.

ABOVE For whatever reason, Mick saw a player in me. I got a good run in the seniors because in 2005 he was promoting youth.

BELOW I was starting to hit my straps in 2006, and had a great game against Essendon in round 19.

ABOVE With Chris Tarrant (Rat Pack original), Daisy Thomas, Shane Wakelin and Harry O'Brien after a round 3 win in 2006. Taz would be traded out at the end of the year.

LEFT The drawn semi-final against West Coast in 2007 was an awesome game. Ben Johnson reckons that's when I arrived as a player. No tattoos yet.

ABOVE At the end of 2008 I was voted into the leadership group, alongside new captain Nick Maxwell and Scott Pendlebury, Josh Fraser and Shane O'Bree. Fair to say I never felt comfortable in that role.

BELOW By 2009 my strength was to play in bursts. We won a nailbiter final against Adelaide and my tattoos were coming along nicely.

ABOVE Cameron Ling was the tagger I had most trouble with. I had to hit the contest at the right moment, try to get the footy on the fly, but it was tough. Geelong smashed us in the 2009 preliminary final.

RIGHT The famous *Coll-ing-woo-ood* chant started in the 2010 prelim final – we could do no wrong and beat the Cats easily.

that 13 years earlier. And in finishing fourth in the club's reserves best and fairest, I won Collingwood's John Wren Memorial Trophy for the highest finish by a listed player in the Seagulls' best-player award.

We won the flag by beating Box Hill at Princes Park in Carlton; I kicked a goal and was named in the best players. Nick Maxwell, my future captain at Collingwood, was also in that team, along with guys like Jarrod Molloy, Glenn Freeborn, Steve McKee and Rupert Betheras, who had all been part of the Magpies' grand final team the year before.

Brad Gotch wrote this review of my season for the club's *In Black and White* magazine, which touched on my sometimes sloppy disposal, a recurring theme over my career:

> Finished fourth in our best and fairest, playing 17 out of the 21 games and if he had played every match he nearly would have won it. He just needs to work on the execution of his kicking as he can be a little bit sloppy at times, but he wins a lot of the football. He is quite a confident kid so he won't be intimidated. Played against Richmond early in the year and did quite well, but players returning to the seniors and a hand injury saw him struggle to get back.

I also managed to play my first three senior games for Collingwood that year, which was a high. My AFL debut happened in round 13 against the Western Bulldogs, and it came as a surprise at the time. I had been an emergency several times, and I was at the game with my gear, as instructed, but not expecting to play, when our full-back, Simon Prestigiacomo, pulled out with an injury a couple of hours before the game. I was then told that I would come into the team. An hour before the game I had to ring Dad and say, 'I'm playing, come in!'

Which sounds a little rushed but in reality, it was not the worst way to play your first game, because it took away any chance that I would suffer from nerves, as well as leaving no possibility that I would play the game in my head before it actually happened.

So I didn't have time for nerves, and in any case, getting nervous is not in my nature. All my career I only ever worried about what I could control, and I have never been one to be overcome by fear of failure. There are a lot of things that I messed up in my life, but not because I feared them. I have more pride in my performance than people realise, and I have always wanted to play really well because I didn't want my parents to be ashamed or embarrassed about me playing badly.

That was my motivational tool. Now, I know that my parents are not going to be ashamed of me, but it was the mentality that I took with me: Play well for your friends and family. I don't want people going around thinking, *That's Dane Swan's mum and dad, he's playing like an idiot.*

My Collingwood guernsey number – 36 – fell to me by chance, and I liked it. I remember a few years later that Mick Malthouse asked me if I wanted to change it to a lower number, and I declined. I just wanted to make it my own, write my own story, and I liked the names of wearers of that guernsey that were on my locker: guys like Rene Kink and Sav Rocca. They were characters, I remember thinking, Sav being a great goalkicker who had more than 500 goals in the AFL, and ended up in the NFL as a punter, and Kink used to be known as 'The Incredible Hulk', he was so big and powerful. They sounded like the kind of guys I would like to follow, so No. 36 it was for me.

My debut was on a Saturday night, 28 June 2003, at what was then known as Telstra Dome (now Etihad Stadium) in the Docklands. I was 19 years and 124 days old, and I had walked into a very strong Collingwood team that had narrowly lost the 2002 Grand Final to Brisbane Lions, coached by Leigh Matthews, a quick rise for the Magpies just a couple of years into Mick Malthouse's regime as coach. Backing up in 2003 we were 6–6 through 12 rounds, hanging in there, when I was picked.

I played only 10 minutes a quarter, which was how it worked in 2003, because the seismic shift towards massive rotations was a few years away. There were four on the bench, and you were basically used as injury back-up and to provide an occasional rest to a regular player. The best players would not go to the bench at all.

My first kick, I remember clearly, was directed to Nathan Buckley, who had a picnic that day in our win over the Bulldogs. I had come on at about the 20-minute mark of the first quarter and we were already on top, and I tackled the Bulldogs' ruckman after a ball-up, grabbed the Sherrin and kicked it in the captain's direction. He was one-on-three, I reckon, but it was the only voice that I heard!

I had eight disposals in that game playing down in the backline, but was dropped for the following week's game, and reinstated for round 16 against Richmond for another win, this time at the MCG, where I had 16 disposals. Then I was dropped again until round 22 against Essendon at the MCG; we had another win, but I hardly played in the game, and it was the last senior footy I saw in that season. When the main players returned from injury, I would cop the knife, and go back to Williamstown.

Really, my impact was limited by lack of time and the fact that I was in and out of the team, although I suppose it gave me a small taste of the elite level. I was not embarrassed and I wasn't a complete failure. I was a bit-part player; I just went and played.

The Magpies shocked Brisbane in the first final, giving themselves a chance of turning the tables from the previous year. David Buttifant, our fitness and conditioning man, asked me if I wanted to train on with the senior squad after Williamstown won the VFL flag a week before the AFL grand final, but I said no. I told Butters that I couldn't see myself getting a game at senior level, and besides that, I wanted to go away on holidays and I wanted the extra week off. I didn't really care what the club thought.

Ultimately the Magpies fell again on grand final day, well beaten by Leigh Matthews' great Lions team who won a third consecutive flag.

The post-season was my favourite time of year, time to let the pressure valve out. It was a different era, and I did things a different way. Thank God I am finished now and not starting. No way would I survive in AFL footy today if I was at the beginning of my career. Not a snowflake's chance in hell …

ROBERT HYDE

Calder Cannons' coach 1996–2006

I remember going to watch him in the Under 16s with Ross Monaghan, our regional manager, and you just see kids who can play, and Dane doesn't look like he can play if you are aiming to pick a role model player. His shorts would be hanging down a bit, his socks would be down and he looked scruffy. Some players look like racehorses; this bloke looked like a bloody Clydesdale, you know, until he started finding the footy all the time, and you realised that he could play.

Then he needed to tidy up his disposal and then work on a few areas. But when they're 16 or 17 you're not looking for someone who's God's gift to footy straight away. We really only had him for a year in 2001 because he was drafted young. He was a good kid, he was no idiot, but he was a lad. He took a while to get himself going and grow up, but there are plenty of kids like that. He needed to work a bit harder at different stages and I remember having a chat with him at one point, we dropped him from the team, and I said, 'You've got to pull your head in and work harder, go back and play good footy'. He did that.

To be honest, he ran like a little waddly duck, you know. But the kid could run and run and run. In the grand final against Bendigo, we played him on Rick Ladson on the wing, and I remember him getting third-best for us at the end of the day, he kicked a couple of goals and he just ran. He didn't look like he could play that much, but every time you looked up he would be finding the footy somewhere else across the park.

He just got the ball, Dane. He's an ungainly kick, but even at Collingwood, every time you looked up he was either down the backline getting kicks, in the middle getting kicks or having a shot at goal. You don't do that naturally, you have to be able to work. So the bloke grew up and he must have trained as hard as anyone else.

When he was with us, he was still sorting himself out. He was 17, he came from a good family, his dad was a really good footballer and, while he hadn't been in his dad's shadow, he'd come from that pedigree of Bill having been a renowned player. He enjoyed lots of things and footy was one of them.

He had a few brushes along the way, at Collingwood, too. Some kids could have gone the other way, Collingwood could have said, 'Stuff you, you're playing up' and got rid of him. But they saw something in him. He's no fool, he's a good person, he's not a dickhead. He's a bit rough around the edges and what you get is what you see.

4

PRECIPICE

'It's bloody hard, when a kid's come straight out
of school, probably doesn't think he's going to get
drafted, and he goes from having no money – because
we used to give him pocket money, he didn't have a
job or anything – to earning some decent money.'

—Bill Swan

I was cruising at the end of the 2003 season. I had broken into the seniors in my second year at Collingwood, albeit briefly, and I was living the life that I loved. Then it all came crashing down over the Christmas period.

On Saturday night 20 December 2003, my friend Kade Carey, cousin Aaron Ramsay and I went nightclubbing in the city, left the club near Russell Street at just after midnight, and grabbed a taxi heading for the Prince of Wales Hotel in St Kilda to continue the session. It turned out to be the night when my footy career could have ended – certainly the closest I came to being sacked by Collingwood Football Club. Ultimately, you could say it was the night that my career really started.

As we turned the corner toward St Kilda Road, adjacent to Federation Square, the cab driver decided to throw us out of his taxi over an argument that revolved around his refusal to change the radio station for us. We were half-drunk teenagers, thinking we could do no wrong, and he chucked us out, right in the middle of the road, not even bothering to pull over to the kerb to dump us.

When we extracted ourselves from the car we had to make our way across a lane of moving traffic, and I nipped across pretty quickly, but Kade, who was in the front, was almost hit by a car shooting through on the inside lane. He ended up jumping on the bonnet of the car, and the force of his body smashed the windscreen. I cannot say whether he did it on purpose, or whether he did it to get out of the way, but the women who were in that car certainly said that he meant to jump on it.

We differed on that, but my instinct straight away was: 'I don't need trouble. Let's run. Let's go.' I took off down towards the Yarra River, but the girls got out of their car and were abusing Kade, and he was arguing back as I did a runner down towards River Terrace, the open area below the Princes Bridge. The key moment for me came when I stopped and looked back to see five security guards around Kade and Aaron, with an argument and then the beginnings of a fight.

Bear in mind that we were all around 19 and 20 years old, and these guys were late-20s or 30s, and they were all carrying those Maglite torches, huge things with a long butt on them, dangerous weapons if you choose to use them in that way. I had to make a quick decision, and it was an easy one because my mates were involved. I went back.

As I was heading back toward the argument I saw one of those guys hit Kade with the butt of his torch and knocked him down, which was a bad idea, because all the Careys can fight. It is no secret that they lived a hard life; Wayne Carey, Kade's uncle, has spoken about the way his mother was abused by his father, and Dick, Kade's father, grew up in that environment, too. On this night, it was about five-on-two, an unfair fight. Someone else's fight, granted, but I know where my loyalties lie.

I got involved in what was a full-on fight by this stage, threw a punch or two, and the argument was taken care of, with those guys copping a hiding. Then I heard police sirens, and I said, 'We've got to go!' Aaron was cool to go, but Kade wanted to hang around because he had been the first to cop a whack. Once again, I tried to shift him: 'Let's get out of here.'

Aaron and I ran off, but he was grabbed and taken down. I managed to get away but both Aaron and Kade were arrested and locked up, and when I went to see Kade the next day, he was pretty badly beaten up. The police who finally arrested him had used capsicum spray to subdue him.

Now I reckon I have a fair grip on the difference between right and wrong, and I am always going to back up a mate when he is in trouble, whether I am in hot water for doing that or not. That is how I was brought up, with loyalty to family and friends first and last. Constant and faithful: the family motto. I think that is how it is and how it should be, because my family and close friends will be there through the hard times, whether I'm playing well or playing badly. Lots of footy clubs will be loyal while you are performing, but if you are not, it can be a brutal environment and plenty have the knife run through them. And with my family, I know that no matter how many times I mess up, getting on the front page for the wrong reasons, they will be there, whereas with a footy club, they have only so much patience.

So while I had initially run that night, I was always going back if there was a real issue, which ended up being the case. I might even do the same again if it happened today, although maybe as an older person you might try to defuse the situation when it cropped up. But when alcohol is involved, your perception changes, and nobody makes the best decisions when they are drunk. That is when the trouble starts. Nobody is getting involved in a fight at a cafe at four o'clock in the afternoon, are they? I went back because I would not have been able to look Kade Carey, my friend and housemate, in the face if I had not.

I had been in fights before, as a younger guy. You would be out, catch the train to the city, sink a skinful of grog and end up in a blue, fights where you have no idea where the punches are coming from, and you hit the first person that you see hitting your mate, like something out of an old western. But you wake up pretty quickly afterwards and that fight near Federation Square is the last I've been involved in, the last punch that I threw.

I have been involved in arguments, a bit of push and shove, but the fight is not worth having, I have learned. The king-hit seems to be more common. Is that my imagination, or is it just that it gets reported in the media? I am not sure, but people seem to be more aggressive nowadays, and I am the farthest point from aggressive.

That fight in the city in 2003 nearly lost me my footy career and ended up in the courts, and the only people who win in courts are the lawyers. The security guards and a cleaner who had been with them made a complaint, and all three of us – Kade, Aaron and me – were charged by the police. A couple of them had ended up in hospital, the cleaner alleged that he had a broken nose and a fractured eye socket, and there I was, facing 14 charges including assault.

The court cases would come later, but first of all there was the prickly issue of Collingwood and my career. The club found out, I am guessing from the media, and they asked me to come into what was then the Lexus Centre, at Olympic Park. It was early January, and my manager, Liam Pickering, rang me, too. At the club, I had to confront all the big wheels: Mick Malthouse, Eddie McGuire, the football staff such as Neil Balme and Mark Kleiman, and the chief executive, Greg Swann.

I flat-out lied to them to start with. 'Nothing happened. I wasn't there,' I told them. 'Nothing will come of it. I didn't do anything.'

This was a mistake, of course, because it emerged sometime later that I had been involved in the fight even though I initially took off. So my trouble had just doubled, and at this point of my footy career I had played the grand total of three senior games for Collingwood Football Club. They did not owe me anything.

I knew I was on the verge of being sacked, and at home in Essendon I cried for the first time about footy. It really hit me because I knew that I deserved to be sacked, the way that I was handling myself, not respecting training and finding the shortest avenue to every end result.

I was told – and I cannot recall if it was by Pickers, or by Dad – that the Collingwood Football Club board had already decided that it wanted me sacked. I believe that to be the case to this day, that the decision had been made.

I was asked to attend another meeting at the footy club, and I was allowed to bring Dad with me, along with Pickers. I was highly emotional; every kid who plays AFL thinks they will go forever, make the money and nothing will go wrong, and I was no exception to that rule. At 19, you think that you can run the world. I had been taking it all for granted and I thought that it was about to end very quickly.

I had a day to ponder this in the early part of 2004. When I sat in that meeting, I did not say much at all. The heavy hitters were there, getting stuck into me, and I was at that point of my career where I felt like I had no right to be speaking out, still earning the stripes.

Dad had been good with this situation. I think, deep down, that he would have been disappointed with me had I kept running away on the night of the fight, because that is how he raised me. He also knew Greg Swann quite well from the time they had together at Williamstown, when Swann was president of that club, and I remember Dad saying, 'Give him another chance.'

They watched the CCTV footage from the cameras at Federation Square, which showed me bolting after the first part of the fight, having a fleeting involvement, and then taking off again. But it was Mick Malthouse who saved me, I have no doubt about that. He spoke last, from memory, and came straight to the point. 'Listen, we're not going to ruin your career on one stuff-up.'

Mick clearly saw something in me, whether it was that he thought that I could play, or maybe it was because we were from the same socio-economic background. He had grown up in Wendouree West, a less-than-swish suburb of Ballarat, and he knew that I was from Broady. He understood that kids make mistakes, and he had a sliver of sympathy for me in the sense that I was clearly standing up for my mates. It was not as though I punched someone for no reason at all.

He said, 'Look, this is obviously your last chance. And you can't live with your mates anymore, because they're causing you issues. This is it, mate. Now prove yourself to me, repay some of the faith I'm showing in you, and do what you're told.' I looked at Mick and the others and said, 'Thank you.' It was a tremendous relief for me, a reprieve that I was lucky to get, and I went back to pre-season training with some enthusiasm, even though the court cases were hanging over our heads.

54

It was not a nice feeling to be in a courtroom, and I remember this much: I found it really tough because when I am nervous and tense, I have this habit of smiling a lot, and I knew that was not going to be a good look when I was up on charges. I think there was an article written that I was smirking in court, but it was just how I deal with a situation that I'm nervous about. Mum and Dad came along with me, and it was a nasty time of my life. Dad was happy that I'd stuck up for my mates, and obviously if we had all had our time again, of course we'd have walked away that night, but my parents were fully supportive. It was not like we just walked up to those guys and smashed them. Yes, we might have been in the wrong at the start, but they started the fight. Kade got hit with a torch first.

In the criminal case, Kade was ordered to perform 200 hours of community service and fined $3000 for criminal damage. According to a newspaper report of the judge's findings in the County Court, 'The judge described his actions as "stupid and arrogant", but questioned the response of security guards who confronted him, acknowledging that Carey was provoked. He said Swan and Ramsay joined the fight to defend their friend.'

Aaron Ramsay was given 120 hours of community service to perform, and I was ordered to do 100 hours' service after most of the charges against me were dropped. I ended up with a conviction for affray, but none for assault.

For the first time in my life – but not the last – I was on the front pages of the newspapers, never a good thing, and when the civil cases came around, I had to pay about $100,000 in compensation to those other people who were involved in the fight. I never had much respect for those guys, because as my profile grew over the coming years the lawsuits would continue to come, and the cleaner should never have been there in the first place. It ended up going for eight years and costing a bomb, and it all left a horrible taste in the mouth.

But I did my community service and extracted something from it, down at the Salvation Army feeding the homeless and out in the van helping people who were down on their luck or on the streets. Actually I drew so much from it that I still do it, every now and then, and Major Brendan Nottle, who is the head of the Salvos in the city, is a Collingwood supporter and the club chaplain who I see from time to time at the footy.

I am not saying that I enjoyed that period because it is not the right word, but it was an eye-opener for me just seeing how hard some people live. It gave me a different perspective on life, and I remember thinking, *Footy's just a game.* You have a crap game and you can get down on yourself, but there are people doing it a lot harder than me. I'd be thinking, *I've got to train tomorrow* and that it's a pain in the arse, but I'm getting the perks of a footballer and complaining. Well, a lot of people are doing it a lot tougher than me.

Years later, in 2010, I gave some talks to young people about violence and fighting, and I cited that story from 2003 when I spoke to them. The talks were about one-punch assaults, and the dangers, and I had two stories that I could relate, great examples of what can happen. That fight near Federation Square had cost me about $200,000, it had gone through the courts for eight years, so it was an easy way to illustrate the dangers of getting involved.

There was another incident in 2010 when a guy punched me in the face at a nightclub, and I had just walked away that night. That was the example I used, because the first fight cost me a lot of money; the second one cost me nothing. Sometimes, it is the stronger man who walks away.

• • •

One of the first changes that I had to make after the meeting at Collingwood at the start of 2004 was awkward to say the least, and that was to move out of the share house that I had been living in with Kade and two other mates. I waited as long as I could possibly wait to tell Kade, and I nearly broke down when I did it. 'I've got to leave,' I told him. 'The footy club wants me out.' It was very hard, because at the time Kade was my best mate, we did everything together, we had been through some crap together, and I loved him.

Kade took it well, like a mate would, and here is the thing. We all have mates who are hangers-on, who want to be there for drink cards and the perks of being an AFL-listed player, but the friends who actually cared about me understood my position. Kade said something like, 'Mate, you have to.' And I said, 'We'll still see each other all the time, I just can't *live* here.'

My parents had backed up the point that Mick Malthouse made when they said, 'If you want a footy career, you need to go.' So they helped me to buy a house in Kingsville, in the inner west, for $385,000. I was spending every cent of the $80,000 or so that Collingwood paid me, so I had nothing for a house, but Mum and Dad said, 'We'll go halves. Down the track, once you start saving some money from footy, we'll buy the house from you for what you got it for.' They believed in me, my parents, and I owe them big-time because, had it not been for that little manoeuvre, I might have moved in with another mate and messed up all over again.

For six months I lived alone in Kingsville, and then Guy Richards, a teammate, moved in with me because he needed somewhere to stay while he looked for a place to buy. That ended up being two years or so, and we became very tight, having some good times in that house.

But I have never been in any trouble with the law since that time if you discount the odd speeding fine or parking infringement. If it happened now, a player would get a talking-to from the leadership group, but I cannot recall that happening to me. I had been in my own little world, out on the grog with my mates, and footy was too hard for me, training was too hard, and I was not ready. Dad was right, I had been drafted too early, and I was not ready.

That incident was a sliding doors moment for me, and I managed to fight my way through it. It was another one of those times when you would have had long odds about me making anything of a football career, in fact you could write your own ticket in 2004. The point was that I learned from it, and I don't even regret it, because it was part of what turned me into the person that I am. Because I reckon if that had not happened, I was heading down a particular track at Collingwood that would have sent me out of the game in another two years or so. Not for the last time, I would come to acknowledge that you learn more from your stuff-ups than anything else.

And walking out of that meeting in the Collingwood boardroom, a little light went on in my head.

MICK MALTHOUSE

Collingwood coach 2000–2011

One of the things that I tried to do is to treat everyone as an individual and give them space to be who they are. I've always found him to be very honest with me, very honest with his performance. Outside of being a very, very good player as a Brownlow medallist, he's one of these blokes – and there are only a few in the competition – who you don't see argue with the umpire or chase extra exposure. He got enough exposure from the way he played, so he wasn't demonstrative in any way in an effort to attract attention. It was quite extraordinary the way that he just got on with it.

59

I twigged early days when I had a shot at him in one particular game that he had pride in his performance, and there's no question that, knowing that, I was able to appeal to that pride from time to time: 'Has this bloke got you?' In the 2010 replayed grand final against St Kilda he was okay, but not having a great game, and I asked him to go on to Brendon Goddard. We were actually walking toward the race at half-time, and I thought, *Hang on, if St Kilda are getting back in the game, it's going to be Goddard'*.

I don't rate Goddard's defence so I thought, *You know what, I'll give Swanny this job*. I just knew that it would prick his sense of challenge. You just knew that was the case even though he didn't say it. He kicked the first goal from the goal square and *bang*, he's back in the game. That's what he had. It was pride in performance, not demonstratively so, but it was there.

Swanny didn't need a lot of training exercises but again, behind closed doors, where no one could see him, in the altitude room on the treadmill, he belted it. It wasn't for public scrutiny, but that's the way he was. For all his tattoos and the way he is, he never demanded public adulation, he just wanted to go about his job behind the wall in that little box where they had the running machine, and he flogged himself, because it was for pride. He knew that they wouldn't keep up with him if he did that running.

The 2003 incident was a catalyst for his career, I believe. He was getting into too much trouble, but once we laid down the ultimatum, he just needed to address where he lived and who he lived with. Remarkably, because I didn't know if I was hitting home or not, he listened.

He went to the extra lengths to make sure it was done. It was an important time because he was young enough to lose it again, but he took it on board because he thought I was right. He wasn't going to challenge me over it, and it was a simple instruction: 'Move.' That's what he did, and full credit to him. He might say that I helped him but I reckon it was his parents. He's got such great respect for his parents and I love that, so between us all, there was a decision to make, he made that decision and that was a turning point for Swanny.

Never underestimate him. When we first got him there was a knock on his kicking, he was a double-handed dropper, he waddled like a duck, he picked and chose when he ran, but what I loved about him was his work. You're a coach and you look up and you see your half-back flanker have a shot for goal on the run from the 10-metre square, and you think, *Wow, this kid's defended well and his offensive play is outstanding. His ability to work is extraordinary.*

Halfway through 2007 we were going nowhere but we nearly kept Geelong out of a grand final. I'd been watching the ice hockey and I couldn't believe how they exploded when they came on, so there was an ultimatum to David Buttifant and Guy McKenna as assistant coach to artificially elevate our interchanges. Our training had to change; everything changed because some players were to come off and some were not.

Scott Pendlebury was about nine minutes on, 90 seconds off, Swanny was about six-and-a-half on, 90 seconds off, and it actually destroyed the opposition's ability to tag them or run with them. But it wasn't about me being comfortable with it; the most important thing was they had to feel comfortable. Swanny gobbled it up, we knew that he could absolutely burst, and the really important thing for him is that he's not selfish. There's a tendency for players who are on for a set time, if they don't get the footy they don't want to come off, but he knew that the whole system would be out if he didn't come off. He's very team conscious and that's an underestimation of people about Dane Swan – he really had his team and his mates at heart, very much so.

He's in the top echelon of people I coached, no doubt. We've had a very good relationship, a strong coach–player relationship. Outside of that, he's got his life and I've got mine, and the age difference is big. It's not like he's fatherless; he's bonded to his family so you don't try to be anything else to him, but sometimes the chemistry is there. I've always said that with some, they're the player and you're just the coach. But with others, there's a bit more of a connection, and he is one of those.

5

RAT PACK

'Awesome to see Allen Iverson in the hall of fame.
The only person (apart from dad) I ever wanted
to be or admired when I was growing up.'

—@swandane 5 April 2016

Allen Iverson is my sporting hero. He has retired from the NBA now, of course, but in 2004, he was at the height of his career with Philadelphia 76ers in the best basketball league in the world, he had been the most valuable player in the league, leading scorer and an All-Star. He also came from the wrong side of the tracks, so to speak.

I identified with Iverson, which requires an explanation. Even before Allen Iverson became a superstar in the NBA he had found trouble with the law. In 1993, he and a few friends were involved in a fight at a bowling alley in his home town, Hampton, Virginia, in the United States. The row was split along white and black lines, and there was an allegation that Iverson, then 17 years old and a well-known high-school ball player, hit a woman in the head with a chair. Four black men including Iverson were arrested despite protesting their innocence.

Iverson went to jail for four months but the conviction was later overturned on appeal for insufficient evidence, and it became the subject of a documentary film called *No Crossover: The Trial of Allen Iverson*. He reflected upon his time behind bars: 'Going to jail, someone sees something weak in you, they'll exploit it. I never showed any weakness. I just kept going strong until I came out.'

Iverson was drafted No. 1 to Philadelphia and won the league MVP in 2001, but he had trouble fitting into the tight structure of professional sport, which is where the famous *practice* press conference came about, a little piece of theatre that has a million looks on YouTube and even has its own Wikipedia page:

> We're sitting in here, and I'm supposed to be the franchise player, and we in here talking about practice. I mean, listen, we're talking about practice, not a game, not a game, not a game, we talking about practice. Not a game. Not the game that I go out there and die for and play every game like it's my last. Not the game, but we're talking about practice, man. I mean, how silly is that? … And we talking about practice.

In 2004, right around the time that I was finding my problems with the law, he was benched by coach Chris Ford for a period, and he came up with this gem:

> I don't know any franchise players that come off the bench. I don't know any Olympian that comes off the bench. I don't know any All-Star that comes off the bench. I don't know any former MVP that comes off the bench. I don't know any three-time scoring champion that comes off the bench. I don't know any first team All-NBA [player] that comes off the bench. Why Allen Iverson?

My point is, this is how I saw myself as a footballer, in that I wanted to do it my way. Not so much that I was a smart-arse or full of myself at all, but Iverson was one of the first big-name sportsmen to have lots of tattoos and to show them, proudly. He had his way, and I loved his attitude; I still do. For instance, I hated practice, but loved playing; I saw him as an example of how finding your own way could work in a professional environment.

It was the boys from the Rat Pack who saved me, finding a way for me in 2004. Of course, they were not officially known as the Rat Pack back then – that nickname would come later – but they were a tight-knit group of guys within the Collingwood footy club already, even before the name was attached, and they put a comforting arm around me. Ben Johnson was there, and Chris Tarrant, Rhyce and Heath Shaw, Ben Kinnear, Alan Didak, Heath Scotland (before he was traded to Carlton), Andrew Dimattina. There were no set rules for entry, although the truth is that most of us had a rap sheet of some sort, or an incident that had made the front pages of the newspapers somewhere along the line. People came and went, too, as changes were made in the club, with the likes of Dale Thomas and Sharrod Wellingham coming in later.

Those guys were the first to get around me when I had my troubles. Looking back, they had something in common with me: they were the guys who had fun, they would take the piss a bit more, have a laugh, and they were my kind of guys, for sure. They worked hard, and they were all great players, but they liked to muck around a bit; they were serious when they needed to be, but not for every waking minute of the day or week. It was a certain mindset, and that is what I related to. That is what I was drawn to, because that's how I am.

Out of all those guys, Benny Johnson and Tazza were the ones who turned me around the most. Over the years, a lot of preconceived notions and negative connotations came out of Collingwood about the Rat Pack, but my experience was that we cared about each other as mates. Yes, we might have gone out drinking and we all had our little rap sheets, but it was more than that. We were buddies.

Benny and Taz grabbed me after the big meeting in early 2004 and Johnno said, 'Every pre-season, you're running with me.' Everyone at Collingwood knew that Ben was one of the hardest trainers in the club, so that would be a tough ask. He said, 'When you can't keep up, try to hold on.' I hated doing the running with him, and I can remember him yelling at me, 'Keep up, bitch! Don't be a bitch, just hurry up!' Johnno taught me what work ethic was about.

As for Taz, he took ownership of my previously non-existent weights program because Ben was the same as me; he despised weights and only did what he had to do. I hated lifting weights, but Taz was a monster in the weight room, and I lifted with him as much as I could. He was a big strong boy and I could not match him, but at least I was in the gym and working.

Previously I might have done 25 minutes; now I would be there for an hour or even 90 minutes. It was the hardest three months of my life, that pre-season, and I was cooked. I would go home and sleep all day, eat, then come back to the club and cop my punishment all over again. Both Taz and Johnno loved boxing, too, and I started to spar a lot, drawing a lot of aerobic fitness from that. We would do three rounds and by the end, you could hardly hold your hands up, you were so tired. It was great training, and we were not trying to kill each other, either, which is what slowly turned the key for me.

I had dodged the biggest bullet of all time and my training standards improved. I didn't have a choice, because Johnno and Taz were forcing me, and the funny thing about that is, if they had gone too far I would have told them to piss off. If it was someone that I did not connect with, if it was someone like Nathan Buckley or Scott Burns or a player or coach who I was not super close with, it might never have happened. But I toed the line because I loved those guys.

It takes all kinds in footy, and I do not think there is a right way or a wrong way to prepare and play. I reckon that if I had tried to prepare like Bucks, or like Scott Pendlebury today, I might have lasted five or six years and then been burned out, totally fried, because my style has always been that I like to sit around with ten mates and drink until five in the morning sometimes, just to let some steam off. I don't mind talking about footy to my mates away from the game, but it is just about relaxing, and really, I would rather find out about their footy or their life than talk about mine. I want to sit there and talk rubbish and get to a point where I am not wound up like a spring. I have always been good at forgetting about my footy outside the club; I want to go home, have a glass of wine and chill. I was never a person to be brooding: 'Shit, that kick I missed yesterday', or 'I'll have 50 kicks to make up for it', or 'Jeez I need to walk in the water, I'm feeling sore.' My style is different: 'I'll be right by game day, I'm going out with my friends to have a great time.'

For me it was about having a work–life balance, which a lot of people talk about nowadays. Except that the *balance* part for me was not about hitting golf balls, or fishing, like some other guys, and I was never the kind of professional athlete who might spend his time walking in water, reading a book or getting massaged. My enjoyment came from a few beers with friends, and it always has.

A guy like Bucks could never operate like that. He was a perfectionist and a great player, no doubt, and when I first met him when we started playing together at Collingwood, I hardly spoke to him. We were okay, but it was just that I did not deserve too much attention because I was flying in the face of what those older guys were trying to achieve, aiming for premierships, trying to get the best out of themselves.

Prior to 2004, I couldn't even care about winning or losing. I was selfish, I must admit, and when I was out of the side I would almost *hope* that we lost, so that I could come back into the team. I don't think it's unusual for a young player to be like that, but looking back, I wasn't giving anything to the group. It was all about me, and I am sure none of the senior players – Bucks, Scott Burns, Paul Licuria, James Clement – would have had any time for me in the first couple of years. They probably would have been saying, 'Who's this idiot? He's just come in and he's doing nothing.' They might not even have known my name, but I didn't deserve their respect, and I was doing nothing to try to earn it.

Bucks was at his best around this time as club captain. He had won the Norm Smith Medal in 2002 when Brisbane pipped the Pies in the grand final, and had won six Copeland Trophies to the end of the 2003 season, as well as the Brownlow Medal in that year. He was a dominant figure around the club, and I remember him and Johnno having rows at training, because he would call for the ball even when he was out of position, and Johnno would yell out, 'Get him off the track, he's ruining the drills! Stop hoggin' it!'

But people gave him the football – I had done it with my first-ever kick in an AFL game – because he demanded it, and he drew the football because he was so good. He had changed from the earlier days of his playing career, when he had picked up the nickname 'Figjam' (translated as Fuck I'm Good Just Ask Me), and he grew as a leader around the club, realising that it could not be all about him, and that he needed to bring people along with him. Above all, he had an enormous desire to win and he loved footy, and he wanted to win a premiership after reaching the big one in 2002 and 2003 but having it ripped away from him by the Lions.

So 2004 was about change for me. It was not like I transformed my lifestyle or sought out sainthood, but I did stop drinking on the night before games, and I had started to make friends within the club rather than only outside. Mick used to call my non-footy friends 'your scaly mates', and he was anxious for me to stay away from them. As much as Collingwood wanted me to leave my old friends behind, I could never do that, but at the footy club I hung out with the Rat Pack guys, and also with their mates. When we went out, Johnno brought his friends, Taz brought his along and I brought mine, and we all merged together into a bunch.

One thing that I hate is when people say bad things about my friends or put out negative ideas about them. I guess the footy club thought that the problems I had with the law were *their* fault, but I knew that I was just as much to blame for what happened, because I probably encouraged them to go out. I mean, they had to work Mondays, but I only had to go to recovery. I could go out on Wednesday night until late because I had Thursdays off, and I would force them to go out because I had the money. I think I have the best mates in the world, like everyone probably does, and I would not be the same person without them. I love them, they keep me grounded, I go away on holidays with them all the time.

I don't want this book to sound like all I wanted to do was drink, but I need to make the point that the culture was different in 2004. It was not so much frowned upon for a footballer to have a beer, and the attention was nowhere near as suffocating as it is today. There was no social media, hardly anyone with cameras in their phones, and as a player, you could get away with a lot more. If you behaved like that now, even if you were innocent, a photograph would be snapped, you would be on Instagram and Twitter, and it would go viral.

Inside the club, Johnno and Taz were becoming close mates of mine, and I was seeing first-hand what it was like to be an AFL player. We went out after footy every weekend, and all day Sundays. Taz was a superstar of the game at the time, and everyone loved him; he was just about Collingwood's biggest rockstar, and I hung with him a lot. There was never any lining up at a nightclub, and it would be straight in for quite a few freebie drinks, too. These guys were huge in Melbourne, you have to remember, and it was Collingwood, the biggest club in footy.

I was making my way, and this was my first look at celebrity, for lack of a better word, the high-profile football life, and I absolutely loved it. A few years later, the *Herald Sun* published a story about what it dubbed the Rat Pack, which offered up a lot of negativity about what we were doing and the impact it had on Collingwood. And there we were, depicted with our heads superimposed onto rats' bodies for the illustration that accompanied the story.

But we embraced it. We were a bunch of mates (and yes, we were rats) who cared about each other, and we are still friends. In the end, we ran with the idea, and at least we stood for something. We stood for each other, we played hard, partied hard, and we played for Collingwood. The way we saw it, the Rat Pack was a positive.

It was a tough year for the club in 2004, but I played 13 senior games in my third year on the list, roughly half-and-half between Willy and Collingwood. I was lucky, in a way, because the Collingwood run had ended after the losing grand finals of 2002 and 2003, and Mick Malthouse was looking for new blood. Some of the guys who had been part of those two grand final teams were moved on, and I was probably gifted games that I didn't deserve, because coaches tend to pick youth until they know whether they can play.

Even the mighty Brisbane Lions, winners of the previous three premierships, had fallen to Port Adelaide on grand final day, reaching the conclusion of their surge. We finished outside the finals, and I played various positions when I was in the senior team; I had certainly not graduated to the midfield group headed by Bucks, Paul Licuria, Scott Burns and company.

Often I played in the back pocket and I started to find a bit of the football – 20 disposals against Port Adelaide in round 6, 21 the following week against Carlton and 22 in the last game of the season, also against Carlton. And I played my first Anzac Day blockbuster against Essendon.

I had kind of graduated from the Williamstown days, and I knew that of all those players drafted in my year, 2001, I was nowhere near the most skilled, the fittest, or the hardest worker. Seventy per cent of the guys would have been better athletes than me. I had started my career quite slowly; by comparison, Chris Judd won the Brownlow Medal in 2004 having been drafted at the same time as me.

But a lot of guys who were picked up never made it, for whatever reason. In my case, I knew by the end of my third year that I could find the ball, and I knew that I could win the footy in a one-on-one situation, no matter what level that I played at. I had issues with using it, but that was a work in progress.

If he had known me at all, Allen Iverson might just have been proud of me.

6

MAKING IT

'People say to me, "What if he was a total professional, like Luke Ball or someone who did everything right? How good could he be?" I always say, "Maybe he'd be really bad."'

—Nick Maxwell, Collingwood premiership captain

There is a saying in footy that you need to go backwards to move forward, and Collingwood had that down pat. We finished thirteenth in 2004 and we were dreadful in 2005, winning just five games and ending up second last, with only the archenemy Carlton below us. The Blues were still suffering the after-effects of the salary cap scandal that had engulfed them a few years earlier, but at Collingwood, Mick Malthouse was rebuilding the list.

At the end of 2005, we picked up Dale Thomas with the No. 2 pick and Scott Pendlebury with selection five, while Travis Cloke had been taken as a father–son pick at the end of 2004 to play centre half-forward, and running defender Harry O'Brien (later to be known as Heritier Lumumba) was a rookie-lister early in 2005.

All the pieces began to fall into place, including our first trip to Arizona for altitude training in 2005 under conditioning guru David Buttifant, who was a believer in that form of training. Eddie McGuire had Collingwood firing off the field, with revenue tripling to $45 million and regular profits of $2 million plus.

The club even made a big-money pitch – ultimately unsuccessful – to recruit Jonathan Brown from Brisbane Lions. Browny has since said that he met with Mick Malthouse and was close to making the move because the Lions had gone into decline, and he wanted to play in another flag. But he stayed put, remaining a one-club player.

I started to feel like I belonged in AFL football, playing 13 senior games in 2004 and 14 games in 2005, mostly in the backline and sometimes as a tagger. That downturn for the club was helpful to me, because it gave me a chance to play at senior level, I had improved my off-field behaviour (not before time) and Mick was promoting youth. For whatever reason, he saw a player in me.

My first 40 or so games were as a back-pocket player, because Malthouse liked my one-on-one ability, but I had a few goals kicked on me. I can recall Adem Yze from Melbourne and Paul Medhurst from Fremantle (who later became a teammate) giving me some nightmares in those years, and in particular Yze's five goals on me in the Queen's Birthday game in 2005 was a defining moment. Mick called me out after the defeat, and I cried in the rooms afterwards. It was a big stage, 65,000 people at the MCG and I was badly beaten, and it was probably the first time I ever had tears welling up over a game of footy.

To this day, a lot of people seem to doubt my care factor for football but it is a myth. Of course I care! I would never have lasted as long as I did without actually giving a toss about it. In my experience, there is nothing worse than arriving at the club on a Monday after a defeat, those moments when everyone is treading on eggshells, no one is game enough to tell a joke and the fun disappears from the game. As a player, you have to watch tape in the coaches' review and you look terrible. When you are flying, as we would be a few years later, the season seems to take about two weeks, and your life is good, but when you lose, you are smacked around in the media and you can be grumpy at home.

It is true that I never lived and breathed footy as such, and when a game was over, I tried to move on. I didn't get angry about it, or stew about it, and that is how I function in everyday life as well, not mulling over things. Yes, it is disappointing to lose a game of footy, but what is the point of dragging yourself around over losing a game? Treat it as a game as much as possible: that was my motto.

I would barely watch the highlights of other games on the television news, and over the years, I watched less and less of my own tapes. I always felt there were more important things in life, although you would not have known it that afternoon at the MCG in 2005 when I was reduced to tears.

I had never played in the backline before Mick tried me there in 2004 and 2005, but as a new player, you will do anything to get a game, and you are hardly about to complain or stamp your feet. Plus, footy was different then, and you did not need to be an elite kick to play in the back half, like you do now, with your quarterback-type players, a guy like Luke Hodge playing at half-back for Hawthorn.

There was no requirement to pierce through a zone, or anything like that, and in fact, teams were flooding numbers back into their own defence so, if you played in the backline, you had plenty of time to get cheap kicks and move the football. Kicking has never been my strong suit anyway, but I got by.

We lost the last eight consecutive games of the 2005 season and there was a big football department review ordered by

Eddie. I had made some ground that year, but one incident left me with a sour taste, as it probably did the club. We played a Friday night game against Essendon in round 16 and I went out drinking with a teammate and friend, Julian Rowe, at Q Bar in Prahran after the game, staying out to about 4 am.

We had a rehab session the next morning and we stayed at Rowey's house in Prahran, setting the alarm so that we could get down to the club later in the morning, but when I woke up it was already after 10 am and I could hear his alarm blaring. When I ran into his room, it was right next to his head, but he was still sound asleep, and when I checked my own phone, there were stacks of missed calls from the footy club. I said, 'We're in deep shit here!' Which we were, of course.

There was a supporters' breakfast that morning, and we missed that, making the crime worse. We raced down to the club, and I remember hurling myself into the pool and saying to him, 'Just get into the water.' As if that was about to save us. We had not even had time for a shower or brushed our teeth; just jumped straight in the car. All the other players were at the breakfast, and then a relative of one of the big supporters saw us in the pool, and reported it back.

We were both dropped the next weekend. I went back to Williamstown, had 40 touches, and came straight back into the seniors to complete the year, but Rowey only played one more senior game. He was delisted at the end of the season, and I have always felt a sense of guilt about that, because I contributed to it.

• • •

There was a watershed coming for me. In 2006, I made the senior team for a round 1 game for the first time. Previously I had never been in the team from the start of a season – in 2005 I didn't play until round 8. In the game against Adelaide at the Docklands I had a career-high 34 disposals playing out of the backline. Later on I'd see that I extracted my first Brownlow Medal vote from that season-opener against the Crows. I recall that I was leading the AFL in marks after round 2 with 26, there were so many cheap possessions available in that style of play.

Playing seniors from the start had been a goal, and I kept the momentum running. In round 2, Sam Mitchell was giving us trouble against Hawthorn, and I went into the middle to play on him for a while. In round 3, I had 22 disposals and two goals against North Melbourne, and I was starting to play some regular footy in the middle. I had to play on man, but my philosophy was that if I had the ball, the other guy didn't. When I found myself about to be tackled, I handballed with my left; I found that split second of difference helped me in tight.

I felt more comfortable than ever that year, and we were pushing up the ladder, winning eight of our first ten games. As a player, there is a moment when you stop looking over your shoulder and start playing, and 2006 was the season for me. But my credits were not so strong, and I did cop one spray from Malthouse when we played the Lions in round 10. My hamstring had been tight in the lead-up, but I did not want to give up my place in the side, and I thought that I could play. Then in the first quarter I remember saying to Benny Johnson, 'My hammy doesn't feel right.'

I will never forget laying down on the ground at quarter time, and Mick breathing fire at me: 'You fucking wouldn't want to have brought that into the game.' I said, 'No, no I didn't.' But later, I admitted my mistake, and fortunately Bucks saved us in that game, kicking six goals as a forward at 33 years of age. I missed two weeks of footy, the only games that I missed that year.

The Rat Pack had its issues that year, with Ben Johnson and Chris Tarrant involved in a fight over a taxi in Port Melbourne. Taz was the first to get involved and Benny, who came to support him when the fight broke out, ended up getting charged with assault, although the charges were later moved to a Magistrate's Court diversion program. They were both fined $5000 by the club, although Collingwood chose not to suspend them, and Malthouse made a statement that would be quoted quite a bit in the coming years: 'The fact that Chris and Ben are crucial to the on-field success of Collingwood has influenced my decision. Had they been youngsters on the fringe of selection, I might have thought a playing ban was in order.'

That was Mick's style. He did not believe in punishing the rest of the team and the whole club because of one or two people's misdemeanours. Having said that, there was an aftermath. Taz would be traded to Fremantle at the end of that season, a little chunk of the Rat Pack that was removed, and Greg Swann was obviously talking about my group when he said to the media:

We don't expect all of our players to be monks, and there's a group – I'm sure there are at every club – who enjoy getting out and being a bit more social than others. We just have to make sure that's done within the confines of … common sense, that they're not out late at night when, invariably, I think, that's when the trouble starts. We take all these issues very seriously. We've worked very hard to get our club and our brand to the level it is. These things don't help us.

I played my first final in that 2006 season, an elimination final against Western Bulldogs at the MCG, in what was Collingwood's first finals appearance since 2003. It was the game when my teammate Brodie Holland came off the line to flatten Brett Montgomery of the Dogs, copping a six-week suspension, the harshest for a couple of years. I remember Mick saying to us, 'Watch out for Montgomery, he'll pick off the mids', and Brodie made sure he did not. We lost and I had a quiet game: 14 touches and no goals, one of the disappointing games you put into the recesses of your memory, somehow.

But it was a positive year, overall. I averaged 24 disposals, by far my best, finished sixth in the Copeland Trophy voting and polled 11 votes in the Brownlow Medal, enough to earn the description 'one of the surprise packets of 2006' in the annual *AFL Season Guide.* I started to kick a few goals; I had 26 touches and four goals against Geelong, then 29 and three goals against the Bulldogs in a purple patch in rounds 8 and 9, getting five Brownlow votes in two games.

The ball-winning ability that I had was coming to the fore by 2006, when I had four 30-plus possession games. I was always aware of my statistics up to a point, and trust me, players keep track of them even if they do not like to admit it. You certainly know when you've had none! I didn't count them in my head like kids might do, but I certainly had an idea, at least until I hit the 25 mark or so. You have a feel for whether you are playing well.

By now I was earning nearly $300,000 a year and life was pretty good. It had never occurred to me that I might earn that kind of coin. I'd paid my parents back for the house that I was living in, and bought a BMW for myself, starting a trend that I have followed ever since. I invested money later in businesses, but overall I was keen to have a good time, not to just park my money away in the bank. The way I looked at it, while I had the chance of living a good lifestyle I might as well live it. I make no apology for spending $30,000 on a watch, or going out on the weekends to nice restaurants.

After all, who knows what will happen in five years? My theory was: pay the mortgage off, then have a good time. I had a nice car, I liked to travel, I bought some property, even though if I had been as frugal as some people I know, then I might have more to show for it. The idea was to have a good time.

· · ·

The 2007 season was Mick Malthouse's last year of contract at Collingwood, and his timing, as ever, was immaculate. Collingwood had a terrific season on the back of the rebuild that had been done, and we were not too far from reaching a grand final.

Geelong was pretty much unbeatable in that season under Mark 'Bomber' Thompson's coaching, playing a spectacular, hard-running game style, but we were highly competitive, finishing sixth with a 13–9 record, then quickly knocking Sydney out in an elimination final. Against West Coast in the semi-finals, we played a draw at Subiaco and then beat them by 19 points after we played five minutes each way of extra time, and I had 38 disposals and kicked two goals, including one right near the end of extra time.

That was an awesome game. I recall myself, Pendles and Leon Davis going into the middle late in the game and the message coming out: 'No one else but these three blokes in the middle!' When the siren went to end the regular time, not everyone knew that there would be extra time, and I remember my teammate Guy Richards actually putting his hands up, thinking we had won. I ended up with 11 clearances and 20 contested possessions for the game, the most on the ground, and Pendles, in just his second year, was awesome too, with 26 disposals.

We loved to travel for our games, and that was a pattern that repeated over the next few years for the Pies. We were close, and we would go in there with a job to do and try to get it done, that was the mindset. I roomed with Johnno, and it was fun, and being booed by the crowd did not worry us. It actually spurred us on, because we knew that if you did not barrack for Collingwood, you hated us. Mick liked that us-against-them idea, too. So we would be thinking, *This is all we have, this is all we've got. We have to rely on each other.*

The win in Perth put us into a preliminary final against Geelong, with Port Adelaide and North Melbourne in the other preliminary final, and we were thinking the same as everyone else: whoever wins our prelim wins the flag!

Geelong was an amazing team, having lost only four times during the home-and-away games, and had won its first final against the Eagles, so we would be underdogs. They would slingshot the footy from half-back, straight down the middle, and they scored heavily if you did not put clamps on them.

Geelong probably thought they would roll right through us, but we almost pulled a rabbit out of the hat at the MCG in what people said was one of the great preliminary finals. It was close throughout, and the final margin was five points the Cats' way, and when the siren went we had a stoppage about 45 metres out from goal. It always makes you wonder, *What if?* Because if we had got over Geelong that night, we surely would have won the flag that year.

In the end Geelong beat Port Adelaide by a record margin in the grand final, deservedly so, and to get so close to toppling them in a prelim was frustrating. Especially for Bucks, who had finished the game on the bench having ripped his hamstring in what turned out to be his last-ever game after 15 seasons, 280 games and half a dozen Copeland Trophies. Our 35-year-old skipper had managed just five games for the season, his body letting him down. He would not have been able to play even if we had we sneaked through to the grand final.

We knew that we were not meant to win that preliminary final, and really, it was a remarkable effort to get so close against the great team of that era. Deep down, we were probably planning for a big Friday night and a good weekend, because we knew exactly how good Geelong was, but it is amazing how well you can play without too much pressure. In that game we had Scott Pendlebury at just 19, Marty

Clarke also 19, Dale Thomas, Trav Cloke, Tyson Goldsack and Harry O'Brien at only 20, all good young players with big futures at the club. Travis won his first Copeland that year, and Pendles was runner-up, which was pretty remarkable for a pair of guys who were so young.

I was 23 and it was the closest I had been to the Big Dance. I had enjoyed my most consistent season, and had 25 disposals in the last final as well as finishing fourth in the Copeland Trophy, my highest finish to that point. But there was one last act for the year, and that involved the Brownlow Medal count, where a certain Spiderman threatened to win.

I was not invited to the count and the glitzy function at Crown, but as it happened I was leading near the halfway mark with 11 votes through round 10, then polled another three-voter in round 13 so that I was in the mix with Jimmy Bartel from Geelong, Simon Black from Brisbane Lions and Sam Mitchell from Hawthorn. At this point I had been enjoying the Mad Monday celebrations at a pub, dressed in a Spiderman suit, and then headed back to Alan Didak's house in Kew to get changed and go out again. People were showering and changing and the Brownlow was just background noise on the television as I soared to the top of the leaderboard.

That's when my phone started ringing. The footy club wanted me to get ready to go into Crown, and my manager, Liam Pickering, asked the same. He said, 'You'll have to go in!' To which I said, 'No way, they didn't invite me anyway. Bad luck, it's not my fault.' The count continued, we had already headed out, and fortunately for all concerned, Bartel ran over the top of everyone to win the medal.

I finished with 20 votes, tied sixth in the game's most famous individual award even though the footy club and the AFL obviously did not think I had any chance whatsoever. It was a bit of a laugh but in another way, it was the first time that I'd attracted much notice in my on-field footy career. I was now on the radar, as they say.

Even teammates were starting to recognise me and give feedback, and I can remember at least two – James Clement and Scott Burns – giving me a pump-up in that season. Clement said, 'You can be anything you want to be, just pull your head in a bit. You're great one-on-one, just get everything right off the field, because if you're more disciplined it'll happen for you.' Burnsy told me that if I changed my ways a little more, I could 'be what Bucks has been to this club'.

This resonated with me. I figured that I must be doing something right if my teammates were talking like that to me, especially the senior guys who I did not have much to do with. They had their families, and away from the footy club I wouldn't speak to them much, but I respected them within the four walls for what they had done. They were legends of Collingwood. It was certainly something to ponder.

EDDIE McGUIRE

Collingwood president since 1998

We have a family connection, Swanny and I. His grandfather and my dad were good mates in Broady, they were straight out of Glasgow, basically. All the Scots in Broady knew each other; we all lived around the corner from each other. His aunty was my fill-in teacher at school one time. She introduced herself as Miss Swan, and I said, 'You're no relation to Billy Swan are you?' And she said, 'He's my brother'. So we became good friends.

I always laughed when I watched Swanny walking and running because he reminded me of a Glaswegian with that rolling gait, where you keep your chin tucked in, just in case something was coming around the corner! He always had that swagger about him.

He doesn't know that in 2003 when he almost got the flick, there was a lot of good cop/bad cop involved. We decided to go hard, and I went hard in particular because I didn't want him to think that I would stick up for him just because I was from Broady too. Mick Malthouse was in strong and Greg Swann was in strong, and we made it seem a lot tougher than it probably was. We had decided to scare him to straighten him out. Fortunately, it worked.

I've always had a great relationship with him. We looked after each other, I've given him a couple of tongue-lashings, and to be honest, it's probably a bit of a Glaswegian conversation that we've had, 'the hairdryer' as Sir Alex Ferguson called it. It'd be, 'Pull your head in. You're going down a dangerous path'. Our respective fathers and grandfathers were not shrinking violets, so you could actually have a frank conversation and know it wouldn't go any further. We thought the world of him, and he was the sort of bloke who if he knew he was wrong, he would cop his whack and move on.

As a lot of footballers find out, there are plenty of people who are pulling your coat, not necessarily taking you down the right road. That's why when you have people around footy clubs who genuinely care, the message can come tougher than in other areas of life and the sentiment is 100 per cent right.

To me, Swanny is one of the all-time greats. In my mind, he is one of the greatest players in the history of Collingwood, right up there with Nathan Buckley and Bob Rose and a couple of others. For straight-out achievements he is in the top echelon with a Brownlow Medal, three Copeland Trophies plus a few other top-two finishes, plus he is a premiership player. And he probably should have won a couple of other Brownlows.

But more to the point, people don't realise just how tough he was with the injuries that he carried and the way he gave himself for his teammates. I'd happily have 22 Dane Swans run out to play for me every week, because you wouldn't lose too many.

He's a craftsman, Swanny, and he thinks about his game. His father was a really good player, his uncle Roy Ramsay played senior football, and all his uncles and relatives were not only legends in the Broadmeadows area, they could handle themselves as well. Swanny didn't need to be taught the side-by-side ethos that we had at Collingwood because he lived and breathed that already.

He was an old-style footballer. He played for the jumper. Every week he went out and there were no excuses and he played hard football, but he was also skilled. He might not have looked as silky as a Robert Flower but he never wanted to be Robert Flower. He got the football all the time, he kicked goals, he was a good mark.

It was not as if he was a dour battler who willed himself over the line. Dane Swan could really play football.

He's an absolute champion of the game, a champion bloke and I just loved him as a true Collingwood style of guy: hard, didn't make excuses, honest and hard for his teammates, loved the supporters, loved the club, played great footy and delivered week-in, week-out. When he kicked that goal in the 2010 Grand Final replay and he jumped up in the air, I just knew how much it meant to him and how much it meant to all of us.

What he hid, that people didn't always appreciate – and I was lucky enough to see it first-hand – was that he had total pride in his performance. While he might have let people think he was a bit nonchalant, he knew what he had to do to get himself right to play. There's a debate to be had – I'm thinking about the swimmers at the Olympics – that the people in sport who have a more relaxed approach to life seem to get the job done as opposed to the ones who are highly strung.

In one of the most successful periods in our club's history, he has been the best player in the club. He and Scott Pendlebury – completely different blokes and different players – have been a wonderful foil to each other. The fact that they have dominated the Copeland Trophy for seven years basically shows their resilience and their respect for each other.

The thing I love about Swanny is that he takes people at face value, and he's been a wonderful character in the game without even *trying* to be a character. It was his own character that came through, and aside from that, he's just a wonderful player.

7

BUILDING AGAIN

'He's been brilliant in this era, but in the 1990s when there was no social media, he might have been an even better player. Training wasn't as intense, the Sunday sessions were all part of it, and everyone was doing it. He would've been perfectly suited to that era.'

—Liam Pickering, manager

Those words from Scott Burns and James Clement were ringing in my ears, and by 2008 I was playing some of the most consistent footy of my career. I was on a guaranteed contract by then and I had the confidence to relax and play. Mick Malthouse wound me up and away I went, week after week, and as a coach he had strategies and plans, but he let me play within that structure. He didn't overcomplicate the game, which is the way I like it.

With Mick, if you flew for a big hanger of a mark on the opposition goal line, that would be okay, but you had better take it, or if you tried to kick a freakish goal from a tight angle, the same applied: 'Make sure you kick it or you deal with me.' We knew our boundaries at Collingwood under Malthouse.

Off the field, I was in a good place. I had met Taylor Wilson, my partner, on the night of the 2007 preliminary final defeat by Geelong, and we clicked. Taylor comes from New York City; she had graduated from university and then flown to Australia for a holiday. By complete coincidence, she had been at the MCG that day. She had been talking to the guy next to her on the plane, and asked what she should do to experience Australia when she got there. 'Go to the footy,' he said, and the preliminary final was the first time she did that.

By chance, we met that night at Baroq bar in the city. We had lost the game and our season was done; she was with some friends having a drink, and I dropped in to collect a couple of mates and take them out. They had told me that they would go their own way and leave me to commiserate with my Collingwood teammates that night. 'It's your deal,' they said. But I said, 'Well, I'll come and get you then.' Taylor happened to be in that very bar, and a friend of mine who was in her group introduced us.

We have been together ever since, although the timing – the night of our season ending – was not necessarily ideal. It was a Friday night game, we hung out for a while, and I remember her saying, 'What are you doing Saturday?'

I knew exactly what I was doing: 'Going to the pub.'

She said, 'What about Sunday?'

My reply: 'Going to the pub!'

Then, of course, there was Mad Monday as well, followed by a planned trip to Las Vegas with some mates. I think that she thought I might have been an alcoholic, not being familiar with the usual end-of-season ritual that AFL footballers have.

But we found our way, and after she flew back to America we kept in contact, and it was a whirlwind. Pretty soon, around January 2008, she told me that she would come back to Australia permanently, and we have been living together since then. Taylor is a great person and it was another sliding doors thing for me, going to that bar when I did not need to in September 2007. It's one preliminary final that I might have been happy to lose, with hindsight.

Setting up our life together was relatively easy for me, to be honest. I was not the one who was giving up my life at home, and I just stayed put while she packed up her life. Taylor works harder than I ever will in her job; she has an incredible work ethic, cannot sit still and she goes above and beyond with anything that she does. Taylor settled me down a little, I think, because all of a sudden I had someone else to consider in everything that I did with my life outside football. I played my best footy in the year after we got together and I don't think that just happened by chance. God knows what would have happened to me without Taylor coming along.

I was still not perfect, of course, in terms of the off-field behaviour at Collingwood. I think that as my career moved on I found ways not to get caught! Plus as I improved as a player, the club would give me a bit more room, because it was a different culture back then and nobody thought it was a crime for a footballer to go out and have a few beers. Soon enough clubs were bringing in rules such as drinking bans when they had a six-day break, that kind of thing, or bans on alcohol when a player was recovering from injury, and sports science started to take over. Needless to say, it was not my idea of fun.

There were a few dramas in early August that year with Heath Shaw and Alan Didak, two Rat Pack life members, suspended by the club over an incident in which Shawy drove home from the Geebung Polo Club in Hawthorn after a few drinks and crashed into two cars. Heath was charged with drink-driving, but the issue didn't stop there. He covered for Dids, who had been with him.

Shaw told the club that Alan Didak wasn't there; Didak had one or two previous indiscretions, and when Eddie McGuire defended him in the media, saying 'he'll be accused of the

Kennedy shooting next', it made our president look silly when it came out later that Didak was, in fact, with Shaw on the night.

Being Collingwood, it quickly became front-page news and talkback radio went crazy. Nathan Buckley had retired and was working in the media that year, and he didn't hold back either, saying on 3AW:

> For those players to be out from a football perspective six days before a game, when they have had an eight-day break is just unacceptable and then to top it off by being dishonest to the people in an environment where you rely on honesty and you rely on trust is unforgivable.

Everyone weighed in with an opinion. Tony Shaw, the Collingwood legend, said he had been trying to tell McGuire for several years that the club had a cultural issue with poor off-field behaviour. He said on 3AW:

> The club's just trying to make an example and they haven't set the scene prior to this – Eddie will tell you I've rung him a number of times about different players doing different things off the field for nearly four to five years and I think that the protectionism that Eddie's trying to give the club to save their image in fact is detrimental to the very thing that you try to build and that's the culture.

It was August and Dids and Heater were suspended for the remainder of the season, which took away some of our momentum over those last four rounds. It was probably the beginning of a new era in footy and for Collingwood, too, with the media speculation and interest soaring, and clubs under more pressure than ever to crack down on what their players were doing off the field.

We had a decent year in 2008, but a loss to Fremantle in round 22 hurt us badly. We slipped from fifth to eighth on the ladder, which meant we had to run with sudden-death in the finals. We beat Adelaide in the first final, where I remember Nick Maxwell tagging Scott Thompson, for a different look, but the Saints ended up knocking us out of the finals in the second week. It was a disappointing finish considering we had gone a week further into the finals series in 2007.

I went to the Copeland Trophy count thinking that I was a chance for the best and fairest after a consistent season, and Ben Johnson told me halfway through that he thought I would win. I was nervous, because it meant something to me. I had Mum and Dad on the table at Crown, and they were rapt when I won – Dad had always said that I kept getting better as a player year by year, and it was true. Overall it was a huge thrill for a No. 58 draft pick out of the suburbs who was not even any kind of star as a junior, a virtual nobody. And my consolation prize for our poor finals series was to win the club's award for best player in the finals.

• • •

There was a big changing of the guard at the end of 2008. James Clement retired and went home to Perth for family reasons, and Scott Burns, who had spent the 2008 season as captain, retired as well. Against that, some of the young players we had brought in over the previous few seasons were becoming stars of the competition, and there was a lot of optimism as we headed into 2009.

I was voted into the leadership group for the first time, an honour that I certainly hadn't sought but I felt that I should accept, at least in the beginning. Back then, it was about the best players being in the leadership group. You were a leader, whether you wanted to be or not. I was happy to try anything once, although it turned out that I never felt comfortable in that role.

Nick Maxwell took over the captaincy, and he was the right guy. Mick loved him and he had been groomed for the job while Burnsy held the position for a year in 2008. I rated Maxy highly, both as a player and a captain, we became good friends, and he was an outstanding captain of Collingwood footy club.

To this day I can't understand that people pot Maxy in any shape or form. Was he Collingwood's best-ever player? No, he was not. But he went All Australian and he was the best captain that I played under. The only other captain I played under at Collingwood for an extended period was Bucks, and to be fair, maybe I haven't given him sufficient credit because under his watch I was young and stupid.

But in my prime, it was Maxy who held the reins. I had become the club's best player, my profile was higher and he went out of his way to make sure everyone was happy. He would say, 'Don't worry, I will do this for you.' He was the face of the group, he made sure that you knew where you stood, and he led on and off the field. He was an awesome captain and he got criticised a lot, but not internally, and he is as well respected inside the walls of that footy club as anyone in my time, ever.

Maxy was as hard as he needed to be. For instance, you would see him and Heath screaming at each other on the field, and in the newspapers people would write that there was something wrong with this. But outsiders didn't understand how the dynamic worked. Those two guys left it out on the field; they were not at each other afterwards. When the arguments and arm waving happened on the field, it came from a place of wanting to win.

Heath is a pointer and an instructor even now that he is with Greater Western Sydney, an organiser on the field, and so is Maxy, and that's what we needed at Collingwood, some organisation and marshalling down the back. Maxy would yell out, 'Swanny, go right!' because he could see what was unfolding from the back half of the field, and I would respond.

I won the Copeland for the second time in 2009, and we went all the way to the preliminary final only to fall to Geelong, again. The Cats probably cost us two flags, but they were so good it's hard to argue with that result. We had lost the qualifying final to St Kilda, which had finished on top of the ladder under Ross Lyon, then beat Adelaide at the MCG on a dodgy free kick to Jack Anthony, who kicked a goal from nearly 50 metres out after the siren to win it. Ultimately Geelong smashed us by 72 on its way to another flag, so there was still a gap that we needed to bridge.

My numbers went up again, and I was approaching the peak of my career, averaging more than 30 touches a game.

I had 48 disposals in round 10 against Port Adelaide, which was the highest count for a decade and the third-highest ever recorded. As a general rule, I always wanted to get to 30, which meant that I needed to get seven or eight a quarter, and that is how I approached it.

In my last couple of years, the numbers did not bother me so much. Of course everyone wants to play well, and I certainly did, and every footballer wants to be best on ground every week. I wanted to have big numbers and if I didn't, I would be upset with myself, especially if we lost. It might not have seemed like it, but I had a big competitive streak; I hated playing badly, I wanted to play well every week.

Having said that, I could let it go when we lost or I played poorly. The first night or the next day in match review I would be annoyed but overall I was pretty good at leaving it alone, worrying about the next one. My mantra was to focus on what I could control, and there is no point a footballer thinking back to that ball he could have spoiled or that contest he could have won. It's in the past. You cannot change it afterwards.

I was a consistent player, and that was something I aimed for. Especially once I got to regular senior footy, I had the belief that I could play well every week, but I was never naive enough to think that I could play well in every single game. Look at any good player, and they will have a bad day occasionally; even the basketball phenomenon Michael Jordan had bad days, and he was a freak of nature. In our game, it can come down to the unpredictable bounce of a ball, and that's just how it is, so I tried to make the gap between my best and my worst as small as possible.

If I wasn't getting a lot of the football, I would try to go forward and kick a goal, or go back behind the ball and mop up and help the defenders out, so there was always a way to contribute. If I was being tagged and struggling to make a big impact, I might go and sit in front of someone like Nick Riewoldt to cut off his leads, or try to create a seven-man forward line because I knew the bloke who was on me would not necessarily go for the ball, just disrupt their forward line, block up space for them. There was always a way to help the side, even if I was not getting my 35 touches.

I was an All Australian for the first time that year, 2009, and runner-up to Gary Ablett in the AFL Players' Association's Leigh Matthews Trophy for the most valuable player. The All Australian selectors slipped me into a half-forward flank position, which was amusing given that I was playing on-ball full-time by then, but I was happy to be wherever they wanted me since it is not picked as a real team to play anyone in particular. Plus, there were some pretty decent midfielders who deserved their positions ahead of me, guys like Chris Judd, Gary Ablett Jr, Lenny Hayes and Joel Selwood.

As an All Australian I had to get used to the idea that taggers would come to me in this period, and often they would turn their back on the play and focus on me, rather than the ball. Cameron Ling from Geelong was the one I had most trouble with, because he was a great player, too strong for me to push off the football at stoppages, and he had a lot of discipline and concentration. Playing against Ling, I had to hit the contest at the right moment, try to get the footy on the fly, but it was tough. Clint Jones from

St Kilda played on me a bit, Brady Rawlings from North Melbourne, Robert Shirley from Adelaide and Ryan Crowley from Fremantle, and they were all difficult to shake off, so much so that I hated it initially.

The rules didn't allow me to do what Diesel Williams did in a previous era, and belt them if they held on to me! But as time went on I started to change my mindset, and I took tagging as a compliment. It was there, they were planning to stop me, so they must have rated me a bit. It was a challenge for me to overcome. I would think, *Let's show them why they rate me.*

Sometimes it made life too tough and I had to accept that my influence would be limited, so I might go to Pendles and run a block for his opponent, or tell Scott Burns, 'Wherever I start, hit it there, and I'll get it out of there.' I love the big numbers as much as anyone, but if I was struggling against a tagger at times I had to think, *I'll do something for the team.*

•   •   •

Interchange and rotations were a big changing point around this time, and Collingwood led the transformation. It came from David Buttifant, our fitness and conditioning man, around 2008 and 2009 and he gave specific advice to me. Butters and I got along well, and he sat me down and told me the story behind increased rotations.

The idea was to keep yourself fresher while you were on the ground. Everyone looks at different sports and how they handle themselves, and in this case Butters and Mick Malthouse had studied ice hockey, how explosive the players were when they came off the bench. They had seen the way that I played and they could see that my strength was to play in bursts, rather than grinding over a period of time.

They told me that they wanted me to come off the ground more, take a quick rest then explode with my running when I came back on the ground, and to repeat that process. They asked me if I was okay with this, saying, 'This is what we think is best for the club. Trust us that you'll get the best out of yourself.'

Of course, back then every footballer wanted to stay out on the ground the whole time, or as much as possible, so this was breaking the mould to some extent. I was no different; I wanted to play. But I trusted Butters and Mick and the sports science staff that it would be best for us, and it definitely helped me, as it turned out. I was never the greatest endurance runner, but the strength I had was speed and power, and I could hold that level for longer if I took a short break, then took off again.

It was about being on the ground for six or seven minutes at a time, and going flat-out in that time, rather than the old way, which was to go steadily but for longer. Secondly, the idea was that I came off just before the fatigue really kicked in. They would say, 'If you've been on three big runs and you have only been on the ground for three or four minutes, get off and rest before you max out, take a rest before the lactic acid comes.'

Lactic acid build-up is extremely common in athletes, especially in power-running sports. It happens when there is not enough oxygen available to burn the lactic acid in your body, causing an aching in your muscles. Our idea was to get off the ground before the lactic build-up came, walk around the boundary to take in some oxygen, then go back on the ground and burst-run again. It was seven minutes on, say 90 seconds off, then go again, and they wanted me to find that place just beneath the threshold of heavy fatigue, and to address it.

Butters and Mick wanted me to lead the change, because I was the main midfielder at the time given that Scott Pendlebury was still growing into his role, and I always liked to think that I listened to the coaches when it came to the game. Sure, I have moved outside the rules when it comes to off-field behaviour, but within the rules of the team and the game, I think I have been selfless and easy enough to manage. I took this on, so did everyone else, and it worked for us.

The increased rotations were across the board, and while Collingwood certainly led, we were not the only team trying it. From 80.3 rotations per team per game in 2008, the AFL figure jumped above 90 in 2009, and then to 117.4 in 2010, and Collingwood's numbers were even higher than the average, sometimes up around 140 a game.

I could see that it would work for me, because late in games I could still feel that I had my running power, enough to run direct opponents and taggers off their legs. As I have said, I was never the best endurance runner but I could surge when other guys couldn't go, and this really helped me when I was trying to break a tag. Plus, when you came off the ground for those breaks – about twice a quarter – the tagging opponent needed to decide whether to coordinate with you and spend his own time on the bench, catching a breath, or keep going. That was another way to break a tag, even if only for a few minutes.

A lot of games I started on the bench, and I would come into the game at about the three- or four-minute mark, with a little of the heat gone from the contest, and I would burst-run straight away. I would do about seven minutes of that; I worked out that seven was around my optimum time on the field, and for two years I was close to the most rotated player in the league, coming out of the game up to 12 times. The GPS figures would show me running, say, 12 kilometres in a game, whereas Steele Sidebottom might run 15, but mine would be in bursts.

In the end, I might play 90 minutes of the 120, so I was still playing most of the time, but I played at a higher level of intensity because I would have had a drink, walked the boundary, shifted some of the lactic acid and then gone again. Unlike earlier, it was not left to, say, three midfielders plodding away all day, it would be half a dozen of us going at 100 per cent for most of the game, and Collingwood ran over the top of teams who could not match that. We would play four, five, six different guys in there and keep them fresh with rotations. Nowadays it would be eight, or even ten going through the middle, but only because of what we did back around 2009–2010.

To coordinate it, our midfielders would come off in batches at the three-minute mark, the five-minute mark, and the seven-minute mark. It didn't matter if you felt like you were playing great footy, you came off the ground because you knew that there was a guy waiting on the bench who was well rested and ready to go. You had to be selfless for this to work.

There was no room for anyone staying on the field just because he was playing well, or remaining out on the ground because he hadn't touched the footy. It was about fatigue and it was about the team, and it was viewed as selfish if you did otherwise. A lot of the media and some of the public hated the fact that guys would run off to the interchange bench straight after they kicked a goal, but it was necessary to keep it coordinated. But I remember a day when Alan Didak had one of his amazing bursts, kicking three goals in about a minute of game time against West Coast and the coaching staff told him to stay on the field, he was so hot at the time!

Butters and I just clicked. He is a good bloke, and while he was making me do stuff that I didn't necessarily want to do sometimes, he had a way about him. Credit to Buttifant for those changes to rotations, because it changed AFL footy and everyone else followed. So much has changed; when I played my first few senior games I started on the bench and would only come on to the ground for about eight minutes in a quarter, and sometimes I would sit on the bench all day unless a teammate was hurt. Buttifant was great for me. He had a way to push my buttons, and he understood everyone's strengths and weaknesses in running. For me it was about speed, agility and power; he and Mick trained it up for us and it was important for us over those couple of years.

Mick Malthouse's game style was well known and well drilled. While Geelong liked to slingshot the ball up the middle out of defence, Mick hated corridor turnovers, so we went around the boundary from the back half, generally speaking. I can remember Travis Varcoe coming into our team when Geelong traded him to us at the end of 2014 and at training, he would ping the ball up the middle and everyone would be saying, 'Whoa, what's that about?' It was so obvious that it was the opposite to what we did over that period.

Mick Malthouse thought mistakes made in the middle of the ground were a recipe for easy goals to the opposition, so we had to go carefully, not slowly, but we had to be calculated in the way we shifted the football. At worst, we were happy to turn it over 55 metres down the wing, or get it out of bounds and start again because in Mick's teams, we always had hard, strong, contested players around the ball.

He had another philosophy related to which goals belonged to who. Traditionally in Australian football (as opposed to soccer, or the rugby codes), you attacked or kicked toward what you considered to be *your* goals and tried to stop the opposition from bombarding *their* goals at the opposite end. Mick's belief was the polar opposite of that thinking. He argued that we attacked *their* goals and *defended* ours – that's what passed on to us. So if Collingwood kicked a goal, it would be invading the goals of the opposition, rather than vice versa. The forward half of the ground, was *their* half. He often talked about that. It's only a mindset but it was important to how we played footy.

Tactically, the game was changing quickly, especially in 2009 when Ross Lyon, as coach of St Kilda, introduced the forward press to footy, a clustered zone of players that pushed forward and tried to lock the ball in, the opposite of the flooding back that was prevalent in the mid-2000s and even before that. It came into play, for instance, when the opposition was kicking out from a behind, or the opposition had the football deep in defence. Presses were commonplace in basketball and other sports, and their arrival in Australian footy was significant. It certainly worked for St Kilda in that season, because the Saints jumped up to finish on top of the ladder, threatened Geelong and ultimately fell just short on grand final day.

Zones had been in place in the AFL for a few years, like Clarko's Cluster that Hawthorn used in 2008, which was a rolling zone that moved across the ground defending space rather than a man. We had seen teams put zones in big numbers behind the ball to close down your ball movement, flooding the defensive 50-metre zone with numbers and clogging it up, but really, what Lyon and St Kilda did was totally different, and new.

As a tactic, it was designed to counter the Geelong style that had been so successful, winning premierships for the Cats in 2007 and 2009. It worked, too, which meant everyone – including Collingwood – was about to copy it.

MAJOR BRENDAN NOTTLE

Salvation Army city coordinator and

Collingwood Football Club chaplain

The first contact I had with Dane came about after the situation that occurred near Federation Square in 2003, and he had been given 100 hours of community service by the court. I was the chaplain at Collingwood, and he was really good in the sense that he didn't have to be pushed or prodded to do the work. He always turned up early, he had a great attitude, and his sense of humour was there. It's one of the things that the people on the streets of Melbourne really appreciated.

So we went out in a van together, handing out meals and blankets to people, trying to connect with people and get them off the streets and into accommodation. He connected with people, no question. It was at the start of his career but they knew who he was. He had this relaxed demeanour and he was very approachable, which was something they appreciated.

At Collingwood we started a program called the Magpie Nest, a housing project, and we have about 35 houses now taking about 120 people off the streets at night, and Swanny went out to one of the houses last year, cooked a barbecue. He was the same Swanny who was out with me in the van more than 10 years earlier. He has this ability to help people to forget about the terrible situation that they're in, they're able to come out of that and enjoy themselves for the time that they're with him.

He often gives me a call and says 'I've got some clothes I want to give you.' I turn up in the van and he's giving us brand new high-end fashion. We got a flat screen TV at one stage. It's not for big-noting purposes, because no one else knows he does this. It happens very quietly, and that's another indication of the depth of the guy.

Dane has come down to the city to serve meals and we have a youth bus that goes out every week, a double-decker bus that we park outside St Paul's Cathedral. A lot of players who we've had down there would hide behind the barbecue, cook some food but not really engage; Dane climbed on the bus, sat down and took over one of the Xbox computer game consoles we've got and started having competitions with the people on the bus.

He's a really interesting character, because he comes across as laid-back, he comes across as laconic, but at the same time I actually think there's a real depth to him and a significant level of intelligence to him as well, which people often miss. He reads people and situations really well, and when you listen to the throwaway lines and the humour, I think that's come from a deep place, and a very thoughtful place. There's a lot more to Swanny than the tatts.

He's the stand-out player that the fans love. Even non-Collingwood fans talk about him as well. I think there's something in him that reminds people of the almost stereotypical Australian larrikin. He's non-conformist in the way he looks, non-conformist in the way he plays football and the way he trains, but there is a real depth about him and a sharp intelligence about him that people warm to.

8

THE BOX

'He loved winning, he loved the challenge and
underneath it, he is a very proud person.'

—Mick Malthouse

St Kilda called it a forward press. Neil Craig called it frontal pressure when he was coaching Adelaide. I heard one player describe it as being like pushing someone off a cliff, gradually forcing them to the brink until they tumbled off (or in footy terms, gave up the ball). At Collingwood, we called it the Roman box, or if we were feeling lazy, just 'the box'. Mick Malthouse turned up in 2010 with this method, taught us, and it turned out to suit our playing list to a tee.

The forward press was a defensive system, pure and simple, aimed at extracting the football back from the opposition. In Collingwood's press, the last bloke in the formation was meant to be no more than 80 metres from the football, wherever it was on the ground, or put another way, we liked to have the farthest player a kick-and-a-half from the ball when it was in the opposition's hands. When we were in our zone, we guarded an area, rather than a man, and we harangued the opposition as they shifted the football, closed up the space and drove them insane.

We did not advertise it or talk about it much but it was our little secret for 2010, and it was brilliant. Combined with fierce tackling and pressure, an extreme physical intimidation factor, it forced the opposition to cough the ball up as they came out of defence, allowed us to lock the ball in and score easy goals from close range.

Mick said much later that he had read about it while studying the methods of Erwin Rommel, the German World War II military leader, relating to frontal assaults on the enemy. Rommel had copied it from the Romans much earlier, which is the way of the world, in that we took what St Kilda showed us and went up to another level.

Mick's description came later, after we had used it successfully in 2010:

> The Roman Legion, which was in a box formation, [was] very
> hard to penetrate and there's always someone to step up. So
> that box can get smaller and smaller, but you've still got heavy
> fighting capabilities all the way through it, which we pushed
> in front of our opponents all the time for the last two years
> and it's come about.

By the end of 2010 we all knew that it was so successful that other clubs would try to imitate it. To this day, teams are pressing forward manically in footy, such is the change from the flooding back of the 1990s and 2000s, but the copying didn't happen quickly enough for the other teams to stop us in 2010.

The press was the first significant thing that happened at the start of 2010. There had been changes of personnel too, with the club trading to bring in ruckman Darren Jolly from Sydney and tough-as-nails midfielder Luke Ball had been drafted after he fell out with St Kilda. These were huge moves for us and they worked a treat. Without those two guys, we probably wouldn't have won the premiership in 2010. We'd never had a dominant ruckman in my time at the club, and Jolly was a big, physical ruckman who worked in conjunction with Leigh Brown that year. Brown was a workhorse and a competitor who virtually reinvented the ruck-forward role that would become popular around that time.

I had played junior football against Ball, and I knew exactly how good he was, so it was nice to have him join our midfield group. We had some class in that area, and he added another layer. He was hard around the footy and he would feed the ball outside to Pendles and myself, and with Jolly being able to compete at the stoppages, for the first time Collingwood did not need to be so defensive with our set-ups.

The other significant thing that happened was that Maxy, in his second year as captain of Collingwood, challenged us to go all the way. And he meant it. As a group, we had played in preliminary finals in 2007 and 2009 without advancing to a grand final, and right from the start of 2010 our skipper laid it on us, publicly stating that our goal should be to win the premiership. It is unusual in our game to be so out there with predictions or statements, and he was crucified for saying it in the media, and was called 'cocky'. But I was in the leadership group at Collingwood that year, we had talked about it beforehand, and I can remember his reasoning for coming out like that: 'At Collingwood, we're the biggest club and we expect to be challenging for premierships more often than not.'

The notion was to just come out and put it on the agenda; we'd done the hard yards, played finals four years in a row.

It was like, 'We're young but we have the talent and the work ethic to do this.' We thought that we were finally ready. From day one of pre-season in 2010, everything was geared toward winning the flag, and no one shied away from it.

Both Jolly and Ball were leaders too and had a lot to say. Bally coined a phrase that year: 'Every decision you make, ask yourself is it taking you closer to a premiership or further away?' That is what we lived by. Thinking back to 2010, it was different to 2007 and 2009, when we were in the premiership mix, because this time we *knew* that we were actually ready. We felt like we just had to take what was ours, whereas in 2007 and 2009 we were up against a Geelong team that was too good for us.

Nathan Buckley had returned to the coaching staff as one of Mick's assistants under the succession plan that Eddie McGuire had pieced together and announced in 2009, after spending two years in the media ranks. Bucks was to act as a line coach in 2010 and 2011 before Mick, who had suffered some health issues, was to hand over in 2012. He didn't coach me directly, but I could see he'd changed; he couldn't have stayed the way he was as a player. The gap had to widen from being best mates to being a coach. Apart from that, he showed himself to be meticulous as a coach, very dedicated, a perfectionist.

The change caused some headlines at the time it was announced, and from Eddie's point of view it headed off moves by a couple of other clubs to hire Bucks as head coach. But the reality from a player's point of view was that the transition seemed so far off that it barely raised a ripple around the club.

We were focussed on the present, and Collingwood won 17 games that regular season and drew another, finishing half a game clear on top ahead of Geelong, the Cats having yet another great year. We extracted so many easy scores as a result of the press that we averaged better than 15 goals a game, second only to Geelong, and way up on the season before; our defensive system was good too, so that we were the second-best defensive team behind St Kilda. Of the main ways to score in AFL footy, turnovers were clearly number one by this time, and we were capitalising on that.

Getting us to adapt to the Roman box was typical of the way Mick Malthouse coached, because he was flexible when it counted most – he could see if there was a need to change. Playing in any sort of zone really flew in the face of what he loved, which was man-on-man mortal combat, because in a zone you are minding space rather than an opposing player.

So it was not necessarily his thing, because he felt that in finals the games tended to revert into man-on-man football. Finals would be tighter, more contested, and if you could not beat your man, you were going nowhere. But trends emerged, this was one worth considering, and we responded. We *hunted* down the opposition, it was aggressive and it was relentless and they cracked, one by one. Even Geelong, in round 19, couldn't handle it. We intimidated teams, and it felt great to have that over them.

We were physically aggressive and even to this day, the pressure that we put on teams with our tackling probably harks back to that time. That year, 2010, was where we probably started it and created what Collingwood became known for. We all bought into it, too, even our outside players like Steele Sidebottom and Alan Didak and other guys – they were involved as much as anyone else. I always say there's no point tackling when you've got the footy, but I must admit, even I laid a few tackles!

Early in the season we beat Melbourne by a point when Heath Shaw knocked a ball away on the goal line, but we lost to St Kilda in round 3 when the Saints shut us down and kept us to only four goals. We lost to Geelong in round 9 too, but we smashed Carlton, and in round 16 we belted St Kilda, clearly one of our main rivals, by 48 points, a game in which I had 36 disposals and a goal.

The second half of the season passed so quickly, because when you are winning in footy, and playing at a massive club like Collingwood, it's never dull. There is no middle ground with the Magpies, and we loved it because the highs were *so* high. The Rat Pack played hard and partied hard. We loved each other's company and it was as tight a group as I've been involved with. Obviously not everyone went out together but usually there would be a big bunch of us. The Rat Pack was at its peak, doing pretty much what we wanted. These were nice times to be a Magpie, put it that way!

We were clear on top by more than a game, even though we lost the last game of the regular season to Hawthorn. Out of ten games away from home we won seven and drew one, showing that we had the ability to travel, and in the first final against Western Bulldogs, we won easily. I had a good game with 39 disposals and three goals, and that win put us into the preliminary final against Geelong at the MCG.

It was a memorable night, that one, because Geelong had caused us plenty of pain in the previous few years, but the ledger had swung around, big-time. We had the Cats covered now, and in the first quarter we played the best 30 minutes of footy that we had played to that point, smashing them seven goals to one to set up the win, like it was a training drill. We owned that half of the ground and they could not shift the football; it was as though the famous Cats' method, the Geelong Highway some called it, had hit a roadblock.

We ended up getting them by 41 points, and our ferocity was such that they could not get the ball past halfway most of the time. I had 33 disposals and two goals, and everyone filled their pockets; we had a dozen goalkickers, which was another part of our method that year, to spread the load.

That was the game that I remember the famous *Coll-ing-woo-ood* chant starting up, and it was an awesome feeling to be out on the ground and hearing that. Of course the club had done a great job in building our membership to record levels, and it was around this time the 'Side by Side' campaign was running, borrowing a line from the theme song. The Magpies' fans were up and about, to say the least.

I always appreciated that the Collingwood fans liked me and backed me. No matter how I was playing they seemed to warm to me, and so many times I have thought, *If I leave or I get sacked, they'll cut their memberships up!* I wouldn't expect them to do that, but I must admit I have read stuff like that on social media, and the first thing that I always heard when I ran out was the fans. I owe them a great deal.

Collingwood had not won a premiership since 1990, under Leigh Matthews, but we all knew that this was our best chance. Guys like Ben Reid, who had enjoyed a great year at centre half-back, and Harry O'Brien, who was All

Australian along with myself (for the second season in a row) and Alan Didak, who was at his best at this time, we were all at our peak.

But we had other guys who just stood up that year, like Steele Sidebottom, who was still a teenager but who stepped in and played brilliant footy, and Brent Macaffer, who was a tackling machine up forward, and Tyson Goldsack, who could play forward or back. Dale Thomas was so electrifying off a wing that Ross Lyon suggested he could be the best player in the AFL, and Scott Pendlebury had already developed into the smooth-running midfielder that we all knew he could be; Pendles also was All Australian in 2010.

The promotion of youth meant that quite a few of our older players, guys who had been there through the difficult years, were pushed aside, but Mick made those calls. It was tough – the likes of Tarkyn Lockyer and Josh Fraser had been the cornerstone of the club – but everyone wanted to win a premiership. And when the time came and they missed out, they were heartbroken but they never let it show. They had every right to complain but we never heard a peep.

St Kilda would be our opponent in the grand final, after the Saints blew away Western Bulldogs in the other preliminary final by 24 points. It was their second year in a row in the grand final and they had the advantage of carrying the pain of a near miss in 2009, when Geelong beat them by under two goals in a cracker grand final. Under Ross Lyon they had that suffocating shutdown style of play that kept teams to ten goals a game or less, and the Bulldogs had only managed eight in the preliminary final.

We were about to experience what it's all about.

LIAM PICKERING

Manager

He has never changed, right through the years. He's been very loyal to me, and I've changed companies a couple of times and he's been with me 100 percent. He's extremely loyal and you can see that with his family and friends. He's loyal to a fault, to be honest.

In 2003 he was basically sacked and his father, Bill, and I went into the club after the Federation Square incident. The initial police report came out with all these charges, most of which were dropped, but Eugene Arocca was Collingwood's lawyer at the time, and my understanding is that his recommendation to the football department at the time was to sack him, based on the charges.

We looked at the vision of the incident and it showed Dane had minimal – and I am talking *very* minimal – involvement. The main fight had finished by the time he got there. He'd taken off and done what the other boys should've done, which is run.

I think the board's perspective was 'This guy's got to go', but once we got the CCTV, we said, 'Where's his influence?' He was lumped into a group charge but he had nothing much to do with it. He'd been loyal to his mates, which I admire, but that incident's cost him a lot of money. I'd hate to think how much. Fortunately it's finished now.

From a management perspective people find this hard to believe, but of all the blokes I've managed - and we've had to deal with some issues - he's the most reliable. If he says he's going to do something, I don't have to follow him up. He'll do it. He doesn't let me down in that regard. He says that he couldn't survive if he was starting footy now, but I don't believe that for a minute. I think he'd adapt, guys like Swanny would adapt to anything.

Obviously Swanny's a great footballer but the interest in him comes from the initial bit of trouble which was that fight, then loading up with the arm-sleeve tattoos which he was the first to get, and then people have got to know him. I often say this, but there are very few players who opposition supporters like, but Dane's done that, he's so knockabout and what-you-see-is-what-you-get, he's achieved that. There are very few people in footy who are universally loved like Swanny is.

There's a fascination in him as a bit of a scallywag but there's also the fact that he's a great footballer to go with it. He's been a remarkable footballer. He hates the weight room but he's strong. It's like Gary Ablett, get them around the footy, and you can't move them. He never falls over and he's quick, and when I say quick, it's power out of the contest. That's why he's been such a great player.

9

OPPORTUNITY

'Of course he marched the beat of his own
drum, always, more so off the ground than on it,
but I always liked the fact that he was an individual.
And whatever he was doing, it worked.'

—Eddie McGuire

Grand final week was a new experience for me, and for most of our players, and it was crazy-hectic, starting with Brownlow Medal night. I had played my best season so far, touching the ball at least 30 times a game and kicking a few goals, and as it happened, I was the shortest priced Brownlow favourite in history. All the media awards had gone my way and I was hopeful, but there was the grand final to think about, too.

I had polled quite well in previous Brownlows – 12 votes in each of the previous two seasons, and 20 in 2007 – which may have influenced the odds makers. I tried not to think about it too much, but footy is such a big deal in Melbourne that it was impossible, because everywhere I went, my mates and other random people would say, 'You've won the Brownlow', or 'You're a moral.'

And when you come down to it, players might tell the world that they are not fussed about the Brownlow, but then there is the downtime, sitting on the couch, and you start thinking, *I could win the Brownlow? Me!* Who would have thought, back when I was a scrubber in my first couple of years, I could possibly win the medal?

Collingwood asked me on the day of the count if I had written anything down in case I needed to speak, and I told them that I hadn't, so they gave me a list of sponsors to mention, should the votes fall my way. I was not about to write a speech, because to me that would have been a bit premature, and it's not my style. When Taylor and I arrived at Crown there seemed to be a thousand cameras trained on us.

Then a woman from Channel Seven came up to me about an hour before the actual counting started, and said, 'Dane, all the five favourites are going to walk up onto the stage as the telecast begins.' The idea was something like this: Will Dane Swan win it? Or will Jimmy Bartel win it? That was the tone of what she was telling me would be said, and she also indicated that everyone else who was supposed to be in the mix had agreed. I was the red-hot favourite and I didn't want to look like an arrogant idiot by saying no, or like I was too cool for everyone else, so I thought that I'd better get up with the others. That was the plan.

The Brownlow is a full-on dinner with about 1000 people there and all the eating is done before the count, which usually starts just after 8.30 for TV purposes. Close to that time, someone from the broadcaster will warn everyone that the live television coverage is about to start, and everyone has to shut up. So with about a minute remaining to the start of the broadcast, the woman from Channel Seven grabbed me and said, 'Everyone else has pulled out, it's just you.'

It was not the news I wanted to hear, and I snapped back, 'You're kidding aren't you?' Before I knew it, they had pushed me up on the stage, and they presented me on my own. I am not easily embarrassed, but right then, I was very uncomfortable to be up there as though I was the only player who had a chance of winning. I could actually hear people in the front row seats saying, 'What's he doing up there?'

It was a fair question, too, and it was a certainty from that instant that I would not win the Brownlow Medal. That was the moment that told me it was not my turn.

As the count got underway, I kept looking down at these cards that they hand out on all the tables with all the games listed, round by round, and little flames beside your name if you played a blinder. I had about 15 games with a fire next to me, but there were nowhere near that many where I actually polled votes. But I had an even better idea that it was not my night when the round 6 votes were read out, the game against Carlton when we won by 53 points.

Judd got the three votes in that game for his 37 possessions, and I got two votes for my 31 touches and a goal. The next day, there was a lot of commentary around the votes that Judd was given for that game in such a big defeat. It is the old debate about whether votes – in particular the three-votes – should go to someone on the losing team. But in my opinion, you cannot take the voting away from the umpires because it has been with them forever, and in any case, there are not too many people who won a Brownlow and you think, *He doesn't deserve it.*

It is awkward, Brownlow night, especially if you are playing in a grand final a few days later, and in my experience, the only players who enjoy it are the players, coaches and staff from the club whose player wins on the night. I couldn't have a drink, and I was first nervous, and then bored.

So while I polled 24 votes, in the end Juddy blew us all away. He had an amazing run of five three-votes in a row from rounds 4 to 8 inclusive and ended up with eight best-on-ground and 30 votes to win his second Brownlow, adding to the one he had from 2004 in his West Coast Eagles days. Gary Ablett finished second and, of our players, Pendles was the other guy who did well, finishing fourth.

I didn't care about it one bit, and actually, Chris Judd is a champion player, one of the best couple that I ever played against, a much better player than I ever was. He deserved his medal; he had missed the first three games in that season and still polled enough votes to win, which is a hell of an effort. I went in carrying expectations that were put on me by other people, and I was glad to get out of there and focus on the grand final.

I played footy for team success and it is a no-brainer that I would hand back the individual awards for a premiership. The Brownlow was never a big deal for me, even though you want to win. Of course you do. You go to the count after a good year and you're thinking, *Why can't it be me?* Then you move on.

It was a heavy week, that one. I won the AFL Coaches Association Champion Player of the Year award the next night, and then the big one, the AFL Players' Association's most valuable player award, the following night, which gave me the full set with the exception of the Brownlow. To me, the MVP probably means more than the Brownlow, because it is recognition from your peers.

Of course, the Brownlow is the most famous, and it stays with the winner forever, the tag of 'Brownlow medallist'. But peer recognition is important for a player, because every year you go into the opening round thinking, *Have I still got it?* You know that footy will not go on forever, and you have seen people lose it.

People say that players do not watch enough footy to be the judges of an award like the MVP, but we are not stupid, we understand the game at its heart, and we mostly get it right when it comes to awards. Show me someone who did not deserve the MVP. So to win the Leigh Matthews Trophy in 2010, that was one of the first times that I sat back and thought that I truly belonged at quite a high level.

• • •

The 2010 Grand Final was the culmination of ten years of hard work for Collingwood, a slow build to the big climax, and while I think that we always knew we would win, it came so close to being a complete disaster. We had played St Kilda twice in that season, splitting the games, but we felt like we were better than the Saints, really better than anyone, smashing quite a lot of teams.

So beyond the Brownlow night it was back to training on Tuesday of grand final week, and the boys quickly acknowledged my failure to win the medal, despite being the favourite. They were saying stuff like, 'You were stiff', but it was never my Brownlow to lose, frankly, and we played touch footy down at St Kilda beach to get the cobwebs out, and it was quickly forgotten. There were 10,000 people at the last training session on the Wednesday at Gosch's Paddock, to show how excited the people were, we had Thursday off, and then the grand final parade through the city on Friday after training.

All through that finals series there had been so many people at our open training sessions that we needed high barriers so that we could get from the Westpac Centre down to the ground without being hassled too much. On the day of the parade there had to be a million people in the city, and most of them were wearing black-and-white, just a sea of people. I went in the back of a car with Ben Johnson, and it was an awesome feeling, the first time I had ever done that. I remember Nick Riewoldt and Maxy being interviewed up in front of Parliament House, and the crowd drowning out the Saints' captain with the *Coll-ing-woo-ood* chant, which was amazing, if a little disrespectful.

I was feeling quite relaxed, even though it was an exciting time, and I remember having my regular Friday-night-before-the-game dinner of chicken risotto, and watching a few of the television shows relating to the footy. I was at home at my new place in the inner-east of Melbourne with Taylor, and we saw a bit of the grand final marathon before hitting the sack. Not even I was venturing out the night before a grand final; nights out on game eve had stopped for me around my second year!

I was never one to get overly nervous. I think what I felt was more anxious to get out and play, because you tend to play the game in your mind, even when you are in bed, but I am a good sleeper, and I slept well that night.

Tickets were scarce, ridiculously so, and I had to sneak a couple of mates into the MCG for the grand final, which was a story in itself. The boys didn't have tickets; I think players were given a couple for free and then access to buy another four or so, but by the time you made sure your family were able to get into the game, it was difficult to help out any friends.

So when I arrived at the security gate in Brunton Avenue around noon, they had no idea that those two guys were in the boot of my car. I drove through, parked underneath the ground, popped the boot once we had stopped in the designated position near the dressing rooms, and they jumped out, undetected. I was a bit nervous about it, though, and I remember thinking, *If I get caught, I might end up in court over this.* But it was fine, and I was not the only player who did that on grand final day. I know a bloke who had bought one ticket, and had an elaborate plan where he entered the ground, then arranged to have a bunch of friends right outside the emergency exit. Then he hit the red button so that a few could sneak through! It was that kind of week, and they could have filled the MCG if there had been 200,000 seats, I reckon.

Simon Prestigiacomo's incredibly gutsy decision to step aside was a bit of a surprise, because he had trained up until Friday, but he knew in his own mind that he was not quite right, especially for the job of playing on a guy as good as Riewoldt. He told Mick that he didn't want to ruin our chances by breaking down on the day, and it was completely selfless, typical of Presti. I don't think I would have done that; in fact, I am sure that I would not have.

I would have played at 50 per cent fit. I consider myself a team man but in a grand final, with the ultimate prize staring at you, I would not have passed up a chance of a premiership medal, all of which shows that Presti is the *ultimate* team man, and I admire him for that. It was the same when he played; he would spoil the ball all day and he didn't need to get kicks. I think his pulling out of that 2010

Grand Final is as selfless an act as I have ever seen in footy, and we will never forget that.

I shook Presti's hand and said nothing; I had nothing profound to say on the day. It is sad, of course, to see a veteran player unable to take his place in the biggest game of all, but from the point of view of the rest of the players, we had to let it go, get on with the job and focus on the game. I just knew right then that Presti was a better man than me.

The warm-ups are a bit skewed on grand final day, because there is so much preamble to get through, and I remember going out on the ground for the first time in the casual clothes and all the boys were saying, 'Have a look around, soak it up, enjoy it, relax because next time we come out, it's on.' The idea is not to let the tension build too much, because there is so long to wait until the whistle blows.

I was never a rev-up type of guy before the game. I preferred to wander around and talk to my teammates about anything but the game, because my style was to switch on at the bounce of the ball, definitely not beforehand. So before the game, I would be chatting about what had been on the TV, what plans we had for the night, and I was no different that day, even though it was a grand final, my first as well.

Collingwood was the favourite, having finished on top of the ladder and then moving comfortably through the finals series, but we respected St Kilda with their heavy pressing and their zoning in defence. They put so much pressure on the ball that you would bang the ball out of your own defence, but Sam Fisher and Sam Gilbert would be sitting there to mark it.

They were extremely well coached by Ross Lyon and they were disciplined, hard to score against and difficult to move the ball against, and they had a few superstar players like Riewoldt and Lenny Hayes and Brendon Goddard who we needed to be mindful of. Riewoldt had kicked three goals in each of their two finals, and been important to both wins. I knew that Clint Jones, their tagger, would come to play on me, and possibly Farren Ray, too.

I had a tough day, not my best, although I laid a bunch of tackles. At one point I tried to break the tag by going to play on Goddard, who was having a huge game for the Saints, and that worked okay for a period. We were 24 points up at half-time and playing terrific footy, and I guess that we probably thought that we had it done, but of course, it is a grand final, and anything can happen, especially if you take your foot off the gas.

St Kilda came back at us, and we kicked 0.5 in the third quarter, a bout of poor conversion that really cost us, and the margin was only eight points at three-quarter time. They had forced a situation where the game was being played in their style, and we were not able to break the shackles, and Lenny Hayes had been outstanding through the middle, and Goddard, too.

Nineteen minutes into the last quarter Goddard climbed onto the back of Harry O'Brien in the goal mouth to take the mark of the grand final, converted with a kick from close range, and St Kilda was in front for the first time all day. Goddard ran back to the middle punching his chest, and for the first time in that game, I thought, *We are in big trouble here.* It was scary out there, and our backsides were twitching, for sure!

Soon afterwards Maxy took a huge intercept mark between half-back and wing on the Great Southern Stand side. He kicked it forward, Brent Macaffer dropped it to the top of the square, and there was a marking contest where Heath Shaw almost pulled it in. Chris Dawes grabbed the footy while he was actually sitting on his backside on the deck, cleverly handballed to Travis Cloke, who turned around and kicked the goal from right in front to put us back in the lead.

But the drama was only beginning. We were a point up, and time was running out when Lenny Hayes grabbed the footy at half-forward for St Kilda and kicked it around his body towards full-forward. And what happened next is really weird, because every time I see the footage on television – and we have all seen it a million times – I get a little knot in my stomach, a pang of anxiety I suppose it is, even though I know exactly what happens in the end.

My great mate Benny Johnson is at the contest with his opponent Stephen Milne, a guy who loves a goal, a really dangerous player. Johnno is in front but it bounces past the pair of them, leaving Milne goal side and potentially running on to the footy to kick the matchwinner for the Saints. If that ball bounces straight, we are most likely dead. I am back on the wing watching it, and it's all in slow motion, the way it unfolds.

Milne props as the Sherrin hits the turf, and then it bounces hard right in front of him and dribbles through for a behind to level the scores. Phew!

If Milne had kicked a goal there, the Saints would have been five points up. There were 90 seconds of playing time left, time enough for us to get another goal, but not *much* time against a team that could defend like St Kilda. No wonder I find it hard to watch that vision nowadays.

It was a remarkable last quarter, as hard as you would ever get playing footy. We could not force another score as the bodies flew into contests, and when the siren went, I was right there around the footy on the members' wing.

I swear, out in the middle of the MCG with 100,016 people in the house officially, plus the others who were smuggled in, you could have heard a pin drop, it was so surreal. No one knew what to say or do. A few guys ventured, 'This is crazy.'

We had played a draw with Melbourne that very year, but this was the strangest feeling, because going into a grand final, the last thing that enters your head is that you might have to come back again. Which is exactly what we were confronting. Collingwood 9.14 (68) to St Kilda 10.8 (68) was the scoreline, just the third draw in VFL–AFL grand final history and the first since North Melbourne and Collingwood could not be separated in 1977.

Interviewed on Channel Seven, Maxy stood up as skipper even though he was spent, and made a point about the fact we had to come back for a replay in a week:

Oh mate, I don't know if we've ever seen 44 blokes go to war like we just did then. That was amazing. It's probably going to take this for the AFL to change the rule because it's an absolute joke. There's no way it should be decided after another game. Blokes come in for a win or loss, and that's what we should be leaving with.

There was no getting around the fact that we were coming back in another week, and to make matters worse, we were told there had been a big sewerage leak in our dressing rooms, and we had to wait for quite a while, then make our way to the old rooms in the Great Southern Stand, where the AFL had quickly set up an area for us to shower and change.

One thing is for sure: that situation will never happen again, because the AFL has declared that in future drawn grand finals, there will be extra time played so that a result is reached. But right then and there on 25 September 2010, we were dazed and confused, as they say. We had no clue what to do next.

This is where Nick Maxwell was such an outstanding captain. As the players milled around in those awful, old, disused rooms trying to find our bags and figure the whole thing out, he walked around the group patting heads, and he said something profound: 'Boys, how awesome is it to get to play and win a grand final next week. What an opportunity.'

Until that very moment, I can assure you that no one was thinking like that. We were all dirty that we hadn't secured the result we wanted, and there was the logistical nightmare of the situation. For instance, I had bought three tables of ten people at the post-grand final function at Crown Palladium at $3500 a table, I had booked city hotel rooms and organised alcohol for what we hoped would be the celebration of another Collingwood flag. At that point, we didn't even know if the function would go ahead; we were exhausted, and we needed to recover so that we could prepare for the next instalment of the grand final against St Kilda.

I had also booked a flight the following Saturday to Los Angeles and Las Vegas for a holiday; instead, that's when we would be playing St Kilda for the premiership. Everyone was in the same boat.

An opportunity. I will never forget what Maxy said that afternoon, and it helped us to get back up. He spun it as though we had just won a preliminary final, and it worked, because while we had all been doing our fair share of complaining, now the group would start the process of getting back up again.

I have no idea how St Kilda handled it, but I do know that our function went ahead at Crown Palladium, and we were required to attend but didn't stay for long. Mick Malthouse had come into the rooms after the game and said, 'You've paid for your tickets, let's go, see your family and friends, and then we'll go back to the footy club.' It had been a big day for my mates, like any grand final, and they were all well-lubricated by the time I got there, but with another game to play, there was no point hanging around beyond Eddie McGuire making his speech, and repeating the idea that we had been trying to grasp. Eddie said, 'What great news. We're in a grand final.'

We had a recovery session at the footy club after dinner, and I was in bed early. As for my mates, they celebrated as though we had won the flag already! I was in bed by 10.30 that night, and they probably got to bed at 10.30 Monday night!

I have since been told that the St Kilda players did not attend their post-match function, deciding to go straight into preparation mode, which is fair enough. But at Collingwood, we took a positive mentality into it, or tried to find a beam of light. We were thinking, *Imagine if we'd lost, how we'd have been feeling by now.*

By Monday, we were up and about again. And I was not game enough to ask the coach if I could take the following Saturday off because I had a flight booked to the US! I guess I have done and said some cheeky things in my time, but even I knew that would have been pushing the envelope a fraction too far ...

10

PARTY PIES

'He's relaxed, funny, approachable. There's something about Dane that when people are around him, they actually feel better about themselves. I don't know how he does it.'

—Major Brendan Nottle, Salvation Army city coordinator and Collingwood FC chaplain

In the aftermath of the first grand final of 2010, we did some reflection and the general feeling at Collingwood was that we had played poorly, and dodged a bullet. We needed to refocus on what made us a good team, and try to execute it better against St Kilda in the replay. I think we knew that if we played *our* footy, we could win, but it was easier said than done, as the first grand final proved.

I probably reflected how we felt as a group, because I was disappointed with my first game, and I knew that I could do better. I had gathered the ball 21 times, had nine clearances and I tried hard, getting seven tackles against a hard tag by Clint Jones, who was fit and pretty much relentless, not allowing me anything easy. I had wanted so badly to have a huge impact, but I couldn't manage it, so I set myself for a big game in the replay.

The way we looked at the draw, it was as though we could not play any worse: 'Shit, look how badly we played, and we still drew. Look how many times we turned the ball over in the back half. Look at our conversion, so bad. Play one per cent better, even, and we win the game.'

We also knew that we were young by the usual standards of grand final teams. The line of thinking was that we should be fresher than St Kilda. Nine of the Collingwood players who took part in that first final were 22 years old or under.

It was a positive week, and well handled by Mick Malthouse. The crowds turned out at training again, and the excitement was there, but it was muffled slightly because there was little of the fanfare that we had the previous week. Just another game, it felt like. In grand final replay week there is no Brownlow, no other awards, no parade; it is completely different.

The AFL was the big winner of that second week, because a grand final replay is a lucrative thing, worth millions of dollars to the league. The pool for players was doubled to $3.4 million as 'recognition' of our efforts in getting up for a second grand final, and the winning team was to split $1.1 million, a nice little bonus for having your holidays messed around!

Tyson Goldsack replaced Leon Davis, who had struggled for us in the first grand final – he was the heartbreak story of that year. I loved 'Maj', who was a star. We shared a poor work ethic in the gym, just getting it done but nothing more than that, but Maj would have a footy in his hands all the time, kicking those little snapshots that he was so good at. They were no fluke. Like me, he would prefer to practise those out on the basketball court than go outside and run in the cold weather.

Maj had played 20 of 25 games in that season to that point, and he was our kick-out guy, the one who took on the pressure of having to bring the ball back into play. He was an amazing spot-up kick, and at one point of that season I can remember that he had hit targets a ridiculous number of times in a row. But he only had six possessions and eight possessions in the two finals he played in 2010, and it cost him his spot in the team.

Getting dropped would have upset him but once again, we couldn't afford to worry too much about individuals. It was about us, the players who were in the team and playing on grand final day. Leon was not the only player who would be disappointed in that week; those guys like Josh Fraser, Tarkyn Lockyer and Shane O'Bree missed out again, along with Presti, who was still injured. Selfishly, you run around and play and don't think too much about them, and what would you say to someone in that position anyway? Fortunately, those guys refused to show it outwardly, and that is why they were great teammates.

Mick didn't train us too hard and allowed us to address the points that we needed to look at. Once again, we were ready, and as it turned out, we came out of the blocks hard in the replay. Travis Cloke should have kicked the first goal in the opening seconds of the game, and Trav had me to blame for the fact that he didn't. Having marked in the goal square with no chance whatsoever of missing, I gave away an off-the-ball free kick to my opponent, Clint Jones, for pushing him in the face, and we never had that shot at goal. I am glad I was nowhere in the vicinity of the coach at that point, and I was petrified: *Jeez, I hope I haven't cost us the game here!*

As it turned out, Tyson Goldsack bobbed up with a snap for the first goal, five minutes in, and I found out later that a few of his mates had backed him at about 80–1 odds to open the scoring. I reckon they owe me some cash for that, because Goldy had only kicked a handful of goals in his career, being predominantly a half-back.

My mate Benny Johnson bombed another goal from outside 50 to help put us well on top early, and St Kilda could not score. The Saints could not get through our pressure and on the one occasion that they did, running the ball the length of the field at the 27-minute mark, Heath Shaw pulled off one of the great moments of that grand final, or any grand final for that matter.

Shawy later christened it 'The Smother of the Millenium', that little sprint and smothering motion that sucked the life out of St Kilda. Nick Riewoldt was on the end of a chain of handballs as he collected the Sherrin at the top of the goal square and was about to break the Saints' drought that had lasted the whole first quarter. Shaw came flying from behind him, appearing like a pop-up sprinkler out of the turf, hurled himself across the leg of Riewoldt as he kicked, and caught the ball clean so it dribbled away for a rushed behind. Riewoldt did not even get a boot on the footy.

I felt like we would not lose at that moment, even though it was just a quarter of the way into the game. It was that significant, from an emotional point of view. I would have given up on the play; I reckon most people would have. It just looked like an easy St Kilda goal but 'Heater' would not surrender, and he came from long range to make the play and go into the folklore of the game and the club.

It put a big dent in St Kilda's confidence, I have no doubt, because as it was, the Saints were struggling to kick a goal. They went to quarter time goalless, we had an 18-point lead, and the tone had been set for the game. As for Heath Shaw, it was an amazing piece of footy that he never lets us forget, which means that we rarely raise it in his earshot. It would be nice to have him at Collingwood now!

St Kilda had missed a few shots when it had chances, and we kept surging, pushing out to a 27-point half-time lead, but we remembered how St Kilda had come back at us the week before, and I reckon we were all thinking, *It's not happening again*. We played an awesome third quarter to close the deal, and I have this vision of Alan Didak smothering Jason Blake's kick, grabbing the footy and snapping a right-footed goal, and then doing this little shimmy out in front of the Ponsford Stand to celebrate.

Once we got past 40 points in front, we knew that we were home. I kicked one myself from a front-and-square situation and we were not going to be stopped. At three-quarter time it was a 41-point margin and the thought in our huddle was along the lines of: 'Five or six minutes of holding the ball and we're home, boys!' It's about letting the year's work come to fruition, and even though we were miles in front, Mick was never going to let us outwardly celebrate on the ground.

Mick was still going off his head at the break and he was stressed, but the players knew it was over. We were not letting this one go. We started with the first two goals of the last quarter to make doubly sure, and about 15 minutes into the term we could hear the *Coll-ing-woo-ood* chant, rising and rising further to a crescendo. The heat had gone out of the game and that was when the real enjoyment came, the *knowing* that you have what you wanted. We chipped the ball around to our mates, ran past and tapped each other on the back: 'We've done it, finally.'

Typically, I suppose, I was already thinking about the celebrations afterwards. I remember saying to some of my teammates out on the ground toward the end of the game, 'Boys, don't get hurt, because we want to enjoy this. Don't get hurt, because you don't want to miss what's about to happen. There's celebrating to do!' I played on the outside, like a boundary umpire running around and trying not to get injured. It was just an awesome moment, an awesome day, the best day of my sporting life by far.

We won by 56 points, Collingwood's first flag for 20 years and the biggest winning margin in a grand final by a Magpie team. When the siren went, I remember Dids had the ball on the wing and the carry-on started as I made a beeline to my best mates, like Johnno.

Those few minutes when you run around the ground with the premiership cup stay with you forever. I was interviewed by Channel Seven, and Tim Watson hinted that I might well be up for a big night:

Tim: 'I've got a feeling you're going to enjoy this, too.'

Me: 'I'm gonna have a fair crack.'

I played much better in the second grand final, having 26 disposals, a goal and 11 tackles, which was a big number for me but reflective of the kind of work rate we brought to that game as a team. I was happy with how I contributed, but everyone played their part. Scott Pendlebury won the Norm Smith Medal for his game in the midfield, although the presenter, former North Melbourne forward Arnold Briedis, dubbed him 'Scott Emblebury' as he called out the name.

We had a really good bunch of players, and they could have given the medal to anyone. Pendles, who had been great, was the lucky one, but it could just as easily have been Daisy Thomas, who would do things that I would never do. Daisy was magnificent in both grand finals; he did things that made you blink and wonder if you were dreaming. You would watch him and think, *How the hell did he do that?* It's such a pity that his body has let him down in recent years, because he is a superstar player, and I hope that he finds his way back to be the player that he was back then.

We were even across the board that year, and our bottom six players – whoever they might have been – would have been a fair bit better than St Kilda's, and better than the other clubs. We had younger guys like Pendles, and Steele Sidebottom (who was runner-up in the Norm Smith voting at 19 years of age) and Dayne Beams who were hungry, we had guys who were matchwinners, like Dids and Travis Cloke, and we had a strong back six firmed up by Ben Reid, who was sensational all year. We also had a strong captain in Maxy, who was selfless in the way that he would leave his man and swing across to help out a teammate.

I never understood why people outside the club picked on Maxy and criticised him as a player, because we never asked him to have 35 touches of the football in a game. He had a role on the third- or fourth-best forward from the opposition, and he would sag off and spoil the Nick Riewoldt or the Lance Franklin or the Jonathan Brown, and he was a great player for us, even if he was not a Nathan Buckley. There are only so many Nathan Buckleys, I can tell you.

Luke Ball was a big factor for us as an inside guy, and we wouldn't have been anywhere near as good without him. When the siren went that afternoon, Bally didn't celebrate it outwardly as much as some of us, because a lot of his mates and teammates were right there in his space. He knew the pain of coming so close previously at St Kilda. He is a class act, Bally, and I know for a fact that he was as happy as anyone on the inside, but it shows the type of person that he is that he did not make a big deal of that or carry on in front of his old teammates. If you think about it, he was probably closer to the St Kilda players at the time than he was to us at Collingwood; after all, he had been with us for ten months and with them for ten years.

As in any long year, there were players who carried injuries, too. Alan Didak tore a pectoral muscle in his chest in the last game of the regular season but kept playing for the chance to win a flag. You could see the bruising on his chest, and the guys who were close to him were worried that he might not be able to handle it, but he fought through. I reckon he could barely lift his arm above his head for that finals series, and people didn't realise how tough and durable Dids was on the field. They only noticed the high skill level and the X factor that he undoubtedly had.

I remember being in the rooms after the game, and some great photos that I have of me, Dids, Johnno and Heath with our medals and the cup, having beers, and me crying a little when I saw Mum and Dad and my sister, my uncle Danny and Taylor, who were all bawling. It was seven o'clock before we knew it, and everyone had been cleared out of the rooms except for the players and staff, and that's when the best moment of all came along.

Maxy grabbed us and called us back on to the ground in the darkness. Just the 22 of us went out to the centre circle, put the cup in the middle and formed a ring around it. We only had the seagulls and the cleaners in the grandstands for company, and Maxy asked everyone in the circle to say what was on their mind, everyone offering different thoughts and letting the emotion spill out. I remember saying something like, 'It's an honour to come this far with you boys. It's forever. This is the most special day of my life. I love you all.'

Then we sang 'Good Old Collingwood Forever' straight after that chat, and it was the loudest rendition of that song that I have ever heard. Even now, thinking about it makes the hair stand up on the back of my neck, because this was an unbelievable part of my life. At that point, it sinks in, and you realise that you are going down in history as part of the 22 who won a Collingwood premiership that day.

• • •

Twenty years had passed since the 1990 Collingwood premiership and the aftermath of our win was crazy. I can remember seeing supporters crying and there were people saying to us, 'I can die happy now that I've seen Collingwood win a flag.' They were telling us, 'I'll remember where I was when this happened.'

It's a bit mind-blowing to the players, because you put yourself in the bubble and focus on trying to win it, and it is only afterwards that you contemplate the whole thing and realise how much it means to the millions of fans. Players don't always think about how important the game is to the supporters and the members; we can take it for granted.

Personally, I'm fond of saying, 'It's only a game.' Which it is, to me, because there are a lot more important things in the world than chasing a footy around. But when you see how much people invest in it every weekend when they go to the footy, it's a gentle reminder that for a lot of them, it's almost their lives. Without looking down on them at all, so many people live like that, with not much else in their lives, and footy gives them a lift.

Young players probably don't understand that, and there was a time when I was a bit the same, but as my career went on, it became pretty clear to me. Yes, it is only a game, but it's important to a huge number of people, *massively* important, as we witnessed that night. I love the Collingwood fans; they have always backed me strongly, no matter how I was playing, or playing up.

At the function that grand final night the *Coll-ing-woo-ood* chant went up, and again at Eve nightclub when we arrived there afterwards – it seemed to go for an hour or so without letting up. Dids repeated his little shimmy up on the stage, which the crowd loved, and we sang the song of course. Then on the Sunday we had a fan day at Gosch's Paddock, and we went straight there from the club. Myself and Brent Macaffer and Ben Johnson and another mate all stripped off and jumped into the Yarra River to clean up on our way to the function.

We sang the song again on the stage, and then moved on to Dids' place in Kew, and it was another awesome day. Mad Monday was at the Rising Sun Hotel in Swan Street, Richmond, where a few of us dressed up. I hadn't slept, but

I knew that I was booked on a plane on the Tuesday when I would catch up with that.

We ripped in, no doubt, because they did not call us the Party Pies for no reason, but it was all too brief in my eyes. Because of the extra week required for the replay, most people had to depart quickly on holidays, but they were the greatest hours in our sporting lives. The players probably all would have liked a couple of weeks celebrating the flag, but we never got it and we never had much time to let it sink in. Just some more time together would have been nice.

By Tuesday I'd gone to Vegas, where my mates had all watched the grand final replay in a bar. From Vegas I moved on to Ireland for the International Rules series that seems to cause so much comment and speculation nearly every year. It was the first and only time I played in the series, and the fact Mick Malthouse was the coach had a bit to do with my presence. I had previously declined to play the Irish series, but this time Mick insisted so I agreed, and I have to say it was really enjoyable. We played two Test matches in Ireland, including one at the famous Croke Park in Dublin in front of 60,000 people, won both the games, and I picked up the Jim Stynes Medal as Australia's best player.

The irony of that was that I was still in full-on premiership celebration mode – it was the end of October! I can remember Kade Simpson, one of the other players, kicking off the week in Ireland by making us all drink a pint of Guinness, perhaps to fit in with the local environment. I sculled mine to take the pain away quickly; I hated the stuff. I was out till all hours the night before both games but was still able to play the hybrid game. I could even kick the round ball okay!

They were good times, playing in the national colours in a game that is fun to play. I formed a friendship with Sydney's champion Adam Goodes, who was on the trip, and we ended up travelling together the following year. Guys like Jack Riewoldt, Patrick Dangerfield, Jarrad McVeigh, Dustin Fletcher and Eddie Betts were there, and it was great to spend some time with some other players in the workplace, so to speak.

To help celebrate the flag, I got a tattoo with 'CFC premiers 2010' on my leg, and my number, 36, in Roman numerals, but it is virtually covered over by other artwork now. In a way, that's how footy is. We moved on straight away, and it is only later that you get to grasp what happened in 2010. Not so long ago, we had a five-year reunion at a bar in Brunswick, and just about everyone turned up, including people no longer at the club like Daisy Thomas and Chris Dawes, Mick Malthouse and David Buttifant.

You sit there with a beer or a glass of red wine, start telling stories and within a few moments it is as though no one ever left. I don't always speak to all of those guys, because that is the way the world works, but within five minutes we were taking the piss out of each other about the same old things. I can't wait for the next one.

They are not easy to win, as the record shows. That is a given. It's true what they say, there is a special bond among guys who win a premiership, and when you get together, you think to yourself, *Yes, that was pretty special.*

11

DYNASTY LOST

'What made Swanny so good? It was talent, hard work and mental toughness to be that consistent. You have to be mentally tough to be as consistent as he became.'

—Ben Johnson, premiership player

We were all thinking *dynasty* after 2010, there is no doubt about that. The 2010 Collingwood premiership team was the youngest in age, at 24 years and 54 days, since Hawthorn's 1978 flag team, and one of the youngest ever. As a guide to how significant this was, St Kilda's losing team in 2010 averaged 26 years, two full years older.

There was not one player in the 22 who contested the replayed grand final who had hit 30 years of age. Fourteen of our team were aged between 20 and 24, still quite young by footy standards, and Steele Sidebottom was just 19, a baby with a competitive streak. I was a comparative veteran at 26 and suddenly Johnno was our oldest player at only 29.

Our average games played was only 101, compared with, for instance, Geelong's 2009 premiership team at 145 games. Usually, the experts will tell you that you need all that experience to win a flag, but we had won the premiership with a young team, and we knew all that. Quite honestly, we thought that we had a lot more shots in the locker.

One of the original Rats had returned to Collingwood in a trade, and it was great to welcome an old mate back to the fold. Taz had turned himself into a top-class tall defender in his time at Fremantle after playing the first half of his career as a forward. There were a few other new players too, like Andrew Krakouer, a sharp, small forward. With our mix of youth and experience, who the hell was going to beat us in 2011?

We thought we'd ended Geelong's hopes of another flag by flogging them in the preliminary final, and Bomber Thompson had left the club a year from the expiry of his contract. The untried Chris Scott, the former Brisbane Lions player, had taken over as head coach at Geelong, time looked to have passed them by, and the same could be said for St Kilda. We thought we had them covered as well. I can remember thinking, *We'll win it again. We might even go undefeated.*

It was to be Mick's last year as head coach. We all knew about the succession plan where Mick would hand the reins to Bucks after the 2011 season, and none of us were bothered about it on our way to the flag. It seemed too far off, and in any case, it was out of our control and Mick had agreed to it. But inevitably, the media played the potential for problems up after we won the premiership, and the flames were fanned throughout 2011 because once again, we were having a great year. In footy, the media dictates just about everything, and they were arguing: 'You're on the verge of another flag and you're going to change?' The media can make a player, bury a player, pump up a coach or a team, and no matter how much bullshit is written, if they throw enough mud, some will stick.

That is how it was for us in 2011. Had we fallen away, missed the finals or had a poor year, it wouldn't have mattered that there was to be a change of coach, but we were the best team in the competition for the second year in a row and that meant that the speculation just rolled on and grew stronger and louder.

• • •

Mick had explained to the press straight after our grand final win:

> I can get away with saying it now, because it's going to take two or three seasons of development, you don't mysteriously wake up one morning and say 'I'm going to play like Collingwood did'. It takes a couple of years of development, understanding it and performing it and then you pick the players around it ... if they're not the right players it won't survive that contact.
>
> That's what we hard-pressed today [against the Saints], that the more we can hit them front-on and turn that ball over and keep that pressure on them in a forward motion [the better]. It's very, very, difficult to break and it's very difficult to perform your skills under that pressure.
>
> It's very difficult therefore to score, because each player knew his role. You don't wake up tomorrow morning and tell your players 'That's how you've got to perform', it will take a long time [for rivals] to put that in.

We won the first six games on end as the defending premier, before a loss to Geelong in round 7, then won the next 14 on end after that before losing to Geelong again in the last game of the regular season. So much for having killed off the Cats.

Mick had underestimated how fast our press would be undone. Under Chris Scott, Geelong was working out a way to combat it, but the first game was close – just three points – and by the time the second game came around, we could not be shifted from top place on the ladder. They thrashed us by 96 points in the last home-and-away game. So we respected Geelong, of course, but we were not fretting about the Cats, even with their slightly tweaked game plan. They ended up being the only team in the AFL to beat us in 2011.

We had an amazing year in 2011, smashing most of the other teams and setting up a 20–2 record that was one of the best ever, historically. For Collingwood, only the 1929 team, which went undefeated and won the flag as part of the unprecedented four premierships on the trot under the legendary Jock McHale, had really done any better.

Although my 2010 had been more consistent, I played the best stretch of footy of my life in 2011, and specifically in the back half of the season after taking a mid-year trip to the altitude camp in Arizona. I took the option of going to the United States after round 11 because I was sore, and we timed it around the game against Melbourne in round 12 and including the bye round. Darren Jolly, Nathan Brown and Brent Macaffer came with me, as well as conditioning guru David Buttifant. The idea had been flagged early in the season.

I was against it initially, because I always took the view: 'I'm paid to play, so I'll play.' But I had nicked a quadricep muscle in the leg early in the season and I had a sore shoulder, too, and my form had tapered off a little. Eventually I figured, *You know what, I could use a break*. It was the first time in my career I had done anything like that, but it worked amazingly well.

Over in Arizona we had just more than a week to kill, and it was high summer and very warm – such a relief coming out of a Melbourne winter, especially for a guy like me who hates the cold. We didn't train all that hard; a bit of outdoor soccer, a kick of the footy, a bit of running, some weights and some time by the pool after lunch. I am not sure if it was the high-altitude aspect of it or whether it was the mental break that helped me, but there was no media, no newspapers (although the drug testers did make an appearance), and no need for the four of us to worry about footy.

There are fads in footy, and altitude training was one. Butters swore by it, and we did it for a few years, whereas nowadays it is the heat that they are chasing, and in the past few years Collingwood has done its pre-season camp on the Sunshine Coast of Queensland. I used to hate Arizona when we first started to go there, but I put up with it. We used to train hard on the pre-season camps, but we were not policed at night which meant that you could go out for dinner, and it broke up the monotony of just training at home in Melbourne.

Plus it was roasting hot when we went there in 2011, we were not getting flogged like we usually were in the pre-season, and we could have a beer and dinner at night. I came home happy and refreshed and played the best string of games of my career. I was in the zone for most of the second part of that year.

We had some injuries in the back half of the season, notably Ben Reid was struggling with a groin injury, and the big loss to Geelong in the final game probably showed that we were not quite firing as well as we had earlier in the year as a team. Then in the week before the first final, a qualifying final against West Coast, I was caught drinking when I should not have been, and was threatened with suspension.

We had an alcohol ban in place because of the proximity of the finals, agreed to by the players, but after the last game of the regular season I went out with Benny Johnson, had a beer, and one thing led to another. I think we just needed to release the pressure valve a little, and we were not intending to go as far as we did, but we ended up rolling drunk. Of course I was found out; I reeked of alcohol after less than an hour's sleep when I arrived at the club the next day for training. It must have been blatantly obvious although Benny, by some miracle, was not caught.

Fortunately it never came out publicly, but it was pretty heated within our four walls that week. Mick called me in and went off his head at me, sitting me down and saying, 'All the assistant coaches want you suspended. But we need you. I'm not going to drop you. You're a fucking idiot, but we need you. Now go out there and remember that you owe us.'

I had 43 disposals and a goal in that final against the Eagles, a blinder. I knew that I had to perform, and there was an element of 'up yours' to the people who wanted me out of the team in that game, and I suppose it's fair to say that I loved the pressure that the big game and the events of the week put on me. I felt like: 'There you go, we only won by a couple of goals, and without me, who knows?'

Luke Ball and Alex Fasolo kicked late goals in that game to seal the win that put us through to the preliminary final with the direct route, and we ended up playing Hawthorn at the MCG in front of a big crowd in an epic final. As I said, we were not at our very top in the latter part of the year, and in this final we were 17 points behind at three-quarter time and in trouble.

But we came again, and when I kicked a goal at the 13-minute mark we were within a kick, and a few minutes later Travis Cloke extracted another goal to put us in front. We were humming by then, but Buddy Franklin kicked one of the best goals you will ever see from the boundary line, the kind of goal that only he could conjure, and they regained the lead. Taz had beaten Buddy right through that game and I was heartbroken for him; it looked like Franklin might win the game off his own boot.

Not only that, Taz had missed our premiership in 2010 because he was playing in Perth with the Dockers, and as a mate I desperately wanted to win one for him so that he could celebrate with us and experience that feeling for the first time. Really, we didn't deserve to win that game, we had played so badly.

But in the end there was one last stoppage deep in our forward 50-metre zone that finished it. Luke Ball was left unmarked by Hawthorn's players, the ball spilled into his hands, and he kicked the winner with his left boot, around the body, cool as you like, 25 minutes into the final quarter. Up in the coaches' box, Mick Malthouse was in tears, which showed us all how much it meant to him. With every game, he was a step closer to the end of his 12-year reign with the Pies.

We were into the grand final for a second consecutive season, with a chance of going back-to-back, and it was a sweet feeling. This time in grand final week, we would be like old hands, and even the Brownlow Medal count on Monday night was not going to distract me. Or so I thought.

Chris Judd was the hot pick this time after a great year for Carlton, which was funny because he'd won when I was the favourite. Although I'd enjoyed an excellent year, especially the second half, I had low expectations and I knew from experience that was the best way to go. I was actually paying about $15 odds, great value! Scott Pendlebury was probably more fancied among Collingwood players, while Sydney's Adam Goodes, another absolute champion of a player, and Carlton's Marc Murphy also had some support. The feeling was completely different to 2010 when all the focus was on me, and the grand final was my main thought as I turned up at Crown alongside Taylor.

I have heard someone say since then that it is not the votes you expect to get in the Brownlow that count so much, it is the ones you *don't* expect to get, and that proved true for me on this night. I extracted two votes against the Bulldogs in round 6 when I hadn't played a great game, when there had been at least three or four of my teammates who were better on the day. After four rounds, I already had eight votes. The umpires clearly liked me!

In my mind I was meant to go cold in the voting through the middle of the year, but Maxy was sitting beside me at the count, and he said at one point, 'You're home. You can't lose!' I just scoffed at him, because it was early in the count, even though I knew that I had some big games late in the season. I was starting to sweat.

I thought that I would need to be within seven or eight votes of the lead coming into the last ten games to have any chance, and realistically, I felt that Pendles had a better chance than me in that year. But my phone started flashing with messages, saying things like: 'You're a big chance here.' A couple of mates even sent texts with dollar signs in them.

At the halfway point I had 13 votes, and I was trying desperately to stay calm, because I knew how it had been in 2010. I was thinking, *This has happened before.* And Taylor was saying to me, 'Are you going to win?' I said, 'Shut up, I'm nervous enough as it is!' Hawthorn's Sam Mitchell was ineligible because of a suspension, but he made a run, and I remember thinking, *I hope I don't win it just because he's suspended. I don't want that to happen.*

I need not have worried because I polled votes in nine of those last ten games. From rounds 19 to 23, it read: 3–3–2–3–2 and by the end of round 23, I had 34 votes and could not be overtaken even though there was a round of voting to come. Apart from a couple of years when both umpires voted on the Brownlow, it was the highest number of votes for a player in the history of the award. Mitchell, with 30 votes, was the nearest player, Nick Dal Santo the nearest eligible player on 28, and Pendles polled 24, just ahead of Juddy and Gary Ablett Jr on 23.

I had nothing planned, of course, as I pulled on my jacket and headed to the stage to pick up the medal from Juddy, the pair of us probably having stolen each other's Brownlow from alternate years! The host, Bruce McAvaney, shifted the champagne glasses away after the traditional toast, and I gave the right answer: 'I'll save them for Saturday night.'

I talked about my parents, and Bruce asked me about meeting Taylor, which was my cue to bring in the comedy routine. 'We met in a bar, actually, funnily enough. [It's] unlike me. She was out from the states, we met in a bar and I couldn't get rid of her!' I said. Bruce suggested she might have been like a hard tag in footy, and I said, 'Hardest one I've had.'

Generally I am relaxed in front of people, and I remember mentioning my uncle Danny in my speech because he asked for a shout out in the event that I won, and I didn't get out of Crown until about 3 am by the time I did all the media commitments. Mum and Dad came in to town from home, and there were a few tears, which is not unusual with Mum.

My phone battery was flat pretty soon after the count, which meant that when I made my way home and plugged into the charger, there were about 150 messages of congratulation. I just left the medal in its box in my suit jacket and went to sleep. The truth is that it probably meant more to those people – family and friends – than it did to me at the time, because in footy, you cannot stop and reflect. I had a grand final to play and the second that you sit back and think to yourself, *I'm a Brownlow medallist*, that's the moment when everyone rushes right past you. That's the reality for me. I don't see anyone holding a reunion for Brownlow winners.

I loved winning it, make no mistake. And look, it's a nice title to have, but not something that I think about too often. When my name is mentioned in the newspapers now, it's often attached as a description: 'Brownlow medallist Dane Swan'. But I thought of it as being just a medal, no big deal, and there are no photos on my walls of me with the Brownlow, that's for sure. In fact in some ways it did me more harm than good because my profile went through the roof and the media interest in me grew a lot after that.

Later on I gave the medal to Mum for a while so that she could show it off, and then there were a few months at one point when I couldn't put my hands on it. Then in 2014, I swapped it for a laugh with a mate of mine Dan Connors, the former Richmond and Sydney player who won the Jim 'Frosty' Miller Medal for leading goalkicker in the VFL while he was playing for Port Melbourne, so that he could shock people by pulling it out. I actually forgot that he had it for a while!

On the off-chance that I was about to get carried away with myself, a trip down to the footy club quickly put an end to that. We had training at St Kilda baths the next morning, and I had some more media to do, and the players sat me on my backside pretty quickly. They are great levellers, football clubs, which applies both ways: if you are down, the players and coaches will lift you up but if you are enjoying your own work a bit too much, they will knock you down a peg or two quick smart.

By the time the game came around, Mick used a bit of us-against-them in the pre-match speech:

We've gone from being favourite because they don't trust us. They reckon we've lost it. But what they do not understand is our friendship. They do not understand how much we care for one another. Show them the courage, show them the mateship, show them the fight, show them the discipline. Give them their two hours. Never, never regret what you're going to do today. Never, never regret what you're going to do today. This is the greatest opportunity … it may never happen again, boys, I know some of you are young and you think it'll happen again. It doesn't just turn up. This is going to take one of the greatest efforts of all time, because they're a good side. You're gonna wear 'em down, and when that whistle goes, you're gonna go together. No one left behind. No one doubting. No one faking. No one. You get up and you go again, and you go again.

He finished with a reference to our regular hike up the 3800-metre Humphreys Peak, during one of the Arizona trips:

This is gonna be 11 degrees, not minus bloody 40 which we've climbed through. This is gonna be ground level, not 4000 metres, there's gonna be a 25 knot wind, not 150 Ks an hour. You've been through it, you've pushed yourself through it, you've got to the other side. Because you've got each other there. NO ONE DIDN'T MAKE IT! Because you've got your teammates there. All the best.

It was the year of Meatloaf's notorious pre-game performance, and I missed the entire performance while I prepared in the dressing rooms, although we all certainly heard about it afterwards. Actually, I was a Meatloaf fan but I gather he didn't have his best day.

We had been the best side through the year but that was not going to count for anything on grand final day, and Geelong had managed to find a way to beat us twice already. It was tight all the way, and if I have an overall thought, it is that Geelong was more ready than we were, more primed. The

Cats had prepared for the finals and hit September running hard, whereas we limped in with injuries and below-par form – a bit like Meatloaf – and they got us. Cameron Ling, my toughest opponent, got me. I had a poor game.

James Podsiadly's exit from the ground on a stretcher in the second quarter was the turning point, which is weird but true. Podsiadly, their big forward, had enjoyed a great year but when he left the MCG with a shoulder injury, Geelong sent a couple of experienced guys in Steve Johnson and Jimmy Bartel forward, and they changed the course of the match.

To midway through the second, Andrew Krakouer had been on fire; he had three goals and we were 15 points up. But by half-time the margin was back to three points, and then in the third quarter big Tom Hawkins got hold of Ben Reid, who was playing hurt.

Worse was to come for us. Geelong kicked five goals to none in the last quarter as we completely ran out of petrol, and Ling, who had been all over me, even kicked a goal late to add insult to injury. It was his last game of footy; he announced his retirement soon afterwards.

Geelong won a third flag for its great era by 38 points, proving yet again what a great team that it was. Chris Scott, who had changed up the Cats' game plan to handle the way that we played, coached a premiership in his first season, an amazing effort when you consider that the club had lost arguably the best player in Australia in Gary Ablett to the new Gold Coast franchise at the end of 2010.

My game in that grand final troubled me for a while. Was the Brownlow win a distraction? I know that there is a history of guys who won the medal not necessarily playing at their best in a grand final, but truthfully, I think that Ling flat-out beat me on the day. He had played on me and done well in the last game of the regular season, but I had heard in the lead-up that he might take Luke Ball. I have since learned that he stayed with me largely because of the previous game and how it had worked for the Cats. In any event, I would have played better if he had not been sitting on me, but he was good at his job – the best tagger I played against – and sometimes, there's not much you can do about it.

It was a funereal atmosphere in the rooms afterwards, made worse by the fact that we all knew that Mick was finishing up as head coach. Any time that a team loses a grand final there will be post-mortems about what went wrong and how; it is hardly ever said that the other team was just better on the day. In our case, we had finished on top of the ladder, so the questions were always going to come.

A lot of people speculated afterwards that the media circus over Mick Malthouse's departure was a cause of us losing that grand final. It's hard to tell, quite honestly, but I do know a few things that are clear. The players had to walk on eggshells all year and while we did a pretty good job of keeping it to one side, it was tricky.

At lunch, it might come up in conversation: 'Our job's to play footy, Mick's got this year so let's go as hard as we can.' But in the media environment we could not escape from it, and every single press conference would be like: 'Dane, what do you think about Mick and Bucks?' And what could we say, anyway? I couldn't say that I wanted Mick to go on, because it would have been perceived as a knock on Bucks, and that would have been a headline for the press.

I couldn't say that I was keen for Bucks to take over, either, because that would have annoyed Mick, so we all went the same way publicly: 'It's a club decision, and we support the club.' It's an impossible situation for a player, where you have to give the stock standard answer and even then, the media is not happy because you are behaving like a robot.

People have said that Mick froze Bucks out in 2011, deferring more to Mark Neeld as assistant coach, but I cannot recall how he handled that. He is only human, so maybe he did. They are probably not great mates, but nor am I close friends with any of my coaches or assistant coaches, and to be honest, I didn't notice it. The only thing you had to be careful about as a player in 2011 was talking in the rooms about it, in case Mick or Bucks came around the corner.

On the inside it was different to the external story. Some of the senior players that I had spoken to wanted Mick to go on as head coach *beyond* 2011, there is no doubt about that, and even a year after the deal was done for the changeover from Malthouse to Buckley, the guys in the Rat Pack and other senior players wanted the club to defer it. I certainly wanted the club to put off the change, to keep Mick going while we were hot. But it never happened that way.

In the rooms that night of our grand final defeat, Mick told us what most of us already knew, that he would not be taking up the position of director of coaching from 2012. It was hard to hear, because Mick is a footy coach, pure and simple. His words to us straight afterwards were heartfelt:

You don't plan for these. It's like I say to players if you're having a shot for goal, 'Close your eyes and imagine you kick a goal'. You never imagine kicking a point. I never even thought remotely that I'd be up here saying, 'Bad luck.' Is it bad luck? I mean, did people come out of the trench? I dunno. A few people did, maybe a couple didn't, maybe a few didn't. As that player said to me this morning, nine years later he still regrets something.

Will there be regrets? Of course there will be. I'm not about to tell you about it. You know it yourself. Is it the playing group, is it the coaches, is it support staff? Only you will know if there was something missing or a shortcut taken. Those who go on in life have to learn from this sort of stuff. It either takes you forward or takes you back. There's little pieces out of the jigsaw that are missing from your makeup, and it was evident out there. They're going to be missing until you realise you need to do something about it.

This football club has been built on the back of hard work, and labour. Don't forget your roots, don't forget how it was formed. Be that type of football club going forward. You can't be anything else. It's in your DNA. I just want to say on behalf of my family what a great pleasure it has been working here for 12 years. I didn't want to make this about me, but I'm not coming back, boys. I'll leave it to Nathan, I don't want to get in his hair, or even the board. There's some great people at this football club; they'll take you forward. It's not because I'm deserting you; I just don't think I can give of myself the 100 per cent that you blokes need. Again, on behalf of my family thank so very, very much.

I've absolutely been enthralled with the journey. Working with blokes … 12 years ago I met Ben Johnson and Leon Davis … it was a progression all the way through with Alan Didak the next year, and several other players coming along on the way. It's just been one of those great times of my life. I'll never forget it. I know deep down that we'll be hurting like hell right now and tomorrow morning, but boys, you've made this football club from sixteenth, broke and shithouse, and you've converted it, you've made it into a powerhouse.

That was hard to deal with, knowing that it was done. We were gutted to lose the grand final, let alone to lose a guy who had been like a second father to a lot of us. Eddie's words were spot-on: 'Mick, we couldn't have done it without you, mate.'

But I was not the slightest bit surprised that Mick was leaving Collingwood after that day. He is a footy coach, Mick, to the core, and he was always going to end up somewhere else.

As for the dynasty we wanted, it vanished right there and then. Did we deserve better? Maybe, maybe not. I am a believer that in sport, you get what you deserve. I have one premiership to tell people about, and I would have loved another. It won't happen now. That's footy.

CAMERON LING

Geelong premiership captain

I respect him. I hope he respected me. I'd like to think I played it the right way: I was there to try to stop him but I was also there to find the footy. I was never big on outwardly sledging or belting blokes, things like that. I just loved the straight-up battle with Swanny, and it was the same with a guy like Simon Black. They did everything they could to help their team and I was there to limit them and try to help my team. You'd go toe-to-toe and at the end of the day, one wins, the other doesn't. They were the fun battles, and there was no bullshit to it: it was simply 'Let's play footy.'

The one thing I loved most about the role I played – or loved *and* hated really – is that I had to be on. My concentration had to be on because these blokes were so good that if they got going, they could absolutely towel me up. So I'd think, *I'll be in the middle of the MCG in front of 80,000 or 100,000 and I'll be embarrassed.* But at the same time, I knew if I was on and my concentration was right, I could stop those guys and that it would have an influence on the outcome.

I had a couple of good games on Swanny early, then as he got better he touched me up badly a couple of times, then a couple of times late I was able to at least control him, in 2011, for instance. But it *never* felt like you were fully in control of him!

There was always that feeling that if your concentration was not spot-on and you weren't doing everything right, he could go from being well-covered to ten minutes later and he's swung the game and cut you to ribbons. With some players you could have them covered and you would think, *I've got them done for the day now, they won't fight through this*, whereas Swanny was capable of getting the ground back.

He was difficult to play against, super smart as a player and then when the higher interchange rotations came in around 2010 and 2011 he wasn't just churning out continuous one-pace running – it was high-power, high-intensity running. He usually ended up in the right spot so that made him so hard to stop. Shaun Burgoyne in his Port Adelaide days would stop and walk and rest, then explode, whereas Swanny was continuous, but it was cruising and then burst, flat-out for five minutes, have a rest on the bench and come back on as though he was fresh again.

He didn't say much to me. He didn't get too angry, even if I was playing him close. I think he thought, *The only way I can annoy this bloke is to beat this bloke*. And he was good at trying to do that!

If you could keep him to 20 disposals, no goals, not much influence at all, then you would be rapt. Some players if you got on top and put them away, you could keep them to single figures. They might only have one trick or they might give up a bit. You would never keep Swanny to single figures, because he just found the ball, and he had sustained power. Plus he had the smarts, so he'd end up in the right spot. Even if he was having a bad day, he'd still end up in the right spot to get the ball at least 20 times.

12

MICK, BUCKS 'N ED

'What he's been able to do as a footballer, and
how he's been able to cope with all the public
interest and attention that he gets, it's made him
all the more remarkable as a player because there's
no one like him at all in this day and age.'

—Nick Maxwell, premiership captain

I'd love a dollar for every time I had been asked about Mick Malthouse, Nathan Buckley and the whole coaching transition at Collingwood at the end of 2011. There have been a few forests harvested to print all the newspaper articles that have been written about it. It's the issue that never dies, and it still won't go away. As recently as the 2016 season, it kept bobbing up in the media, and when I do talks at sporting clubs, it is always on the agenda at question time for the punters. They never miss.

When the transition was first announced in July 2009, it was pretty much universally praised – that's before we'd become a premiership team. At least two AFL clubs were interested in hiring Bucks as their head coach after he retired as a player and was working in the media, so the succession was Eddie's way of keeping two good footy people at Collingwood, both men he respected: 'It has been a humbling experience to see two of the great personalities, the great minds of AFL football, coming together with a single-minded objective to get the ultimate success for the Collingwood Football Club.'

The timer was set for the end of 2011, when Mick had agreed to move into the role of director of coaching as Bucks took the coaching reins for 2012.

It was a new concept, the succession plan, although Sydney Swans were in the process of doing something similar with Paul Roos and John Longmire. Roosy coached the 2010 season with full knowledge that the job would pass to Longmire, his assistant. Roos put that arrangement to Longmire himself, and then the pair of them went to Sydney's board to ratify it. The difference at Collingwood was that it was driven by Eddie.

With hindsight, the problem was always going to arise if we had success, and that is exactly what happened. I've heard a story that my mate Benny Johnson said to Ed on the day of the announcement in 2009, 'What if we win the next two flags?' That makes me smile now, because it is almost exactly what happened. We were absolutely flying through those two years, and that's what made the whole thing difficult.

I loved playing under Mick and I wanted him to stay on as coach, definitely. That was the case right through 2011, his last year – I wanted him to stay on in 2012, and I was not alone in that. The senior guys that I raised it with mostly were keen for him to keep coaching and while it was not an issue in 2010, our premiership year, it was everywhere in 2011. There is no doubt about that. I can remember rumblings within the playing group about forcing the issue and there was one instance where it was raised with Mick directly.

At round 16 of the 2011 season a couple of players discussed the issue and at least one – it wasn't me – ended up approaching Mick in his office at the Westpac Centre, our headquarters. I am told that they said to him quite clearly that the players wanted him to remain on as head coach beyond that year. In other words, they asked him to help seek a change to the arrangement, to delay the transition to Bucks. The idea was for a petition to be signed by the players and taken to the board.

I have a good idea which players were driving this, and I was on their side with it, but the problem was that it was not Mick's decision to make. It was Eddie and the board who created the transition arrangement, and in any case, Mick sent the players away and told them to forget about it after they knocked on his door that day. The transition was something that he had agreed to, and signed up for, and Mick felt obliged to go along with his word, and that was that.

It was Mick who hosed down the talk. But the way we looked at it, arrangements can be broken, or deferred at the very least, if it is in the interests of the footy club. That's why the approach happened. It wasn't out of spite for Bucks, I should add, and that is the truth. It was done out of concern that Collingwood was about to make a change at a time when we were in with a chance to win back-to-back flags. We thought it was tampering with fire, in the sporting sense, the old ain't-broke-don't-fix argument.

Never ever was it about Bucks at all. I never had a real problem with Nathan taking over; it was purely about timing and it would have been the same issue for anyone who was coming in to replace Mick.

The players' approach to Malthouse didn't come out publicly at the time, but the noise was deafening outside the club, and the media would not let it go. Even during the 2010 finals, Leigh Matthews had flagged a potential problem with the News Limited newspapers: 'Mick is a fantastic coach, but when he hands over the reins to Bucks, I don't think there is any great value in Mick being really hands-on around the place to be honest. It just creates "Who is in charge?" issues.'

In mid-July 2011, Mick was very up-front about his future, saying on *The Footy Show*:

I will not rule out coaching [again]. I'm very aware if I have any ambitions at all to coach, it has got to be earlier rather than later. I can't turn the tap off. It's something in me after 28 years. Nathan Buckley will certainly be coach next year and I would like to be director of coaching at the football club.

I can't say categorically. I can, but I'd be telling a fib. It's a minimal chance that I won't be at the football club.

Mick had coaching in his blood. The coaching director job that had been discussed was never going to do the business for him:

I don't want to be at a football club that I'm going to be paid well at, to do a job that is insignificant and doesn't help the club go forward. I can't be categorical because I haven't got the contract in front of me. I haven't got the actual job description totally ticked off.

Mick was writing a newspaper column in *The Australian* at the time, and later in the season he penned an article in which he said that he would coach again one day, which poured more petrol on the fire of media speculation, given that he had agreed with Collingwood to step aside and play a mentoring role.

Leigh Matthews bobbed up again, when we were flying and on top of the ladder. And pretty much everyone in footy listens to Leigh:

If Collingwood win the grand final, they've won two in a row, Mick's coached the two in a row. I think there's every possibility – and it would have to be initiated by Bucks – to say, 'I know I've got the right to take over, but I'm not sure whether this is the right thing given the circumstances that apply.'

But it's only one of those things that would ever apply if the grand final was won. Even then, it might not happen, but I think there's some chance of that.

This was exactly what myself and the senior players were thinking.

Mick Malthouse was the only coach I had ever played under at Collingwood to this point; he had saved my career, turned me around, made me the player I was. We all loved him, and we would run through brick walls for him. He had the team at the point where we had won a flag and we were tearing the AFL apart in 2011. So if you said to anyone in footy that there was going to be a change, they would say, 'Why change it? Why change the coach now?'

Us older blokes loved Mick because he let us play good footy, doing it our own way. He found out the best way to motivate us, and he let us do that. For instance Ben Johnson might not do many weights, because he hated it, but Mick didn't care about those things, and he allowed the players room to find their method of preparing if they were delivering on game day. He knew that we needed to find what made us feel good, and to enjoy coming to the footy club, and he had bonds with guys like Dale Thomas, who later left the club purely to join him at Carlton. Mind you, he also demanded that you performed, and he delivered a few almighty sprays if you did not.

We thought it was unfair on Mick to effectively put a time limit on his coaching when Collingwood was dominating. I have heard people say that he was finished, but that is rubbish. I don't know how anyone could say that. He had just coached us to a premiership and taken us to the next grand final.

As for the Rat Pack, we wanted him to stay because we had a great bond with him. I cannot speak for everyone, but the people I did talk to – and it's not hard to figure out who – were happy for Bucks to take over when we thought it was time. We understood that no one was bigger than the footy club, and that Mick's time was coming to a natural end. But our feeling was: 'Let's try to win another flag, let this play out, and then Bucks comes in fresh, with no expectations on him.'

Were *all* the players against the change at the end of 2011? Possibly not. The ones that I spoke to wanted Mick to go on as head coach, but I would not be the slightest bit surprised if some of the younger guys were keen for the change to happen and for Bucks to take over. There would have been a few guys who were out of the swim under Mick's coaching who would have been happy to see a change of environment.

If we had missed the finals, or dipped to seventh or eighth, it would have taken the pressure off Bucks, any bad blood would have passed, and I would suggest even Mick, who is a coach first and last, would have understood that it was time for a change. It would have been a win-win situation.

Bucks was working hard at the club already as he waited to take over. It was not like he sat back, knowing that he was inheriting the job. He loves footy and he would play today if he could. He worked a lot harder than I ever did, Bucks.

The players all understood that someone would eventually replace Mick Malthouse, and more specifically, that Bucks was going to coach Collingwood; that was a given. It is not even that we did *not* want Bucks to coach the club. It was about being on the verge of a dynasty and tampering with that, and no matter what people said about our culture at Collingwood, it was a *winning* culture.

We knew that a footy club needs all different types of people, and we had the glue that held us together, made us strong. We were the dominant team in the competition right then, so our thinking was: 'Let's just play this out, let it run its time out. If it's one more year, two more years, so be it, and eventually Bucks will take over, which is great. But let's first wait until the run is over.'

We also understood that contracts had been signed. Mick had agreed to stay at Collingwood for three more years starting in 2012, and Bucks had a contract to be head coach for three years. He had declined other offers from AFL clubs to sign it, so of course it was going to be difficult to get around that, we knew. No doubt it would have been hard on Bucks after the commitment was made, but you have to ask what's best for the footy club. As players, we could not sook about it, so we had to move on, and we got to a grand final.

Did it cost us the flag in 2011, all the distraction? It's hard to say. Geelong was flying when the finals came, and we were in front going into the third quarter. I could not actually blame the situation throughout the season for losing that game. But I know one thing for sure. Unfortunately, no matter what Nathan Buckley does with Collingwood, the issue is always going to be there.

He has never had the clear air to coach the football club as he wants to. The only way to put it away is to win a flag, and we know that's not easy. And no matter who it was that took over from Mick – whether it was Ron Barassi or Leigh Matthews or Jock McHale or Bucks – it was always going to be the same, a hiding-to-nothing situation. And we all know what has transpired.

• • •

What made Mick Malthouse such a great football coach? Well, his game style was clear, that's for sure, and it was about defence first. He wanted us to take the ball around the boundary out of defence for safety reasons, and if the ball was turned over to the opposition, get it back, or knock it out of bounds and start again. He would say, 'If you want to kick it through the middle, the receiver must have time to drop it, sit down, pick it up and go again.' So you had to be pretty sure of your foot skills if you went down the middle, and it suited me, because I tended to go down the line with my kicks.

We would play a loose man behind the ball sometimes, but mostly it was man-on-man, and fierce, that was our brand. Fierce at the ball, hard tackling, hard bodies, win the clearances and contested ball and if you make a mistake, make sure that it was near the boundary line. Mick hated the ball turned over in dangerous positions, leading to easy goals for the opposition.

He always said that we *defended* rather than attacked our goals, as they do in soccer, and because he is such a devoted war historian, he would often talk about what the Germans did or what the Spanish did, although half the time we had no clue of what he was referring to. He loved the annual Anzac Day game against Essendon for that reason, and he gave some of his best speeches on those days.

Mick never confused us with the way he coached, and some of his pre-game talks were awesome. I can remember one of his Anzac Day speeches, for instance, where we all had tears welling in our eyes, and you would almost run straight through the door of the players' room to get out and play. He might read the story of an 18-year-old boy at war who had written back home to his mother, then he might talk about war and he would smash the whiteboard with a hand, BANG! 'That's what *camaraderie* is about!'

Mick had been around footy clubs all his life, and he got it that they function best when people's differences are acknowledged. He knew that it takes all types and he would accommodate players in that way, me being a good example, because I was never a great trainer, and that was well known around the club from the start of my time at Collingwood. But Mick knew that I would do enough to get ready, and from about 2006, I also performed on the field, which kept him happy. My motto was: 'I'm playing well, so leave me alone.' Mick understood that and let me play.

He is the best coach that I ever played under, a father-figure to me (although I have a great father already!) and along with Dad, the biggest influence on what made me the player that I was. We were close (although not socially, since you would not find Mick in a nightclub), and a lot of the players from that time were close to him; it was the reason we wanted to play for him so badly. He had empathy for the players, he loved family and after a Friday night game, he might say to you, 'How are you feeling? See you Wednesday, go and spend some time with your loved ones.' Twice a year he might do that with the senior guys, and it was appreciated.

Mick was intimidating, of course. The younger guys had to earn their stripes, that was the way he operated, and there was a strict and tight regime until you earned his trust, and after that you might be given some leeway. If you were outside his circle, that could not be good. The circle was drawn in close.

We all laughed about the way that he handled the external world, especially his dealings with media. Mick just didn't care for them, and he would say to us, 'Watch this!' Then he would head into a media conference before training or after a game, laughing as he walked out the door, and he would wind the journalists up chronically. He backed up his players to the hilt and at times he would go berserk at us, but in the public arena he was always supportive.

Behind closed doors, it would be quite different, for instance, if a player pulled out of a contest. I don't think that would fly with any coach at AFL level, but Mick would have no hesitation in calling you *weak*. I remember a player, Tristen Walker, who was drafted in the same year as me, copping it one day because he had a cramp. The runner came back to the bench and said to Mick, 'Tex wants to come off. He's got a cramp.' And Mick said, 'That's it, tell the umps to stop the game. Get *her* off. She's got a cramp! Get her off!'

One day, Shannon Cox came to the bench and Mick wanted to speak to him with the headphones on. Mick said, 'Shannon, can you hear me?' And Shannon said, 'I can't hear you, Mick.' And after two or three tries, Mick launched into, 'Can you hear this, Coxy? I'm gonna come down and kick your fuckin' head off!'

Another time he nailed Chris Dawes at half-time. He said, 'Dawesy, what are you doing?' And Dawsey said, 'Fuck all, Mick.' To which Mick replied, 'You're not doing fuck all. You're doing *fuck all* of fuck all!'

He could be hard on me, too, but that was because he had time for me. I remember being told 'you're killing your teammates' and that kind of thing, and he might show footage of me slacking off or leaving my opponent to run free. Maybe he thought I responded well to it, I am not sure.

He even made me play with my socks pulled up, at least early in my career. He'd grab me and say, 'Pull those socks up.' He was deadly serious, 'If you can't play like a footballer, at least *look* like one.' It was a bit of a joke around the club, and when I was playing in the AFL our runner 'Ace' used to bowl past me on the ground and he would say, 'Swanny, Mick said to pull your socks up!' So I would sit there in the middle of the ground and yank them up over my legs.

ABOVE One of my favourite photos: the Rat Pack with our premiership medallions.

BELOW The best moment of all ... just the 22 of us with the cup, letting the emotion spill out.

LEFT When I won the 2011 Brownlow Medal, Bruce McAvaney suggested Taylor might have been like a hard tag in footy, and I said: 'Hardest one I've had.'

RIGHT After the Brownlow I didn't get out of Crown until 3 am but still had to front up to recovery at St Kilda Baths early the next morning.

BELOW No one could catch me in 2011 – we beat the Bombers by 5 goals on Anzac Day.

TOP LEFT The famous 2012 Anzac Day belly rub: 'Stick that up your arse if you think that I'm fat.'

TOP RIGHT Beach recovery sessions were not my thing – I hate the cold.

LEFT 2013 was good for me, not so good for the team. My legs were still a work in progress on the tattoo front.

ABOVE Ben Johnson's body gave up on him mid-2012 and Chris Tarrant retired at the end of that year. A couple of original Rats chaired Taz off in his 250th game in round 20, 2011.

BELOW Heath Shaw was traded out at the end of 2013. By the end of that year, I was the last Rat standing and the oldest on the list.

ABOVE Another Anzac Day, another medal. Apart from that, I had a putrid year in 2014.

BELOW As coach, Bucks had his own idea of what he wanted. We had different ways of going about it but we got on well.

ABOVE My 250th game was in round 15, 2015 at Adelaide Oval.

BELOW I love Collingwood, I love the club and how big it is and I love the fans – this is how they turned out in round 16, 2015.

danes84 Been an honour and a privilege to represent the greatest sporting club in the world 250 times. Hopefully a few more to come yet. Just wanna thank everyone who have wished me well this week and all the football fans who have supported me and my career so far. Much love and have a beer for me this weekend 🍺🍻🍺🍻🍺

ABOVE I played less than a minute in my last game of footy in the first round of 2016. In the rooms they confirmed the news: 'You've broken your leg', but worse than that, my foot was like it had been in a car crash.

BELOW The x-ray shows the plates and wires the surgeon used in my foot.

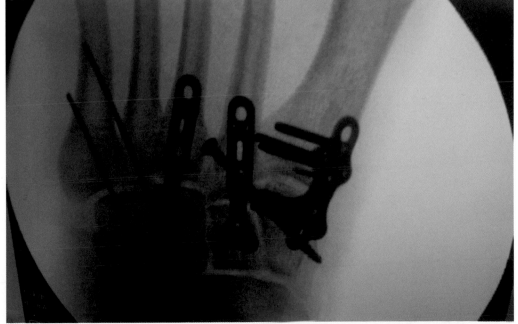

ABOVE The Swan family went to Bali for a week in 2016 to celebrate Dad's sixtieth birthday.

BELOW I've never done anything wrong and nothing was ever my fault – just ask my grandmas!

He would stride up to you at quarter time and yell, 'Get in here!' And as a player, you would be like, *Uh-oh*. 'Yes, Mick?' He could look right through you if he was angry, which was often, but you were desperate to play well for him so that you were not on the end of one of his bakes.

Ben Johnson was a favourite of Mick's and he had it right; Benny always said that if Mick baked you, it meant that he cared, and if he said nothing to you, then he did not. Mick rode nearly all of us hard, including me, but only because he saw something in us, and we played for him.

Some of Mick's sprays were so huge that they were funny, and everyone would burst into spontaneous laughter in what was meant to be the most serious situation. I remember once that he called Sharrod Wellingham 'The Fifth Beatle' because he had not been playing too well as part of the midfield group. When I went to Arizona for altitude training in 2011, Sharrod had come into the midfield group to replace me, and played well in one particular game. But the following week when I came back he struggled, and Mick hit him with, 'Sharrod, who's the fifth Beatle? Who remembers the fifth Beatle?' Everyone laughed at that.

Once, Paul Licuria stood up at a team meeting or in a half-time break and said, 'I'd die for ya boys, I'd die for this footy club.' And Mick just deadpanned it back at him, 'Come on mate. That's a bit ridiculous!' The ice was broken, and laughter came all round.

• • •

The transition is used against Eddie McGuire by people who want to whack him – and there are a few of those – because we haven't won another flag since the changeover. But hindsight is a wonderful thing to have, isn't it. I wish I had it when I made a few poor decisions along the way.

I have certainly questioned it myself. But I have no doubt that Ed and the board were trying to make the right decision for Collingwood. It was never done because Eddie McGuire is closer to Nathan personally than he is to Mick, or anything like that, it was never about mateship. Nobody loves Collingwood more than Ed, and he did not have the benefit of hindsight when he made that call. I don't blame Ed, and I never went to him to express any concern about it at the time, because I didn't think it was my place. I kept my head down and played; he and the board had their reasons, and that's just how it was.

If we had gone backwards as a club straight after the deal in 2009, it would have looked like a great decision. Even now, the club would probably say that the decision was justified, but from the outside, it's too easy for people to look at Collingwood and say, 'They've gone backwards.' Fair enough, it is not a great look when we miss finals for three years in a row from 2014 to 2016. Would we do it again with the benefit of looking back? Maybe not.

I love Ed, he's an awesome person. We hail from the same side of town, Ed being a Broady boy, and we have connections beyond that. My aunty on my dad's side taught him at school, for instance. He has always supported me, even though we've had our moments, and any sprays that I copped from him were well deserved. Ed does a good line in sprays; if there was a final, he would be in it alongside Mick Malthouse!

He barrelled me in 2003 when I was involved in the fight in the city, and again in 2014 when I did an interview with *The Footy Show* that the club hadn't authorised. I will never forget that one. I was in a meeting in the office of club chief executive Gary Pert with Geoff Walsh, the director of football and Ed, and my manager, Liam Pickering, went in to bat for me, saying something along the lines of 'it would be nice if the footy club supported him'. Ed absolutely lost it that day, and I was sliding down under the desk as he unloaded: 'That's *bullshit* we don't support anyone!'

If I was caught for drinking when I was not supposed to be, which happened quite a few times, he would be pretty matter-of-fact with me. He might say, 'You stuffed up.' Then he would move on without holding any grudge. There were half-a-dozen times in my career when Collingwood could have sacked me and probably had every right to, but they stuck with me, and Ed must have had a say in that.

It came to the point for me that whenever I had messages on my phone from Ed – and the same could be said for Bucks, for Geoff Walsh, for Neil Balme – I would panic and think that I had done something wrong. Once, Ed left me a message: 'Call me, ASAP' and I was really worried. It was after the 2015 Grand Final, and we had thrown a party, then been over to Taz's home all Sunday, and I kept thinking, *What's the latest thing I've done wrong?*

When I finally tracked him down, he said, 'Have you heard the news? Your pub's burned down!' After the shock kicked in, I said to him something like, 'Is that all? Thanks, mate!'

A few friends and I had bought the Albion Hotel, and there had been an arson attack that morning, unbeknown to me. So I went back to bed, and dealt with it later!

The great thing about Ed is that it's never personal. If he's upset about something, it comes from a place where he loves the footy club so much, and from the fact that he actually cares about the players and wants the best for them. He gets it off his chest and then moves forward. He has blasted me, of course, but as soon as it was done, it would be like, 'How can we help you, support you?'

In Ed's eyes, if you become a Collingwood player, then you are a Collingwood player forever. He does what he can for you away from the field, he looks after you and takes an interest in you outside of playing, he talks to you about life after footy, helps you to put plans in place. He's done all that with me.

• • •

Mick and I keep in touch but we don't see as much of each other these days, or talk all that often. Now that I have finished playing I would hope to catch up with him a few times a year. In Mick's own book he wrote that friendships had been broken and his own family was bitter about the end of his time at Collingwood, which is sad, in my eyes. I hope that everyone breaks bread one day and lets it go. I would certainly like to see Mick back at Collingwood more often, and I believe that can happen. I know that Ed would welcome it. I think that all will be forgiven in the end, because footy clubs are like that. Ed's been a remarkable president for

Collingwood, and Mick will go into the AFL Hall of Fame, as he should, absolutely.

Footy clubs can be challenging places, and I have been involved in some really robust conversations with Mick, Bucks and Ed over the journey. But I never carried any of them with me, and I understand that everyone was just trying to do their best for the club. It was never about me. Decisions get made, and some are good, some are bad. If you can't get over it, then you are in the wrong sport. And at the end of the day, what is the point of holding a grudge?

I certainly never hated playing under Nathan Buckley, as some people seem to think. If I hated it, I would have left. With free agency, it would have been an easy call to make.

I never even thought about it.

13

RELEASE VALVE

Hey @kanyewestÐÐ if you need some help with ideas to change the world I'm your man … Tell your mate Zuckerberg too

—@swandane17 February 2016

I love tattoos, or more accurately, I am *addicted* to tattoos. That will not surprise anyone, but it is a fact, and tattoos are my way of expressing myself. They are my way of saying that I don't conform, although there is an irony in that, because tattoos have become so popular in the last ten years that you could almost argue that the non-conformist would *not* have tattoos! Actually on the latest statistics about 19 per cent of Australians have at least one tattoo (and it's a much higher figure for younger people), but I'm running with it anyway.

I was not the first in my family to have some artwork done; my sister had one when she was only 16, tried to hide it from our folks but eventually had her backside kicked. I had my first around 2008, a set of big tribal wings on my belly, and then another smaller one on my right upper leg when Collingwood won the premiership in 2010. After that, we worked down my arms and legs. Mum and Dad are not tattoo fans, but they have given up telling me what to do with my life at 32. Mum just says, 'Please, not the face and neck.' Which I have abided by, for now, at least! Although I do have a sneaky 'Where's Wally' tattoo behind my ear.

A lot of people hide their tattoos, and I was the same at the start, even though I was an Allen Iverson fan. Iverson was the guy who really started the trend towards big, bold tattoos in the NBA, and apart from that he was a great player, and a bit of a rebel, which of course I loved. So I was inspired by him, no doubt.

For a long time I remember thinking, *While I'm playing footy I won't get any where you can see them, because I don't want to be known as 'the kid with tattoos'.* But that soon went by the wayside, and I have a snake on my right ankle, a dragon on my ribcage, I have an octopus and a pirate ship and a woman's face. I also have the Swan family motto: Constant and Faithful.

On my knuckles I had the letters forming the words 'Good Life' tattooed a few years ago in Las Vegas. A few of us had just been to see the rappers Kanye West and Jay-Z play their Watch the Throne Tour live – Kanye sings a song called *Good Life* and it just seemed to fit that I had it done there and then. It's self-explanatory, that one, because I want to enjoy myself, and now when I look at my left hand I can see GOOD and on my right hand I can see LIFE to remind me of what I aspire to.

Around the same time a group of us had our names tattooed – mine is on my stomach – with Brett Finch, the NRL player, Dustin Martin of Richmond fame, Gerrard Bennett, who used to play for the Swans, and Harlan, another mate. We had a house party in Vegas and someone called a tattooist to the party, and we went with the names. It was Benno's first tattoo, which he had done on his foot.

My tattoos mean different things to me and often, I just let the tattooists loose with their own designs, although one is the result of a bet. I decided to skip the Brownlow Medal count a few years ago, and bored as usual, I ended up having a wager with Sam Newman that Collingwood would finish ahead of Geelong the next year. I lost the bet, and the penalty was a tattoo of Sam's face … on my butt cheek! It's there, in all its glory.

Having tattoos drawn is extremely painful, and anyone who says otherwise is a liar. By 2014 I knew quite a bit about the pain levels on different parts of your body and shared a bit of advice on Twitter: 'FYI kids – getting your knee tattooed hurts a lot. In other news game of thrones tonight and that …'

Being tattooed is also painstaking and slow, and some of the more intricate works can take up to 16 hours to draw. I used to sit for six or seven hours at a time, and most of mine have been done by Pedro, a friend who is also now a business partner, and other people who work at the tattoo shop we run in Moonee Ponds.

We started the shop, called Renegade Art Society, a couple of years ago with another friend, Rick, who does the financials. Pedro had done my early tattoos at a place called Devil's Ink, and I felt comfortable with him, and with my profile getting bigger, I started posting photos of his work on Instagram. Then at one point, I said to him, 'Have you thought about doing your own thing? Let me know if you want to open your own shop.' Then one day he said, 'It's time, let's do it.' The whole thing has been fun and it's something for me to focus on after footy.

For me, tattoos are a part of my creative side. I am not especially artistic, but I do like art, and it was not as though I had lovely olive skin to start with! I had one tattoo done, I thought, *That looks good!* and the rest is history. I'll run out of room on my body soon enough, I guess. My favourite tattoo? I always answer that in the same way: my next one.

It started out as a fun thing to do but in the end, it kind of defined who I am, and I don't mind that. For a long time there was a taboo – a kind of a stain – about tattoos in Australia, with the older generation especially, and they were associated with criminals. I remember when I started getting my sleeve done, people would look at me as if to say, 'What a weirdo.' But everyone is getting tattoos these days, and the stench is not there anymore.

Personally, I am not about judging people by what they wear or what tattoos or piercings they have. We all express ourselves in different ways, and mine is with tattoos, and we should appreciate each other's differences in my opinion. If someone wants to get a bullring through their nose, that's fine with me.

To be perfectly honest, people recognise me more for my tattoos than anything, even more than my footy, and it probably boosted my profile and my image in a mostly positive way. Against that, I know that if I want to get around unrecognised for some reason or other, I need to cover up. It's trackies and a hoodie on those days.

I've had piercings, too, although one of my first experiences was nasty. I got a nipple ring when I was 17 and playing my first year at Williamstown, and I stupidly played with it in one day and had it ripped out. A guy tackled me – I had protective tape over my nipple but it must have caught – and I looked down and saw blood all over my jumper. When I checked the damage, half my nipple had gone with the piercing. That was the last of the nipple rings, but I do have piercings in my nose and ear.

The message is about independence. I've always done what I wanted to do, whether people liked it or not, and if they don't like it, they can stick it. If I tried to fulfil people's expectations of me, or change their opinion of me, I would be running around in circles all day and night. A long time ago, I decided to live how I wanted to live, do what I want to do (within reason), and while I'm sure it has rubbed people up the wrong way sometimes, I am fine with that. It doesn't bother me.

I didn't change for anyone and in the end, I hope people actually appreciate that I'm just being me; I've never tried to be anything else, or pretended to be something else, or put on any airs and graces. I refuse to be a robot and be what other people tell me that I need to be. I've been reasonably successful at doing that, too, I reckon, while eking out a decent footy career. Of course there were hiccups along the way, but I did all right for myself considering I was a law unto myself, as they say. I had to fit within the demands of the footy club, and for the most part, I did that. I had to toe the party line a lot, otherwise I would not have played for so long.

People often say to me, 'You're different to the usual footballer.' But it's not strictly true, in my eyes. I'm just like a lot of players – and I've had this conversation with a lot of footballers over the journey – but I am who I am. Those guys are told what to say and what to do and they do it. Supporters don't see the real person behind the robot.

The problem with modern footy is that the clubs are not giving their players access to the release valve. Everyone needs to have an out; some people play golf, some people spend hours on PlayStation. In my case, I've always been social; I like going to dinner or a bar with friends and having a few drinks to relax. That shouldn't be a problem, but in the modern environment they want everyone to be the same. They breed robots.

With footy coaching too, they should accept that there are different personalities in the group, and that different things make people tick. Some people need a rocket, some people need to be cuddled to get the best out of them. The way that football is structured today, I would have played half as many games as I eventually did if I was coming into this system. I would have been suspended a lot more for drinking, and for pushing the club's limits and boundaries.

It's the scrutiny that kills you as a player. There's no end to it, and no release, apart from those moments, say, at the end of the season when players tend to go berserk because they have been cooped up for so long. Of course, I understand that in AFL footy they worry about the bottom line, about winning and losing, and they care about the members and sponsors, and it's bad for business if someone messes up off the field, but the game is too nannied nowadays.

Where is the room for individuals? Where is the room for people with personalities? As soon as a player says something controversial, he gets canned in the media, so he just can't win. I came to be regarded as a bit of a party animal, I guess, but put this in perspective. I would drink one night a week after footy, and the rest of the time I'd be on a six-day break (no drinking allowed). Even if I was injured there would be a drinking ban. So out of 22 rounds in a year, I might drink 15 times, and that's tough for someone who enjoys a beer, or a red wine (at dinner) or a vodka (when I am out). Compare that to the average 25- to 30-year-old out in the suburbs and tell me who's the party animal!

I read an article about this once, and it argued that the modern sporting clubs' tough stance on off-field behaviour was basically driven by dollars; that they're petrified of the social media and phone shots. It quoted Professor Keith Lyons from the National Institute of Sports Studies, and he was on the right track:

Sport is a very strange place at the moment. It is very concerned about its public profile. AFL has a particular problem ... becoming particularly scared of losing sponsorship. The rules are to try to bring about conformity so there's no public difficulty for clubs.

He went on to say that the tighter the boundaries, the more transgressions occurred: 'If you have a black and white code, it seems to miss the grey occurring in our own living. Instead, how do we help them grow up and be responsible people?'

What I mean by heavy scrutiny is that there is not much rhyme or reason to it. For instance, in 2014 I made the front page of the *Herald Sun* for speaking at a lunch at a restaurant that was owned by the brother of Mick Gatto, the underworld figure. I didn't even know who owned the restaurant, because the speaking gig was organised for me and I just turned up. I've met Mick Gatto, but I don't have his phone number; if I walked past him, I'd say hello and I'm sure he would say hello back to me. I treat people how they treat me, and if people are nice to me, I'll be nice back.

So it was a ridiculous story that absolutely smashed me, made me appear like some kind of gangster. Do I need to find a list of all the people at a lunch that I'm asked to speak at? Mick bought a ticket for the lunch to hear me speak, and asked for a photo with me. I obliged. End of story.

Later on, Mick Gatto told the ABC:

Dane Swan is a real champion of a man, he has spent time with elderly people and with children. He came over briefly and said hello to me, I asked him for a photo and that was it. I can't understand why the carry-on with all this nonsense. There is never a problem until the media makes it a problem.

I couldn't understand the fuss either but that's the kind of thing you have to put up with if your profile is high. Now I know that AFL players are not going to get much sympathy in all of this, because after all, we're well paid. I get that. The average salary in 2016 was $302,000 and many are earning a lot more, but when you play a game as public as AFL, where you feel like everyone wants a piece of you, your world can cave in when you're not playing well. You have to be pretty thick skinned for it not to affect you.

The criticism comes and it can be vicious, especially on the self-published areas, like the internet forums, places like bigfooty.com or Twitter. Players' families read it and worse, players can actually read it and that's quite dangerous if it targets the wrong player. For me and Ben Johnson, it was a laugh. We used to get on there when we were rooming together on an interstate trip, and it was hilarious, especially after we had lost.

'Swanny, you're a fat piece of shit', would be the general tone of the discussion. Not very imaginative. But the keyboard warriors can be vicious, and not every player is like Johnno and me. One point that I'll make is that I never reply to those people, because that's exactly what they want. They love to get under your skin, and they're the same people who would be down at the club, patting you on the back if you were going well. It's so fickle.

That's all very well for me, but to some players, the constant feedback can be hurtful and it's the kind of thing that can lead to bouts of depression. I have a clothing line, Ratbagg, and not so long ago my friend who runs the brand's Instagram account posted a photo of me modelling one of the hats, which happened to go up online just after Collingwood had lost a game against Melbourne. Straight away, in the comments section, they started to can me with things like: 'Fuck you, Dane, you should be with your mates.' It was so bad that my mate had to put up a post in my name: 'The timing was not great.'

Just because you lose a game of footy should not mean you have to lock yourself up inside four walls for a few days and meditate, but sometimes people seem to expect that. They want you to be hurting badly, just as much as it is hurting them. They will take it personally if you don't seem to feel as much pain. As for me, I always thought footy was a game, and it hurts if we lose, yes, but not enough to drag me down for too long.

It has become ridiculous, but this is the way footy is going. People hate it if a player on the losing side chats to someone from the opposition afterwards, and they might smile or laugh. But to me, if one of my best mates is on the opposition team, we might have talked trash all week to each other, then after the game of course we will talk to each other. Yet in today's world of social media, that can quickly become: 'He doesn't care.' How would anyone know if I cared or not? Do I have to cry in the rooms to show that I care?

Rhyce Shaw's departure from Collingwood is an example of how footy can get on top of a player. Rhyce was part of the Rat Pack, and he is still a friend, but he copped an enormous amount of stick from fans in the early part of his career. Rhyce had the family name – his father, Ray, was a former captain of Collingwood, and his uncle Tony was the 1990 premiership captain – so he was always going to be noticed. When he fumbled a ball in the 2003 Grand Final against Brisbane Lions and had to watch Alastair Lynch pick it up and kick the goal that pretty much sealed the game and came to symbolise that loss, he was branded.

Rhyce was savaged over the fence and it went on for years, even when he was playing down at Williamstown. He was hard done by, and I am not sure if he ever quite recovered at Collingwood, so the best thing ever for him was going to Sydney at the end of 2008. Fortunately, that worked out beautifully for him. I love Rhyce and I was rapt as anyone when he finally picked up a premiership medal in 2012. He was so much more relaxed playing at Sydney, and he learned to love footy again.

When you're in a rut, you can start to hate footy pretty quickly; you are in a goldfish bowl environment with no way out, and the game ceases to be fun. And that is exactly when depression can kick in. People outside of the game tend to dismiss it, but I believe that it's a real problem in footy. I have heard people say, 'They're weak as piss, if I was playing AFL, I wouldn't care less if someone criticised me because I'm playing AFL.' They have no idea what the pressure is like when things are not going well.

The armchair critics will say, 'Give *me* the chance to play in the AFL. I'd love to get big money and get bagged on Twitter.' But then you play for a long time and the scrutiny is there, and you go out in front of 80,000 people and in the back of your head you are thinking, *Don't drop the first ball that comes to me, because they're gonna boo me if I do.* It is a lot harder out there than those people think.

•   •   •

I am one of the lucky ones. I survived and I never let it get to me, maybe because I had interests outside of footy, and it was never the sum of me. People came to have a certain perception of me, but they have no clue, really. I am interested in a lot of different things.

For instance, my music. I like rap best, but I also like folk, I like chart music, house music, electronic music, it just depends which album is out at the time. Seeing Jay-Z and Kanye West in the Watch the Throne Tour in Vegas was a particular high for me, but I also loved Childish Gambino in Austin, Texas, and Machine Gun Kelly. I love live music and will probably go much more now I've retired.

Anything live will get me, whether it is music, theatre or sport. I often take in old-fashioned musicals; I think they are great and I've seen probably 20 of them, from *Jersey Boys* to *Wicked* to *Mary Poppins*, which was awesome, *Aladdin* and *The Lion King*, which was amazing. I was once invited to a premiere and loved it, and now every time I go to New York with Taylor we try to hit Broadway to see something. I've seen *The Book of Mormon*, *The Rocky Horror Picture Show*, *Chicago*, *Avenue Q*, for instance, and *A Gentleman's Guide to Love and Murder*.

I've seen NBA basketball, my favourite of the overseas sports, and one of the best sports to watch live is ice hockey. The Super Bowl is on my bucket list of things to see post-footy, and I'm a New England Patriots fan. I love Tom Brady, the greatest quarterback of all time, who leads the Patriots. To go to something like the FIFA World Cup of soccer would be amazing. Every time I see an event live, I think to myself, *I should do this more*. But of course when you're playing, you're often tired and sore and can't be bothered.

I like to read books, especially autobiographies, although I am easily distracted by television. Certainly when we're away I'll churn through a book or two, and Taylor is one of those people who can sit on a beach all day and read. We went to the Bahamas and she read from 10 am to 4 pm without moving other than to dunk herself in the water every two hours, but I was getting antsy and would head off to the sports bar to have a bet.

People would probably be surprised to know that I've taken some piano lessons recently, while I was recovering from the foot injury. Taylor had given me a bunch of lessons for my birthday because it was something that I'd always wanted to do and the injury meant I had the time to actually do it. Becoming good at it is another matter, because I have zero experience playing music, and the whole thing hurt my brain when I started. I'm not good yet, but I want to keep trying. The funny thing was, when I went down to have my first lesson I was more nervous than I have been in quite a while, as uncomfortable as I've ever been, a 32-year-old man in a moon boot trying to hit the notes on a keyboard. But there is something in this, because I wanted to get out of the comfort zone that I've been in.

By gifting me the lessons, Taylor threw me in the deep end and suddenly I was trying to tinker with the first few notes of Cold Chisel's anthem *Khe Sanh,* then moving on to the very familiar *Changes* by the American rapper Tupac. It's all about learning new skills and changing myself as I move into a whole different phase of my life. For 15 years I have been in the comfort zone of footy, a game I love and something that I knew that I could do. What new skill did I ever learn? My brain hasn't been challenged since I was at school, so I'm trying the piano, and if I am completely hopeless, then I will drop it. But I enjoy it, so we'll see.

I have tried to prepare myself for life after footy by investing in some businesses. A couple of years ago some friends – Matt Darcy (brother of former AFL player Luke), another mate, Danny, and Robbie Kearns of Melbourne Storm NRL fame – bought the licence at the Albion Hotel in South Melbourne, with big plans for refurbishment.

The Albion was an old haunt of mine; it used to be the Motel nightclub, and I drank enough there, so why not invest in it? That was the theory! Me and my friends were there all the time so we thought it was a good fit – I loved that place. But in 2016 the place was badly damaged in a fire that was lit by an arsonist, which was a shock. We were only six days away from opening it, a full renovation with three levels, and while the facade is still there, it delayed the whole project.

The police eventually drew a confession of arson from the builder who had been engaged to do the work. The case went to court while it was being rebuilt, with a big opening planned for 2017. That will be my biggest project but there's also my clothing label, appropriately named Ratbagg, which I started with two mates in 2014. I have always been interested in fashion. We sell street clothes, stuff like hoodies and T-shirts and flat-peak caps and beanies and drop crotch pants, all the kinds of street clothes that I love. The gear is made in Bali and marketed online. At the moment we don't do any shops, so we just use social media to promote it.

So as it stands I own a pub, a tattoo shop and a clothing brand, which to my way of thinking is pretty stereotypical for an AFL footballer! On the field, I guess that I was the exact opposite of the modern professional player in some ways, but I fit the mould in my business activity, and really, it's all about finding things that I enjoy doing. If I throw enough darts something will stick, and I might make a living post-footy. I'm always on the lookout for new products: 'Sporting team themed toilet paper so you can wipe your ass with the team you hate. Your welcome.'

And this: 'Lollie jar you can open from both ends … your welcome. #whyarethegoodonesalwaysdownthebottom'

As you can see, I'm more of an ideas guy and fortunately I have some mates with business savvy, which is helpful. I like drinking, I like tattoos and I like fashion, so they are my business areas right now. They are passions of mine, so the idea is that what I invest in doesn't feel like work. Going to footy training was work to me, but these kinds of things feel like they are my passions. Maybe I will get sick of it in 15 years, but right now the possibilities are all exciting, and I love it.

Travel is my other big passion. I used to love the organised footy trips we did as a group when I first started at Collingwood, but they were shut down a couple of years into my career, meaning that I had to generate my own travel. In my first year with the Pies we went to a resort in Cancún in Mexico, about 30 of us, and it was the first time in my life that I had travelled without Mum and Dad. My eyes just lit up, and I remember thinking, *How good's this? This is all I want to do!*

The following year we had to play an exhibition game in London and after that Ryan Lonie, Ben Johnson, David King and I went to Barcelona and Amsterdam. Isn't that what you play AFL footy for, to go on footy trips? But in all seriousness, I have never missed a year even though the organised footy trips stopped around 2005, and nowadays, I tell the young boys at the club, 'While you've got the cash, don't go home to Adelaide or Perth! Go to Europe or America, or at least to Bali! Have a proper holiday!'

I used to go away for a fortnight; once I could afford it, I tended to go for more like a month and post-footy it will probably be two months. I've become the organiser because all my mates are useless at planning travel. I am really good at switching off, so on holidays I might go out for lunch somewhere on a Monday arvo, sit in the sun, drink a few beers, and I don't have to worry about anyone taking a photo of me or saying on Twitter or social media: 'What are you doing eating a bowl of chips?'

I would hate to think how much I've spent on end-of-season travel over the 15 years, but I love getting away so much that I even put wrist surgery off so that I could travel one year, around 2013. That's probably why my wrists are so bad, and with hindsight, those surgeries should have happened a few years earlier. I kept saying, 'It's okay, it's okay', and putting it off, but it was not okay.

I had torn scapholunate ligaments in both wrists, carried the problem for a while to the point where I couldn't open a door, they were so sore. They have both been reconstructed, the second one in 2013, but my wrists are good for nothing because they're so stiff. I can't do push-ups, and certain things in the gym like squats, because I can't hold the bar.

But the way it works, if you don't have a proper end-of-season break, you're back in Melbourne before you know it, the footy season is on and all you've done is go home to see the folks. What you need is the mental release, and that's especially the case once you get a bit of an AFL profile, so I say, 'Go out, get to a place where no one knows you, do what you like, carry on and no one has a clue.'

Getting away actually helps your footy. Players come back, they catch up with the boys again and some might have even half missed the training and the regimentation. We tried something different most years, but it is usually Vegas and Los Angeles or Europe. I spend a lot of cash in that month away, even though I barely gamble at all, even in Vegas – I might gamble with my life, but that's about it!

Vegas is awesome but it's hard; I used to go for a week, but by then I was cooked. You don't sleep much and even when you do, you come back to earth in some sort of pain, so these days I might go for a long weekend, something like that. I think the recovery time is getting slower for me in my thirties. When I was 25 or so, I could go out on Saturday and not sleep until Sunday night, wake up for training on Monday morning and have no problems at all. If I did that now, I would be a zombie at training, I wouldn't be right until the Wednesday.

From about 2014 I was smarter with my drinking, whereas when I was young at Willy, I didn't care about the rules. I remember one game we played up in Ballarat, and a few of the boys went up the day before and got hammered. One of them was my mate Heath Scotland; he ended up having 35 touches in the game the next day, and the coach, Brad Gotch, praised him for his professionalism in coming up to the country a day earlier.

I used to drink heavily on Thursday nights and a little on Fridays, but in my later years, I only drank on the weekend, other than the odd glass of wine at dinner during the week. I tended to drink where I wouldn't be fingered by someone; that's the way we have been forced to do it, as players. I drink red wine, especially with dinner, and vodka if I am out after starting with a few beers, but I am maturing a bit. These days going out might be dinner on Saturday night with another couple.

While I was playing, I tried to stay within the rules as much as I could, but every now and then I'd think, *Stuff this, I'm doing it. It's my life.* Why play AFL, which is such a great life, and not enjoy it? I wasn't going to sit in my room like a prisoner. I love going out on weekends and enjoying myself, so sometimes I did just that. I didn't want to look back in 15 years and think, *Gee I wish I'd spent more time with my friends, I wish I had done this or that.*

You only get one life, so you might as well have a good one, that's my view.

• • •

No doubt I would have been difficult to deal with when I was playing. Once, at Arizona, we were walking up Mt Humphrey, which is quite a trek, and Mick Malthouse said, 'No headphones today!' I heard him but I just thought to myself, *No way that I'm getting up here without headphones.*

So I put the headphones on and took off, in clear view of everyone, and headed up the mountain. I knew that I would be punished, which I was, but I hated going up that mountain, and having my music helped me. The one or two of us who disobeyed the rules were flogged by David Buttifant. And as I was taking my punishment, I told myself that I would not show that I was hurting. The boys were watching and laughing and I laughed right back at them, saying, 'This is worth every bit of it. I'll do this all day, and next time, I'll do it again.'

Another time, Chris Tarrant and I couldn't get to a rehab session because we were locked *inside* a bar! It was Bar 161 in Prahran on a Sunday night, early hours of Monday, and there had been a shooting outside the club. Security closed the doors and wouldn't let anyone out, and Taz ended up trying to ring people to explain why we were going to be late. The thumping music that was reverberating through his phone would have been a dead giveaway!

A lot of these things never came out publicly, like the situation at the end of 2014 when a hotel room in the city was trashed. I didn't do anything in that instance, but I had booked the rooms for some friends who were having two nights out to celebrate one of their birthdays. Heaps of people came through the rooms in that time and a lot of damage was done.

I ended up with the responsibility because they were booked in my name; I had to cough up a couple of thousand dollars and then the footy club found out, because the hotel rang them. Collingwood told me that if it came out, there was a chance that I might be sacked. Fortunately, and by some miracle, it did not.

Sometimes, I would just get away with what I could manage. When Collingwood went back to the Holden Centre for post-match recovery sessions, I'd sometimes sneak some vodka into my lemon-lime Gatorade bottle and have a few sips while I rode the stationary bike! No one ever knew and I did it more than once. It made recovery more enjoyable, and it tasted delicious!

Other times, the trouble seemed to find me rather than the other way around. A day before my 250th game against Port Adelaide at Adelaide Oval in 2015, I thought that I was going to end up missing the milestone because I was locked up. Me and Gerrard Bennett, a good friend who lives in Adelaide, were out driving in his car and suddenly we were surrounded by two of those big SWAT vans, with police yelling at us to get out of the vehicle.

I said to Benno, 'What's going on, what have you got in this car?' But he had no clue. All I could think at the time was that this was going to be an interesting call to Bucks. 'Sorry coach, I'm in the lockup. My mate has stitched me up.'

One of the cops recognised me straight up and he said, 'What the hell are you doing here?' They told us that they'd been tracking some bikies that night, and let us go, but not before a few of them joked to us, 'Lock him up. Don't let him play tomorrow night!'

• • •

I have no doubt that if I was starting as an AFL player now and the game was structured as it is today, I would have played half as many games. I would have been suspended a lot more for drinking and for testing the club's limits and boundaries. The scrutiny is so fierce, that's the thing.

I mean, you hear some terrible things said about the culture of Collingwood and my own behaviour. I really hate the label 'bad boy', but that's one that gets thrown around a bit. Or you will hear people – I reckon Caroline Wilson, the journalist, was on about this – say about me, 'He's terrible for the culture of the football club.'

Well, the fact is I have been in trouble with the law once, in 2003. In the scheme of life, I got in trouble once, I paid my price, I went through the legal system and copped it sweet. According to my grandparents, I've never done anything wrong.

The 'what ifs' are there, of course they are. Maybe if I had done those 500 ice baths that I dodged, the extra training sessions, ate better food, looked after my body in a more professional way, did not drink as much red wine and vodka, who knows what I might have become as a player? But just as easily I could have gone the other way and burned out earlier.

I had a bit of fun with a hashtag in March 2013 and it got a great response: 'Why?? I spose cause we can. So lets #BlameDaneSwan'

People got right into it and before too long I was responsible for the weather ('heat wave, your fault'), for people rocking up to work late ('No worries boss just #BlameDaneSwan'), for sunburn ('I got really sunburnt today. It's your fault.') for football results ('no Ball, no Thomas and no Didak. Lost to lions #BlameDaneSwan') and a whole lot of random stuff ('my kids wont sleep can I #blamedaneswan?') and even politics! ('Can Labor blame the WA election result on you too?')

Here's the message. Never ever lose your sense of humour.

I can sit back now and ponder: did I give my football career absolutely everything? The answer to that question is, no I did not. Did I have the best time that I could possibly have while playing footy? The answer to that question is yes. It was the right way for me, I thought, and I don't have any regrets about the way I handled it.

Everything I've done, including the times I messed up, has made me the person who I am. I can sit here quite happily and say, 'I'm proud of what I've done, I'm proud of who I am.' Whether people like it or not, I am very content with how life is, and what I've accomplished in footy and how I am perceived in the general public.

Because in the end, the footy club is a straight line from which I deviated every now and then. The way I see it, ten years ago I had a choice. If I was to end with a regret, which one would I rather confront? Giving up the life I wanted, or not giving football my best shot? I chose the second option, quite clearly, and took a risk in doing that. But happily, I ended up with no regrets at all.

People might think this is stupid, but the game comes and goes and it has passed me by now. I am glad that I played for Collingwood, and I owe the club an enormous amount. I will be indebted to the Magpies forever, and I have met some amazing people. But it was my way that I chose, and I am glad that I did.

BEN JOHNSON

Collingwood premiership player and Rat Pack original

To be honest, my helping him had nothing to do with footy ability. I just liked him as a bloke and we were knocking around a bit, we became close mates, and I just wanted him to have a career. Not for a second did I think that he would do what he did as a player. I knew he was good enough to make it, but I had no idea that he could end up as good as he did.

I liked him because he was exactly like us. He comes from a good family and he enjoys himself, he doesn't take anything too seriously and we all had a really good time, just living life, really. We pretty much liked his style. Back in those days, it was normal to go out every Saturday night, and I can remember every Saturday night I would bump into him. I didn't have to try; I'd just find him every week. It was never planned, at least for the first six months. We spent time together, we had a few mutual friends, and it happened from there.

Swanny wasn't alone in wanting Mick Malthouse to stay on at the end of 2011. Look, we just loved Mick, and I think [the transition] mucked things up a bit. We all spoke to Mick, I reckon, and I certainly had a chat to him: 'What should we do? What do you want us to do?' It was actually Mick who said, 'Nothing'.

People don't realise that, but it happened. There would have been eight of us who had the conversation with him, it wasn't any one person, we all did it. I said to him, 'Let's change it, let's get this fixed'. But he said, 'No mate, it is what it is. Just leave it.' And as soon as he said that, we left it.

We had a good time together. In 2011, Bucks wanted Swanny suspended for a final in Perth. We'd been out together for a meal on a Sunday night, and a couple of beers turned into some double vodkas, then we went to Hotel Barkly in St Kilda to a mate's birthday, and of course we knew the owner, who served the drinks in water bottles. We were drinking out of the water bottles and it looked like we were having raspberry and water, but it was full of vodka.

I left Swanny at six in the morning, we had training, and I said, 'Whatever you do, don't you fuckin' be late!' Of course, he sleeps in, and I was in Mick's office that morning with [football director] Geoff Walsh, and they were saying, 'What happened to Dane? Was he out drinking last night?'

I said, 'We went out for dinner, then to a mate's birthday, and not once did I see him drinking.' But I think he got dobbed in by a certain teammate. I think Bucks wanted him not playing the next final, but Mick was good for that.

I could always go home, go to training without any sleep and I was normal, but Swanny didn't hide it that well. It was probably his downfall. Once, I sent him home and the next day I had a phone call from a mate saying, 'I saw Swanny out at Love Machine.' I said, 'That fuckin' idiot.' He didn't even remember it!

That's the era we grew up in, and Dane was only a couple of years younger than me. You trained hard, played hard, partied hard. As young men, our group didn't want to sacrifice our social life or lose those years, and we thought we could do everything; obviously Swanny did it a lot better than what we did. You look back on it now, and I don't regret a thing, and I'm sure he doesn't either.

Footy's a drainer, these days. It's not even footy anymore. It's like a business, a job. That's why Mick Malthouse was so good. He said to us, 'Boys, I know you like a beer. Do your own thing, just keep it controlled.' You've got 40 players and everyone's different. Good coaches nowadays work with all sorts of personalities, and the ones who can't will never make it.

I rate him as the best I've played with. It was always in him and then he started working hard, he got his fitness to the level of an AFL player and after that, it was all him, really. I reckon it all started around the drawn final against West Coast in 2007, which was when he stood up as an elite footy player. He'd been good in '06, but that was on another level that game, and it started something. That elite A-grade player came from that game, and what he did between the finals of 2007 and probably about 2012, I don't reckon Collingwood's ever had a player who had a period like that on the field.

14

UNDER BUCKS

'You can go back and you can look as far as you like, but in the end, it all boils down to one thing, and that is we need to improve. The first step of that will be analysing where we got to this year, what worked, what didn't.'

—Nathan Buckley, post-preliminary final 2012

We had a decent season in 2012, Nathan Buckley's first year as head coach of Collingwood, despite the ructions of the year before. Everyone knew that Buckley's rise to the head coaching job would bring change with it, as any change of coach does in footy, and Bucks had his own clear idea of what he wanted at Collingwood. I will never forget how it all started, at our first team meeting at the end of 2011, when the first thing that he hit us with was, 'Let's talk about the elephant in the room.'

And right there and then before he said another word, I knew that Bucks was talking about my drinking, or more specifically, the fact that I had got away with a bit under Mick Malthouse. *This is about me, nothing surer,* I thought, and then he looked at me. 'Your drinking, that's not going to fly this year,' he said. 'You'll be dealt with.'

Of course he was referring back to the incident at the end of 2011 when Mick had chosen *not* to suspend me before the final in Perth, despite saying that the assistant coaches (of which Buckley was one) wanted me to be stood down. It could not have been clearer to me, although with hindsight I realised that it wasn't personal, it wasn't directed only at me. It was about the whole club, and it was about saying, 'This is how we roll now.'

I knew from right then that the discipline was going to be tighter, because that's the way that Bucks operated himself; not that it's wrong, it's just how he is. Not only that, but the scrutiny was squeezing tighter everywhere in footy with each year that passed, right across the industry. It was reaching the point where a sly fart might be seen as an attack on the Collingwood brand, or any club's brand for that matter.

Collingwood now was a very *serious* club. Partway through the year, there was an incident that started with a group message that turned ugly. The message was sent by one of the conditioning staff about training changes, some banter built up, and this transformed into some of those crude memes that go around. It was only meant to be seen by the boys in that group message.

Unfortunately, Darren Jolly took it all seriously, and he texted, 'Boys, it's game day, let's get serious here.' When that happened, I hit reply and sent him a shocker of a picture, because I actually thought he was joking. But he wasn't, and when we got to the game that night, he brushed me. We usually warmed up together, but he wouldn't speak to me, and he played one of his best games for the year. The next week, we all had to front the leadership group, and Jolly demanded an apology from me.

He told me that he had shown the picture to his wife, and to a neighbour, to check if his concerns were valid. I said to him, 'It was for just the boys. That's the point. It was never meant to go that far!' I would not apologise to him; I didn't think I had done anything so wrong. But it was an uncomfortable time around the club.

I was no longer part of the leadership group in 2012 after being part of that senior group for a couple of years. The leadership group had been expanded to seven players – Nick Maxwell, who remained on as captain, Scott Pendlebury, Darren Jolly, Luke Ball, Dale Thomas, Travis Cloke and Heath Shaw – but excluding me on players' vote.

Frankly, I was quite happy to be relieved of the responsibility, because I knew by then that it wasn't really me. I was never cut out to be captain, or part of the leadership group, because I was one of the boys. At the time, I just said to them that being a leader didn't change me one bit. It didn't make me prepare more professionally, and it didn't change me on the field, plus there were a bunch of extra meetings that I hated. I said, 'I don't wanna come in here on Monday morning and have another two-hour meeting. I'm not doing it. It doesn't change me. I'm going to be exactly who I am.'

I also despised the idea that I had to punish my teammates, which was clearly part of the leadership group's job. That is the way footy has evolved, whereas in the past, the coaches and the administration would handle all the disciplinary matters. I was always compromised, and I ended up going to the players first and warning them of problems coming their way.

There was one minor incident when Steele Sidebottom and Jarryd Blair had been drinking at a time when they weren't supposed to, I think it was on a Sunday night or on a six-day break, and I had actually been with them. Now that makes it awkward! Before they were brought before the leadership group, I had to get to them and say, 'Boys, they know you were there.'

That's how I handled my time on the leadership group at Collingwood. I would go out to the players and say something like, 'They know this. Your best bet is to say that you did it, and I'll try to make sure nothing happens to you. If you don't admit it, you're stuffed.' Or I might say, 'They don't know, so don't admit it, and they can't prove it. If you stick with your mate, there's no way they can touch you.' So those boys would completely deny any wrongdoing.

My style was to protect my mates, and it was impossible for me to sit on the leadership group and punish people who I liked and who probably hadn't done one bit more than what I was guilty of myself. I hated the hypocrisy of that. *Who am I to get up there and punish people?* That is how I thought about it. *If he's playing good footy, what's the issue?*

It worked the other way, too, because the boys would come to me with their off-field issues, more so than they would with Maxy back when he was captain, or Scott Pendlebury as skipper in my last couple of seasons, because they knew that I was in their camp. They knew that I wouldn't lag on them, so I would get guys coming to me saying, 'Man, this has happened, what do you reckon?'

I guess my approach was the influence of Dad, the union rep, coming out in me to some extent, and I know that people might think it's the wrong behaviour to encourage and not good for the culture of a footy club. A lot of people believe that a player who does something wrong should immediately confess and be honest, but my style is to look after people around me. So blokes would be telling me, 'I went on the piss last night and I wasn't supposed to.' Or I would get a text, 'Come for a drink.'

I also know people in the nightclub scene, and I found out stuff, so I might text a player, 'Be careful man, because I know!' So in most ways it was right that I was no longer part of the leadership group, although when Bucks introduced the new guys at a media conference, he was asked straight away why I was no longer among them:

> Title is one thing but influence is probably the main thing you measure leadership on. We've got a mix of strong characters and different characters in our leadership group and throughout our team in general. You know, Swanny will do what he's always done, and he'll lead by example primarily with what he does on the field, and his form has been of such a high standard and so consistent in recent years that we expect that to continue. But the players believe the guys they've chosen are the guys to take us forward.

Bucks was different to Mick in the way that he wanted to see the footy club run, and in time he would bring in the Leading Teams organisation to address the culture, but on this day as he talked up the leadership group, he explained what had happened over the first few months of his tenure:

> We've also spent a lot of time examining what a Collingwood footballer looks like, the qualities and the values that he lives by and behaves by and he prepares for his football by. I think the playing group have chosen wisely in regard to the guys who they see as standard-bearers for that.

Bucks was just trying to make his tweaks to the way the club functioned, and at the start of that year he had added Rodney Eade, the former Sydney and Western Bulldogs coach, as a football and coaching strategist in the role that had been earmarked for Mick Malthouse. In terms of players, Leigh Brown and Leon Davis had retired, while Brad Dick and John McCarthy were delisted.

We had basically the same team as we had in 2011 and at the season launch, Bucks set the challenge for us:

We're fortunate to have a lot of talent in this footy club but there'd be other clubs who boast the same. We're fortunate to be well resourced, but there are probably clubs who would say that as well. We believe we provide a great environment for every individual representing our club to make the most of that talent, but there would be others who would say exactly that right now. The facts are the team that wants it most, the team that believes in each other and the team that carries a single-minded determination to ride the inevitable setbacks and challenges is the team that will prevail.

I adjusted quickly to having him in charge. After all, he had finished playing a few years earlier, he had already been an assistant coach in 2010 and 2011, and I was not stupid enough that I would fail to grasp that we would have a different relationship as player–coach than we had as teammates. It was what it was.

We started well, and in the round 5 Anzac Day game against Essendon I won the medal for best afield. When I kicked my third goal, I ran back to the centre rubbing my belly in mock celebration. That was because of an article in the *Herald Sun* a few days earlier suggesting that I was overweight, and too casual.

Actually I have always been okay with weight, other than for a few days at the start of a pre-season when I might carry a couple of stray kilograms, so I would like to see how the media people define *overweight*. It's true, I was never ripped and lean, but I'm not fat either, and if someone saw me walking down the street now I would like to think that they wouldn't see me as overweight by any stretch of the imagination. It's just body shape. I naturally have strength and power, I can't do weights and I can't do loads of running, but I come back strongly, and I am naturally quick and powerful. That is my body, whereas some people are unbelievable runners, guys like Steele Sidebottom and Scott Pendlebury.

But people just like to pick holes in you when you're not doing that well, and that article popped into my head when I kicked my third goal that afternoon at the G. The message was, 'Stick that up your arse if you think that I'm fat.' Usually I don't like to play to spite people, but that was one occasion where I'd copped it for a week, and I ended up having a great day in one of the biggest games of the year.

We were flying through round 14, on top of the ladder. We fell off a bit, losing to Carlton and Hawthorn, and then, on the day after our round 19 win over St Kilda, I ran into trouble for drinking again. It was a Sunday night, six days out from the game, I guess that I tried to test Bucks' patience, and he was true to his word from that first team meeting.

I was with Benny Johnson, who was injured at the time, although he was never caught by the club. He had actually sent me home that night, but I made one of those decisions that you tend to make in the fog of alcohol; I came home, then went straight back down my stairs and out again.

Ben and I had been at a friend's birthday party at Hotel Barkly in St Kilda, and neither of us was meant to be drinking; in fact the whole playing group had agreed to an alcohol ban for the rest of the season as a gesture to show that we were dead serious about the challenge ahead. But because I knew the owners of the Barkly, I arranged to be served waters that were part-filled with vodka so that we were not exposed.

Later I went to a party and another mate's place, and I can remember getting in the taxi in the early hours, thinking, *Why is there so much traffic?* Then I realised it was about 7 am Monday, peak hour traffic had hit, and I had a bit more than two hours to get to our Monday training session. I had a shower, tried to get a few minutes' sleep, but felt worse by the time I got to the club.

I had to get in the boxing ring and spar with Jarryd Blair, and I was probably still drunk, so they quickly figured out that I was the worse for wear. One of the first things that occurred was that the leadership group spoke to my mates, Ben and Taz, to check out what had happened. Johnno rang me later, and I said, 'What should I do?' He said, 'They know. They said you won't play again for this team until you admit what you did. I'm telling you, mate, you have to go in there and say that you were drinking.'

So I confessed, and they suspended me for two games (against Sydney and North Melbourne), the first internal suspension of my career. It was also made public, which caused a free-for-all in the media. The leadership group was forceful, and it was heated. I remember Darren Jolly telling me, 'I can't trust you on the field anymore'. I just said to Jolly, 'Look at the year I've been having, how can you not trust me on the field? *Please!*'

If I had been having a bad season, or if he'd said that he couldn't trust me *off* the field, I might have copped it sweet, but I was playing well in 2012. 'You're kidding,' I said to Jolly. 'Just worry about how *you're* going. I'll be all right on the field.'

There was some push back from me, and I questioned their right to punish me, although I copped it sweet. I just felt that I should be able to control the way I operated. At the time, I'd been All Australian four years in a row and I'd won the Brownlow Medal and three Copeland Trophies, so I felt like I knew how to handle myself. I had no doubt that I could continue to perform on the field. My thinking was, *I've done this all my career, and look at the footy I've played. Just leave me alone, get off my back, and stop hounding me!*

Ultimately I was made to stand before the playing group and apologise, and Bucks, who had also had quite a bit to say to me, told the media that I had expressed remorse for putting the club in a bad situation:

The club's protocols around alcohol are very clear. For as long as I can remember, our players know, no drinking on six-day breaks, no drinking when you're injured, and above all else when the playing group get together and decide we're going to make a stand and find an extra little bit of investment for the last part of our season, and we're not going to drink, you don't drink.

He was backed up by Eddie McGuire, who said on Triple M, 'If everyone puts their hand up and pledges, takes the pledge and it's one in all in, then it's one in all in.'

I had never been in favour of the alcohol ban in the first place, and I had made that clear when the players talked about it a few weeks earlier, because to me, it only impacted on a few players. I said to them, 'I don't understand it. Fair enough if we all have to make sacrifices, I understand we're a footy club, but there's 45 on a list, and say 25 who want to go out on a weekend and have a beer, and we'll sacrifice that. But the guys with wives and kids who don't go out, what do they sacrifice? Do we say they can't see their kids on the weekend?'

Of course I was not suggesting it literally, but the point I was making was that we were only penalising half the list. They said, 'Don't be stupid.' So it cost me two games of footy, against Sydney and North Melbourne. We lost to North in round 21 and then Hawthorn in round 22, and momentum had gone. We'd slid to fourth, meaning we had to play top-of-the-table Hawthorn in the qualifying final.

It was a really difficult time, an emotional time, and my mate Chris Tarrant announced in August that it would be his final season of AFL footy. Taz could have played on; he was a sensational athlete and looked after himself well, but he felt the time had come, as he said:

A couple of people were surprised but I've always thought if I could go out on my own terms, that's the way to do it. I've been around for a while where you do see people hang on that little bit long I suppose and play that extra year, and end up playing in the reserves and end up resenting football a bit.

We were well beaten by Hawthorn in the qualifying final, and not long afterwards learned that our former teammate John McCarthy had been killed in a terrible accident in the United States while he was away with the Port players on an end-of-season footy trip. Apparently he was disorientated after being at a nightclub, and found himself locked on the roof of the Flamingo Hotel in Las Vegas. 'JMac' was only 22 years old when he fell to his death after 5 am, trying to jump from the roof on to a palm tree, plunging 9 metres to the pavement.

A lot of the boys were absolutely devastated. He had been with us before moving on to Port Adelaide for the 2012 season, and guys like Brent Macaffer, Nathan Brown and Blairy, who were extremely close to JMac, were really cut up. I was close to him myself, too, used to see him socially a bit, and his locker was near mine, but everyone loved JMac. He was that kind of guy.

Our grieving was played out through the finals and while we got over West Coast in a semi-final to reach the prelim against the Swans at ANZ Stadium, we found out that the funeral service was to be held at Sorrento on the day before the final, which gave us a decision to make, since we were scheduled to fly to Sydney that day to prepare.

It was an easy decision. As Nick Maxwell said, we were not passing up the chance to say farewell to a good mate, and I have always felt that friends and family come first, no matter what. I reckon a few of our guys wouldn't have played the preliminary final at all if the funeral had been on the same day. We went as a group to Sorrento, paid our respects, then jumped straight back on to the bus to Tullamarine Airport and up to Sydney to play the Swans at Homebush on the Friday night.

Not surprisingly, we lost that game, and our season ended there. The boys were drained after a whole week of coming to terms with JMac's death, and the manner of it. The thing is, the people who run footy want to make it seem so serious, but in the end, it's just a game. In weeks like that, things go straight back into perspective. You head into a big final, and you are thinking, *We're going to play a game of footy and one of our best mates has lost his life.*

It made everyone think. You go home, see your loved ones, tell them that you love them because you never know when it'll be too late. When something like JMac's death happens, the loss of someone so young who had so much in front of him, it's like 'Who really cares about winning or losing? There's more to life than footy.'

We tried to honour JMac in that final, as we'd done against West Coast, and he would have wanted us to play well. We talked about playing on raw emotion that night, and about using the game as an outlet for what we were feeling after his funeral, releasing some of the sadness and frustration. But Sydney was too good, Lewis Jetta ran half the length of the field to kick a goal for the Swans, and we just couldn't rise to that particular occasion. Sydney's team included Rat Pack life member Rhyce Shaw and later we would be pleased for him. In the end, a lot of the boys were very emotional because of the defeat ending our season, the end of Tazza's career, and JMac's death.

Bucks told us in his address afterwards in the rooms:

We're all feeling different emotions at the moment, not a lot of them good. I urge you, at some stage, to go and ask Taz how quickly 15 years pass. Most blokes in this room, most, have got one of those little medallions around their neck. Fifteen years and he had 15 chances but he didn't get one. That's all we play for. That and being able to look each other in the eye when we come off the field …

As we have for the last four weeks, as we have throughout the year, we go up, we go down, we stagnate … [we're] side by side together. In particular the last couple of weeks I'm really proud of this group, in particular the last couple of weeks I'm proud of the leaders, I'm proud of our ability to do what we needed to do, not just for ourselves but for our mates, for the club, for the competition, but predominantly for our mates.

We are where we are because of what we've done, we've got to prepare better if we want to avoid this … In real terms, it's a fruitless year because we finished top-four, yes, but we're two hurdles shy of where we wanted to get to, but that doesn't mean we don't acknowledge the work that's been put in along the way.

We've got to work harder, smarter, longer. That's exactly what we're gonna do …

Sydney went on to win the flag, so there was no shame in losing to such a strong team, but unfortunately, it was the start of the slide.

• • •

Bucks showed himself to be a calm and collected coach when he took over. He knew what to say and I think that his time in the media probably helped him. Sometimes the television will show him ranting in the coaches' box but by the time he gets to the rooms, he will be calm. He might raise his voice sometimes but overall he is relaxed and he is a great speaker.

Bucks got his message across really well. He liked more handball to get out of traffic, he was not as wedded to the boundary line as Mick had been, and I liked playing under him even though Mick Malthouse was my favourite coach. When he took over from Mick, Bucks didn't really have his own team, and that was a process that would take a few years.

But he and I connected okay as player and coach. We had our issues, of course, and at times I did feel like I was unfairly targeted in meetings, but it was all about footy. In the end, those hard conversations came from times when I stuffed up. He didn't just pot me for no reason. He was my coach; he had to address problems. We'd talk about it: 'Here's your penalty.' I copped my whack, then the next day, you move on. He didn't carry a grudge and neither did I, and once I copped what I knew was coming, all the people at the footy club supported me. It wasn't like I was hung out to dry or frozen out or anything.

We did okay in Nathan Buckley's first year, a year when there was a lot of change to adjust to. More changes were coming, and quickly. And unfortunately, it was the start of the slide.

NICK MAXWELL

Collingwood captain 2009–2013

I can think of at least half a dozen times in games where it got really tight, and as the captain I grabbed him and said something like, 'We need you, this is on you. You're the one here.' And every single time Swanny would win a clearance, kick a goal, do something. He has always been a big-game player.

Even though he's never wanted the responsibility of leadership, or to be the serious one giving a talk or something like that, he took that responsibility on whenever I looked him in the eye. He would find a way to drag us over the line. That is a great player.

He knew that certain things were non-negotiable, and I'd like to think he had enough belief and respect in me as the captain that he would pull his head in when he needed to. I remember when he didn't [in 2012] it possibly cost him his second Brownlow Medal. He went out drinking on a Sunday night, and I had to confront him the next day and say, 'What were you doing?' We suspended him for two weeks, and he was really good about it. He knew that it was his choice, his decision and it went against team rules. He copped that one and in the Brownlow, he was only five votes behind Jobe Watson.

People ask me how good he could have been if he was a total professional, like Luke Ball or someone who did everything right. I always say, 'Maybe he'd have been really bad.' He's just someone who needs to not put extra pressure on himself, not take himself too seriously, someone who needs a release outside the club. I say to them, 'We've got a pretty good player here. Why would we ask him to be something that he's not?' He wouldn't survive in the industry if he became a footy head, doing everything right. He's just different. It's a good lesson for the industry and the coaches.

He changed the game, a lot. I remember David Buttifant and Mick Malthouse talking about the ice hockey, how they came on and off and went on the burst. Dave put up some stats and said, 'This is what we want to do and this is how it works.' He had the top ten disposals in the league, and he said, 'It's funny how the guy who gets rotated more than anyone has had the most disposals'. It was Swanny. It changed the whole mindset.

He's obviously relaxed and very laid-back and everyone gets that part of him, and he's very dry with his humour. But he worked hard in his own way. Through his peak years, I would be at the club late and you'd walk past the treadmill and you'd see him in there going hell for leather with no one else around. As much as he was one of the cool kids, he still worked his backside off. Swanny cares about footy, absolutely. You can't survive in the game if you don't care. Some things did sting him and he wouldn't let you know about it, but you could see it.

He is also very generous, both with his time and his money, shouting people lunch or dinner or paying for people's trips away, I would hate to know how much he has spent on everyone else. A lot of people wouldn't know that with all the sick children who come to the club and people who want jumpers signed, he would do anything you ask and he would do it for anyone. Often I'd text him and say, 'Mate, can you do a quick video message for this person's birthday?' 'Get well' or whatever it was – it was never too much trouble. He would do anything for other people.

A lot of people say to me, 'How did you and Swanny become mates?' Because we're so unalike, they wonder how this is possible. I always say, 'We're different, but we respect where each other comes from.' I don't try to change him. The expectations and standards I had for him were the same as for any other player and the same as I had for myself, but I also let him be himself. I think that was important to get the most out of him.

One of the first things I say to the young players who come in for their induction is, 'One of the most important decisions you will make is which player you are going to follow. Which player are you going to connect yourself to and copy, train how they train?' But at Collingwood, I used to add, 'Whatever you do, don't pick Swanny!' Because a lot of the young guys would've been drawn to him, just for the reason that he's so different. I've never seen anyone be the way he is and still perform the way he does.

15

THE SLIDE

'The fact is, in many ways mate, you epitomise what we want to turn everyone here into, and that is the best version of themselves. You're really true to who you are. I reckon you've been the same bloke the whole way through, but at the same time you've been able to retain that integrity of who you are, but then fit in with what the club is asking of you.'

—Nathan Buckley, on Swanny's 250th game

Chris Tarrant wasn't the only member of the Rat Pack to depart at the end of 2012; Sharrod Wellingham was traded to West Coast. In fact, it was as if Taz's retirement was the trigger for a mass migration in Nathan Buckley's first few years of coaching.

Was it simple coincidence? I highly doubt it. I think it was a combination of things but it was pretty clear that the club, under Bucks, wanted cultural change. I was disappointed to see my good mates Taz and Sharrod go, but this was only the beginning of the breaking down of the Rat Pack.

There were a huge number of changes in this time. Midway through the 2013 season, Ben Johnson's body gave up on him and he retired. At the end of that season, Alan Didak was delisted and both Dale Thomas (to Carlton) and Heath Shaw (to Greater Western Sydney) were traded out, all of them Rat Pack life members along with Dayne Beams, who was traded to Brisbane at the end of 2014. Darren Jolly and Andrew Krakouer were both delisted at the end of 2012, and Chris Dawes was traded to Melbourne on a four-year deal. By the end of 2014, Nick Maxwell had retired mid-season after a bad ankle injury, Luke Ball retired and Heritier Lumumba was traded to Melbourne.

This is the kind of stuff that happens in football clubs as they try to improve on-field, so it wasn't *all* about the culture, but that was certainly part of what was going on. There was a clear-out happening, and by the time Beams – winner of the 2012 Copeland Trophy – moved to Brisbane Lions at the end of 2014, the Rat Pack didn't exist anymore.

Beamsy is a superstar, he was a big loss. His brother, Claye, was already at Brisbane Lions, and his dad was ill, so you couldn't begrudge him leaving, but I always felt like he wanted to get out of Collingwood anyway. I've no doubt that he had a few issues with Bucks, and the way it works in footy is that when those things happen, another club swoops. Brisbane offered him great money which made the decision easier for him, because as a player, you reach a point in the middle of your career where you can make your best cash. Dayne was at that point.

Sharrod was a Perth boy and he had family issues that were dragging him home to Western Australia, so when the offer came from West Coast he was almost bound to take it. Johnno was done, he kept breaking down, whereas Taz's body was okay, but he was ready to go, and he's made a good fist out of life outside the game.

Alan Didak had more in him, I have no doubt; he was delisted at only 30 by Collingwood, but Dids couldn't see eye-to-eye with the club about the changes, and in any case, we all came from the place that said footy isn't everything. Dids never hid the fact that his relationship with the club had deteriorated by the end of 2014, when he was cut, telling the *Herald Sun*:

We didn't have the best relationship, but at the end of the day, he [Buckley] is the boss and makes all the decisions. My career at Collingwood didn't finish the way I wanted it to, but it is what it is. I always wanted to be a Collingwood man and to stay a Collingwood man forever, but it hasn't ended up like that.

It was hard for me, because I spent so much time with those guys. In particular Ben Johnson had been alongside me right through my career. I did warm-ups with Johnno, I roomed with him, I did weights with him, in fact anything that was to be done in pairs, we did it together for more than ten years.

Rhyce Shaw had needed a fresh start when he was traded to Sydney at the end of 2008. With Heath, his younger brother, there were different reasons. Heater had to go because he didn't get along with the powers that be at Collingwood anymore. Heath had lied to Eddie McGuire and covered for Dids a couple of years earlier, and the one person in the whole footy club you do not want to make look stupid is Ed. He will support you, that's one great thing about Ed, but if you have messed up he will let you know. Then as soon as that rant passes over, he is back in your camp.

But I think that the footy club thought that Heath Shaw was a bad influence in the club, a cultural problem. That's what I gathered from his departure. Mick Malthouse loved him – would never have traded him – but once Mick had gone, it was going to be a problem, because Heath had a history of biting back at the coaches, and he would argue a point. This was the issue at the time, but in my eyes, it never came from a bad place with Heath. It was really about him wanting to win, wanting what was best for the boys.

In the end he was given an amazing deal by the Giants, much more money than he could have extracted from Collingwood and five years of security, so he took the chance to go to that new club and become the Pied Piper with the kids. They follow him around, those boys up in Sydney, and I'm not surprised. Heath and Alan Didak are by far the funniest blokes that I ever played footy with, it was a non-stop comedy routine around the club and, being good mates, they bounced off each other perfectly. They left a big gap at Collingwood with their carrying on; we used to be in tears they made us laugh so much, and they were sorely missed.

In the space of a few years nine of my best mates left the club or were moved on – Maxwell, the Shaws, Johnson, Didak, Tarrant, Wellingham, Thomas, Beams – and I just needed to find a few more close mates at Collingwood. I tweeted around that time about having to find new lunch partners, but it was not as though I was completely on the outer with the younger guys. For instance I have always been close with Scott Pendlebury and Steele Sidebottom and more recently with Marley Williams, too. My core group of friends had gone and I just moved on, even though I am still friends with that original group, the old Rat Pack.

Did Collingwood deliberately break up the Rat Pack? From the outside it probably looks like that. What I do know is that I would have loved to have Heath Shaw, Dayne Beams, Sharrod Wellingham and one or two others in the team in my last few years at the club.

We all had rap sheets in the Rat Pack, there is no doubt. My fight in 2003 and a bunch of drinking incidents were on the record, Sharrod had been done for drink-driving in 2008 and the club was furious, because the TAC was a major sponsor of Collingwood and it withdrew the money after that. Sharrod was only 19 at the time, and it cut him up. He told *The Age* a few years later:

> Initially, I didn't realise the severity of the situation ... I went into the club on the Monday and was just sitting in Lloydy's [then Collingwood development boss Simon Lloyd] office, having a chat and said, 'Bloody hell, I got done DD on the weekend, you wouldn't read about it ...' Well, eventually we did read about it.
>
> I remember Eddie just absolutely tearing shreds off me in his office. He sent me out, I sat down outside, then he called me back in and he quite literally sat next to me, put his arm around me, and said 'We're here for you. We will deal with what's going to happen.' But I wasn't really sure what was going to happen.

It was the same with all of us. Benny Johnson and Chris Tarrant had had their issue over a taxi, Heath Shaw had been fined and suspended for illegal betting as well as his drink-driving incident, Alan Didak had made the front pages for being in a car with a Hells Angel who was alleged to have gone on a shooting rampage in 2007. An appearance on the front page seemed to be a prerequisite for joining the Rat Pack.

The *Herald Sun* had given us the tag around 2008 and we ran with it, and the supporters embraced it as well. I know that people say footballers should be role models but we were normal boys, not robots, and we bled for the footy, loved the footy club. We stretched the rules every now and then, and pushed the friendship with Collingwood, but we played hard on the field, we were all good players and we had a great time together. We were lads, and you could see us enjoying it.

We even kicked the ball to each other on the field, looked after each other. I knew where Johnno was before I knew where I was, because he played off half-back and he would scream as soon as I got it in the midfield. I would give it to him even if he was in the wrong position, and then he might give it straight back. It was the same with Dids, I knew exactly what he was doing if I came out of the middle, and I would hit him up.

I think people actually liked us because we had time for everyone, and we cared about each other, and if we stuffed up on the field we would tell each other about it, but we also backed each other up to the point of lying to protect each other! There was a camaraderie to the Rat Pack that no one else really had, and Mick Malthouse loved it. He was far from stopping it or changing it.

Over the years the Rat Pack legend had grown legs. Guys from other footy clubs, out in suburbs or the bush, would send us photos of a group and say, 'This is our Rat Pack.' Groups like that exist in any footy club, bunches of guys with something in common, and I certainly loved it at Collingwood.

When we're together we might put out a photo of us on Twitter or Instagram, like eight of us at Alan Didak's wedding in January 2014 for instance: 'The rat pack all back together for Dids' wedding. #goodtimes #memories'

There we were, me with Heath, Rhyce, Dale, Sharrod, Dids, Johnno and Taz, all scrubbed up for the occasion.

And there was the five-year premiership reunion in October 2015: '5 year premiership reunion today for the party pies. can't wait for the 6/7/8/8 and a half/9/10 and so on reunions … Awesome to see all the boys.'

Or after I injured my foot, when I caught up with a few of the Collingwood gang in April, I shared this: '7 cold pies and 1 mildly warm one. Quality lunch with quality (using the term loosely) people.'

People loved that stuff, and whenever I mentioned the Rat Pack, they knew what I was on about straight away. Mateship. Good times.

I would rather be a bit off-centre, not quite straight down the line, than be a robot. I never wanted to be a generic guy, a beige kind of person who got lost in the mud, and at least with the Rat Pack we stood for something. It's one rare thing that we can thank the *Herald Sun* for, that one.

• • •

It was through this time that the Leading Teams organisation came back to Collingwood. They had been inside the club before, back in the time when Tony Shaw was coaching, around 1999, but Mick Malthouse was old school, and he got rid of them not long after he took over the job in 2000.

Leading Teams is a company that does leadership development through what it calls a Performance

Improvement Program; it's in place at a lot of AFL clubs. It was started by Ray McLean at Central District in the SANFL in the 1990s, went to St Kilda briefly under Stan Alves' coaching, then really exploded after Paul Roos brought it to the Sydney Swans from 2003. It is about fostering good culture within the club and encouraging open dialogue and strong feedback, those kinds of things.

Bucks wanted it at Collingwood and I didn't like it, even though I enjoyed Ray's company. He came down to the club as the facilitator, and he was good at what he does; he is a decent bloke, pretty funny with some of his lines and he has this ability to make the meetings go quickly. I came to understand how it helped some people, probably some of the young guys. But it did nothing for me. I understand that giving feedback to people is relevant, but I also know that the feedback is always the same and besides that, I was never going to change. I heard the same old stuff I had been hearing for years: 'We're worried about your off-field behaviour' or 'Can you start to impart some knowledge to the kids, come out of yourself.' Later on it was feedback like: 'You need to manage your body properly.'

I could understand the advice I was getting about helping the kids, because previously I had probably operated in my own little clique, even kept to myself a bit. They said, 'You've got a knowledge of the game, and we'd like you to impart that to some of these new guys.' I was happy doing it, especially with guys I had a relationship with, like Marley Williams. I might talk to them about off-field things as much as on-field. Early in my career I just wanted to get in and get out but later on I realised that I needed to do things like that. It was understandable. Everything that the other players said to me through the Leading Teams stuff, I got.

Sometimes the idea would be to go away and write down the strengths and weaknesses of other players, and what you would like to see from them, and then you would do the same for yourself. We would come back together after that as a group and compare the two documents, and only rarely would they be miles apart.

It was done peer-to-peer, not so much from Ray McLean up in front of the group, so players would split into small groups and go away to talk about each other. Since the Leading Teams program became popular, it's the peer reviews that have had the most publicity; guys like Jason Akermanis when he was the Western Bulldogs, and Barry Hall at the end of his time in Sydney, have been critical.

I do agree that the reviews are a bit of a licence for players to bag each other, and even the young guys were allowed to have a crack, because everyone is equal in that way under the model. But I'd learned my trade under the system where you earned your stripes, waited your turn to speak out. When I was a kid at Collingwood, I said virtually nothing until I was good enough, and later on, if a first-year player came to me and said I needed to pull my head in, I'd be thinking, *Are you kidding, mate?* Although for the harmony of the team, I wouldn't say anything back to him.

I've always cared about winning and I don't want to mess up the team. People always said to me that I wasn't hard enough on my mates, that I would rather be liked than respected. But being hard on my mates is just not my style. On game day I might have something to say, but I could never criticise anyone for going out or drinking or stuffing up, because I knew that I did that myself.

So I never complained about Leading Teams. For all the hot water I found myself in over the years for drinking, when it came to game day I like to think I was selfless, that I did the right thing by the team. So I went to the meetings – and I *hate* meetings – and I participated, not too loudly, but I was involved. I didn't bag anyone.

Through that phase I was also protecting other players and under the Leading Teams model I probably should have been making that public at the time, dobbing the guy in, but I didn't like that style at all. I was not about to bury a 20-year-old kid who was playing good footy when he was only doing what I was doing. Instead I'd give advice to those boys, something like: 'If you want to have a drink, just stay at home, or go to someone's house where you won't get in trouble.'

But truthfully I never got anything out of the program. It would take more than Leading Teams to change me as a person – I didn't want to change who I was!

Bucks had his idea of what he wanted, and to be honest, it has probably taken him until 2016 to get near what he was looking for. By the start of the 2016 season, we only had seven players on our list who had played in the 2010 premiership, which is a big turnover. We went backwards for a couple of years, but who is to say that we wouldn't have declined had Mick Malthouse remained on as head coach for a year or two longer? But we're dealing in hypotheticals here ...

• • •

Another big change at the end of 2013 was the club's elevation of Scott Pendlebury to the captaincy ahead of Nick Maxwell. It was done by vote, but what I found strange was that Maxy won the players' vote, but they still gave Pendles the job.

Now Scott was always going to end up as captain of Collingwood; that was a given. We're good friends, and I rate him the best player I ever played alongside at Collingwood. If people saw the work he does around the club they wouldn't be surprised at how good he is. He is just the perfect professional, he's so driven to be the best he can, and he has the bonus of great talent, so much time to work his magic.

But my point is that Maxy had more votes, so why go to the bother of voting in the first place? It is not a knock on Pendles, but the way it happened caused Maxy to struggle. Maybe it would have been easier if the club had come to him and said, 'Listen, we're thinking about handing it over.' But to hear it outright one day would have been tough: 'Mate, you're not going to be captain.'

Under the Leading Teams system, you have to nominate a group of players who you want to be your leaders, and you have to do it in front of the group. You can pick who you want, and I certainly voted for Maxy. I thought that Pendles would take over the captaincy, say, the following year, and I had no problems with him getting the job. But I did rate Nick Maxwell and I don't think it was right, the way it happened.

Bucks' game plan was a little different, too. Mick had been about hitting the boundary, and at worst we would take the ball out of bounds and start again, backing ourselves to win the contested ball. With Bucks, we tried to move the ball a bit more freely, and a touch more through the middle of the ground.

Bucks is great at articulating what he wants, he has always been excellent at getting his point across, and he knows what to say. That kind of stuff has never been an issue for him, and that's why he was so successful when he spent time in media. That time in 2008 and 2009 was great for him; he formed relationships and got some well-deserved respect.

Also before he coached Collingwood he had worked two years as an assistant to Mick; he got to see the pressure of coaching a big club like Collingwood, and how it worked. So overall, he was better prepared than a guy who'd come straight out of the game to coach based on his playing ability.

With some clear air, putting 2012 and its tough end behind us, we had high hopes for 2013 but we slipped backwards slightly. We lost two of the last three games to miss the top four, finishing sixth with a 14–8 record, and had a home final against Port Adelaide. They beat us and we were knocked out of the finals in the first week.

I hurt my ribs in that game, possibly even broke them, and ended up playing forward and kicking three goals. It was friendly fire from Ben Reid that caused it when he crashed into me as I was running back with the flight of the ball, thinking that I was right. He just smashed me and I couldn't breathe afterwards. I must have sounded bad, because my opponent was saying to me, 'Are you all right?' and I could only say, 'I can't breathe.'

I couldn't run much in the last quarter (thanks Reidy!) and Port blew us away in a big surprise, in what turned out to be Alan Didak's last game for Collingwood, just his fifth of an injury-plagued final season. Port had jumped up under Ken Hinkley's coaching in that year, and they played a high-speed game that was hard to stop. I couldn't laugh without pain for a couple of weeks as the dust settled on our quick exit from the finals.

• • •

I think the players knew that Mick would coach again in the AFL; coaching was part of his make-up. He wasn't finished and he just couldn't let go. I always knew that he would coach once the year's grace he had given Collingwood after he was released from his contract was up. So we weren't surprised when he signed on to coach Carlton from 2013 after the old enemy sacked Brett Ratten to make room for the master coach. Mick had been big in the media, and he'd come back to see if he could turn around the Blues and have a crack at breaking Jock McHale's all-time record of coaching 714 games.

At the end of 2013, Dale Thomas took up a big offer to go across town on free agency. No doubt, it was all about rejoining Mick and David Buttifant, who was also crossing to the Blues, and the offer he had was way better than he could have got at Collingwood. Daisy had suffered a bad foot–ankle injury and only played a few games in 2013, but I remained convinced that he would find his way back to his best.

We had introduced some new players like Jamie Elliott and Marley Williams, while the old warhorse in me kept going with an average of 31 disposals and 21 goals for the season. I was chosen as an All Australian for the fifth time in a row, won the Bob Rose Trophy for best finals player, and was runner-up to Pendles in the Copeland Trophy voting. At the Copeland awards night, there was no hiding the fact that all my old mates had gone: 'I thought I was going to be sitting at a table on my own but I managed to find a couple of friends.'

I also finished third in the Brownlow Medal behind Gary Ablett and Joel Selwood, polling 26 votes. I was a vote from the lead, held by Selwood, with a round to be counted but there was a game against North Melbourne to come; we'd lost, and while I had touched the ball a few times, I didn't expect to get any votes, and I didn't. Ablett polled a three-voter in the last round for Gold Coast to win it.

It was a good year for me, personally, but my body was aching. I had reconstructive surgery on my right wrist in the 2013–2014 off-season to fix a problem I had been dealing with for a couple of years; I had actually had the same operation on the other wrist four years earlier. They were both shot, and I have no idea why, but I knew that, finally, I would need to have the second wrist fixed.

For a while I had held off, and my thinking was, *I can be All Australian with a wrist that won't allow me to tackle or hold a plate, so what's the issue?* But it got too hard, and I was in a cast for ages, even going away on my usual holiday with the plaster on. When I got back from overseas I could at least start running in December, but I didn't feel myself – something wasn't quite right.

It started with night sweats for about ten days, drenching the bed. I had to get up in the middle of the night, towel myself down and line up towels underneath me when I went back to bed. To be honest, I thought it was just the alcohol toxins pouring out of me from the footy trip away. Then one Monday we had a 2-kilometre time trial at the club, just for the guys who were in the rehab group, and I ran last.

I ran 7:23 or something like that, and while I was never a super endurance athlete, I had previously had the power and speed to get past a few of the stragglers at the very least, but this time Jarrod Witts went past me, and Ben Kennedy, and a few guys who I would normally have covered.

The club thought I was being lazy, and I remember Scott Burns, Bucks' assistant, having a go at me: 'That's not acceptable!' But I told him to push off, that I would be right to go by round 1. It was my usual stance: 'Leave me alone and let me do my thing. If everyone gets off my back I'll be the same player I've always been.'

But that night I had two episodes of the night sweats at home, and Taylor, who had been at me to have it checked out, finally insisted that I see a doctor. The next day, I was tested and found out that I had glandular fever, and that I had been training with it for a fortnight! I did not feel horrendous any of that time, but I wasn't hungry, and I was tired all the time, so the diagnosis did make sense to me. I had figured it was just fatigue from the grind of pre-season, but I must admit the hot–cold alternating temperatures were a worry, and I am glad that Taylor made me have it checked.

Scott Burns was not the only party who had been interested in my fitness. My old sparring partner, the *Herald Sun*, had weighed in (pardon the pun) with a back-page story headlined 'FAT CHANCE' in big, bold letters in which the journalist, Sam Landsberger, questioned my preparation and my commitment to the task. Having acquired a taste for social media, I nailed him using my Twitter account. I especially enjoyed the hashtag:

@SamLandsberger really?? Fark me slow news day. Didn't think it could go much lower. You're down there with shark shit at the minute.

I'd appreciate the Herald Sun stop using me as clickbait and to sell papers. It's becoming absurd. #IDFWU #imofftosmashsomekfc

I found out later that Landsberger hadn't even written the story, that an editor wrote it off a picture that made me look fat, and put Sam's by-line on it, basically.

When I went back to the club, the first person I chased down was Burnsy, saying with a smirk, 'Mate, you can piss off. I did that with glandular fever! Imagine how well I'd run if I didn't have glandular!' But it did limit my pre-season quite a bit; until Christmas I was only walking or jogging a couple of laps. I thought, *This is the life, come back in January and I'll be fine!*

Of course it wasn't that simple. I did some running just before the practice matches to build my fitness up, but straight away I contracted Achilles tendonitis and also patella tendonitis in the knee. I didn't want to miss any footy, so I kept going through the pain, but I could hardly walk, let alone run. With hindsight, the 2014 season was coloured from the start. I started to get back problems that related to the sciatic nerve, with pains shooting down my back and right into my hamstrings. I had turned 30, and old age was kicking in.

I had to sit down on an angle or the pain would shoot through, and I had to sit on my right butt cheek all the time, even when I was driving or on the toilet. It turned out that I had three slipped discs in my back, I couldn't bend over to pick up the footy and I couldn't run. Then later on in the season I tore the intercostal muscles in my rib cage in a game, and to top it off, I missed three games late in the year because of plantar fasciitis in my right foot.

I had to stand out of five games with injury in that season, the most I had ever missed, but even when I played, the injuries were there. To be fair to the coaches, I didn't tell them anywhere near the truth about what was going on, because in my head, I was thinking, *I can still do better than a young kid coming in, even when I'm not 100 per cent.*

I had my moments in 2014; in the Anzac Day game against Essendon I won the medal for best on ground with 26 disposals and four goals. I loved those games, the crowd, the atmosphere and the fact it was Essendon as an opponent. I averaged 25 disposals across the games that I played, which was the first time since 2009 that I hadn't hit the 30 mark, but I felt like I was playing okay considering that I was not at full fitness.

It was after the second game against Essendon in round 17 at the MCG that I finally confessed the full extent of my problems to the fitness staff. They were walking around the group in the rooms straight after the game, asking each of us how we were. When the physiotherapist Dave 'Scruff' Francis got to me he probably got a shock when I said, 'I'm no good. That's it for a while.'

I had some scans on my foot and the medical staff weren't happy with me: 'Mate, you can't play with this.' So I missed three games as Collingwood continued to fall away badly in the second half of the year. We went 8–3 for the first half, then 3–8 for the second portion of the year to miss the finals for the first time since 2005.

I had three epidurals in my back that year, and I reckon that I had ten painkilling jabs in both knees, as well as both heels. I just chased my tail all year, and with hindsight, I should have taken eight weeks or so off and tried to get my body right. But as much as I moan about footy sometimes, the one thing I have always loved is game day, and I miss it when I don't play. My attitude was: 'I'm a professional, this is what I get paid to do. This is the one day of the week where it's actually where I can express myself, do what I like. This is why I get paid what I get paid. It's why I am who I am.'

I hated standing out, and at the same time, I started to cop heat in the media. Terry Wallace, the former player and coach, is one media person who I can recall writing me off in that year. It's not an easy game, and what I find amazing is how quickly ex-players forget that. In their eyes, they never stuffed up a kick or made a mistake, and they have to justify their role in the media by potting blokes. I don't ever envisage doing media as a job but if I did, I would like to think I'd have some sympathy for players and that I'd remember that no one is perfect.

I couldn't win; if I played with my injuries I was getting criticised, both inside and outside the club, and if I didn't play, it didn't help the club. I reckon half the players in the AFL would have been happy with 25 touches a game but inside, I was copping it for not chasing my opponents, which was never a strength of mine anyway.

It was a shocker of a year and it finished on a sour note – a 10-goal defeat by Hawthorn in the week before the finals, as the Hawks went on to win the premiership for the second year in a row. They had found a way to win again despite losing Lance Franklin to Sydney on free agency, but Collingwood was in a difficult place. The 2010 premiership suddenly seemed a million miles into the distant past. We just lost too many players, on reflection, too many good ones to sustain what we had built.

It is just amazing how quickly footy changes. In those five years from 2009 to 2013, I'd been All Australian, won three Copeland Trophies, a Brownlow and a premiership, and the sun seemed to come out wherever we went. The time seemed to pass so fast. Suddenly the Rat Pack was down to one Rat. And I was the oldest player at Collingwood.

NATHAN BUCKLEY

Collingwood coach from 2012

It was going to take something like that injury to stop him, really. He's been amazingly durable. One thing that I think people forget when you look at the champions of the game is that they make it look so easy and because it looks easy, like it's coming naturally, they look like they're not under duress. When you look at Swanny and the way he carries himself around the game, you think he's uncomplicated and there's no duress or trauma at all, but he's carried so many things into games in terms of injuries, and he's also carried the pressure of being the best player in a really good side. He's carried high expectations around finals and he's welcomed that in his own way, but it was going to take a train to stop him and the injury he got in the first round was horrific.

He's always gone about it his own way and he's been true to himself, but there have been times that my personality or Swanny's personality versus the club's values and professionalism meant we've had to have discussions about 'what this looks like and where we go from here', as a captain and as a coach. But Swanny's a smart bloke, and the club is fair, because when you've got a high performer like him, you have to look for some common ground. Sometimes the club needed to put the foot down and sometimes Swanny said, 'I can't bend that far.'

I suspect that he would have adjusted if he was starting out now. There was definitely some tough love early in his career, and times when he didn't look like a patch on the player he became. Even he

255

would have doubted whether he was worthy, whether he wanted to do it. He comes across as a bloke who's so genuine and true to himself and they're the things I often use to describe him, and you get the impression that Swanny's the same as he has always been. But the fact is, he needed to make sacrifices to go from what he was as an 18-year-old to become the player he was. It's not as if he just kept being the same bloke. He's made compromises and he's invested in himself and his footy and the football club to become what he became. He made those judgement calls as a young bloke and at some stage he would have asked himself, 'Do I want to do this?' But he made those decisions and he became a champion through them.

We suspended him in 2012. The players had got together and said they wouldn't drink for the last six weeks, and Swanny was part of that, and then a week later he's been caught and we're talking, and he's like, 'I know I stuffed up, but I think you need me.' That was pretty much where Swanny was coming from. 'You still need me to play, don't ya?' You look at him and say, 'Given everything we've decided, I don't know that we can.' The leadership group was involved in that, but there was a lot going on behind the scenes at that time, settling down after the handover, and Swanny was in the middle of that.

What you want is an open enough relationship and a strong enough connection where you both understand where each other is coming from so that you both can have real conversations about their contribution, where the club's going, what you need and where you're going with it. But outside of the footy club, there is a want to label people. Swanny is labelled as a larrikin who couldn't give a toss about anything, and I'm a hard-nosed, unmoving, uncompromising maniac, basically. But he's not that and I'm not that. Swanny plays up to it and he loves poking fun at stereotypes and playing up to them for a laugh and maybe he perpetuated it in some ways, but no, we've never had a problem.

He keeps his competitive streak well hidden. I've always said I don't reckon I've seen many blokes who've had as much pride in actually playing the game. I mean, he couldn't care less for training, although he does what he has to, he couldn't care less about meetings or ticks and crosses. He gets all the information he needs from playing the game, what works and what doesn't and then he stores it in the back of his mind and rolls out and fixes it the next week. The other thing that is really clear about Swanny is that as his career went on, he wasn't always turned on by your standard home-and-away game. He needed to believe that there was something more riding on it than just four points against any old opposition. The bigger the game, the more turned on he was, and that became evident at the peak of his career because he played his best footy on the biggest stages.

16

#BLAMEDANE SWAN

'A lot of the media had written me off. As much as I say I don't read it, it does come across your desk – not that I have one.' – Swan

— @CollingwoodFC 16 March 2016

AFL football was swamped by talk about drugs for most of the 2013 and 2014 seasons, as the Essendon–ASADA affair rolled on and the media speculated about changes to the league's separate policy on illicit drugs. The Essendon drama was everywhere, with 34 players being charged and found guilty of using the performance-enhancing drug thymosin beta 4 by the Court of Arbitration for Sport in Switzerland.

Essendon had been banned from playing finals in 2013, fined $2 million, and coach James Hird had been suspended for a year, meaning that Bomber Thompson had taken over as coach for 2014. It was the story that would never go away, and it led to a lot of talk about illicit drugs as well, the non-performance-enhancing type.

At the end of November 2012, our chief executive, Gary Pert, had gone on record with his concerns about players in relation to illicit drugs:

> There is volcanic behaviour which is what you are talking about. We have had experts and consultants talk to us, and psychologists, and there is definitely a concern that has been raised to all of the club CEOs and the AFL are very aware of this.

On 29 November, journalist Caroline Wilson used her column in *The Age* to voice the argument that Collingwood should sack me. Caro seemed to think she knew a lot about me.

It is true that Collingwood's chief executive Gary Pert genuinely believes that illegal drugs have infiltrated football clubs to a dangerous and damaging degree – a degree that the current AFL illicit drugs policy cannot hope to adequately address.

But it is equally true that Pert, his president Eddie McGuire and Magpies coach Nathan Buckley are desperately worried about what is taking place in their own backyard. Pert has been telling friends for weeks that he is tearing his hair out with concern over the behaviour of certain players at his club.

Further down in the article, after suggesting that the club should get rid of me, she hammered me:

Swan is not the only player at Collingwood who has been a law unto himself during his end-of-season break but he has been a dreadful influence for some time and to take a stand now could prove the correction required as Ray McLean moves in to rebuild the erosion of discipline and dedication and bring together what appears to have become a team divided.

The club has asked Swan whether he has been using drugs and he has denied it. St Kilda has unofficially confronted Sam Fisher with the same question in recent days and he denied it also. So did Ben Cousins for two years at West Coast. Even if

Swan is telling the truth about drugs his cavalier behaviour has helped create a culture which is not healthy.

I glanced at the article, but I don't have much time for Caro, and it was damaging to me, as well as hurtful. She probably sticks by her story, I know that she said she had been speaking to people at the football club, but I thought that it carried an underlying dislike of me that I could not understand.

From what I was told, her negative opinion of me came from an incident at Flemington races the year before, an Emirates Stakes day when one of my mates was involved in a punch-on with her son. It was nothing to do with me, though. We were in the nursery area, and my friend had a party going with his clients and there were all age ranges there, from kids to 70-year-olds, and in the marquee next door there was a bunch of teenagers who were carrying on a bit.

At the end of that day, one of the blokes from their group was sitting on a chair that belonged to us, and we were packing up, and someone asked him if we could take the chair. The guy refused, and said, 'I'm sitting on it.' Which escalated into a blue in which punches were thrown. Again, I was not involved in that fight in any way, but from what I heard, Caro believed that I'd hit her son.

If I had been involved, there were people with phones everywhere, and from experience I know that someone would have snapped a picture or some video of me, but nothing came out because I just stood and watched. I knew exactly what would happen if I became involved.

That was the first of a lot of pretty nasty things that Caroline Wilson said about me, and to this day that's the only explanation for the grudge that she seems to hold against me. We have never met. Fortunately, Collingwood was quite supportive after the original article appeared in the newspaper. Bucks went to his Twitter feed: 'Still waiting for your call Caroline … not a quote in sight. Don't ever presume to speak on Collingwood's behalf.'

What you have to realise, and what we know very well, is that Collingwood sells newspapers, especially if it is a Collingwood drama, or a Collingwood stuff-up. Throw in the fact that I've been one of the highest-profile players, and you have stories that get traction, stories that will hit the front page.

So I had to lay low after that; a mate of mine had a buck's party and I couldn't even turn up, because it was everywhere in the media. I spoke to the club about it, and Eddie came out on radio to defend me:

> What we don't want to start doing is having a witch-hunt.
> We don't want to start having the burning at Salem, but we
> do want to take action to eradicate this issue. People like
> Caroline today have made a quantum leap from turning this
> into a police issue if you like, or a sanction issue, this is still a
> health issue. I don't know if there's been any strikes against
> any players at Collingwood, certainly we don't have any
> players on three strikes because we'd know about that.

It didn't affect me greatly, and I was never going to change because of Caroline Wilson, but what hurt was the impact that it had on my family. My mother was in tears when I saw her, and my grandma, too, and that's when you realise that anything like that can be written, without any real foundation, and it can hurt people.

I said to my parents, 'Don't worry about her. It's a bullshit story.' But when your mum hugs you and starts crying, it's hard. She said: 'You're my son, we hate people saying that about you.' I think my grandma even wrote a letter to Wilson, and Mum certainly did, and I don't think Caro is getting an invitation to the Swan Christmas party.

How would Wilson know about my private life? If someone at the football club told her those things then it would be disappointing, no doubt, but I cannot remember being asked questions about drugs directly by Collingwood, and I don't think it was a big part of my life.

I just thought the attack was unnecessary. I mean, I'd been overseas, as always, and the only time people knew what I was up to was if I posted a photo on Instagram. I actually think it is a great idea for players to get away and have a stress-reliever, get out of the bubble, whether you go to Japan for the food or the art, or you go to Vegas to party, or Alaska to see the whales, I don't care. Everyone should do something.

I had played for 14 years, and it is tough to grind it out, thinking nothing but footy for that long, and my style is to get away and forget about it. Which is not for everyone, but it can work, and I should not have to defend myself on that point.

• • •

I will put this on the record. I have experimented with what some people call recreational drugs, but have never taken performance-enhancing drugs or what you might call 'heavy drugs'. I have been tested far too many times to even think about anything that would enhance performance, and in my eyes it is not part of our game's culture anyway.

I also have never received a strike against my name in 15 years of AFL football. Not one positive test under the AFL's illicit drugs policy, which, given the amount of times I was tested, proves that drugs have never been an issue throughout my career, despite what some people in the media have implied through various articles and commentary.

When I was about 16, I smoked some marijuana, and I hated it. I was hanging around with some older blokes who smoked, and I thought that I would try it, but my lungs couldn't handle it; to this day, I hate any smoking. But I have experimented with substances, and there is a context to put this in, I reckon. Plenty of 30-year-olds in Australia have.

The culture has changed, and people have to understand that. Back when I started playing AFL footy, if you walked into a house party and saw cocaine or an ecstasy tablet, you would be shocked. Now, if you go to a house party and see people using cocaine, it doesn't raise an eyebrow. I know that it is illegal, but if you go to a party now and there is no cocaine, people will say, 'Shit party.'

That is the reality of Australia now. On the latest figures, for instance, 8 per cent of Australians used cocaine once or more in their life, 35 per cent of Australians have used marijuana and 10.9 per cent have used ecstasy. These are not small numbers. I am not promoting it, or encouraging it, or glorifying it, but that's the way things are, and it's changed a lot. Of course I have tried drugs but it doesn't mean that I have a habit or a problem, it doesn't mean that I do it every single weekend or to the extent that people have speculated about.

Everyone in Australia would know someone who has done some drugs, unless you're a priest (and I am sure that is not unheard of, either). So why would you be surprised or shocked or outraged to find out it happens in footy?

From what I've seen, it is nowhere near as big an issue in footy as it is outside the game. I can only speak for myself, and I have a reasonable clue on what happens in the big wide world, but I believe that drug use is certainly not as common in footy as it is in general society.

No way do the AFL players use to the extent of the guy next door who is not drug-tested, not scrutinised and does what he wants. With the amount of testing of AFL players, including the hair testing that they now do, they will know who is using drugs. In my opinion, it is nowhere near as rampant in footy as people say it is. We're just in the spotlight, in the headlines because we live in a fishbowl.

I have been tested at least 80 times, to the point where I played a few subtle little games with the testers from ASADA. Once, they came to my house at 6 am about a week after I had already been tested during the pre-season camp in Arizona, and I tweeted: 'Stop sending out drug testers at 6am. It's starting to piss me off. What's wrong with the afternoon? You can't catch me anyway. Too clever.'

Another time I posted an Instagram photo of the ASADA tester at my table, handling the samples, and all I did was put a big target on my back. It was a stupid thing to do, I realise now, because they came for me after that, testing me all the time. But it wasn't meant to piss them off; it was about telling the world that it was 6.30 in the morning and I was getting tested.

The ASADA guy complained to Collingwood about it being an invasion of privacy for me to post that photo, and I thought that was a bit rich. I mean, it was 6.30 in the morning, my partner was asleep in the next room, I am doing a drug test but *I* am apparently invading someone's privacy? In the end, I had to apologise to ASADA, or rather the club wrote a letter and I signed it, but I thought it was ridiculous.

At Collingwood at the start of 2015 we had our own suspensions, after Lachie Keeffe and Josh Thomas tested positive for the steroid clenbuterol. Needless to say it was a bombshell in the media, because this was a performance-enhancing drug, and Josh and Lachie ended up being suspended for two years by the AFL.

But what happened to Josh and Lachie could have happened to a few people. We had a break after our pre-season training camp, and they were at the St Kilda Festival. From what I understand, the clenbuterol was laced into some cocaine that they used in St Kilda the night before, which Josh admitted to the media: 'We can only assume it occurred in a night out prior to testing, when we took illicit drugs. At no stage did we knowingly take clenbuterol.'

Now you can argue that they shouldn't have been using cocaine, but they did not deserve what happened to them, in my view. They are both good kids, and I don't consider them to be drug cheats, even though that label will be attached to them. I would be surprised if there are any actual drug cheats in the AFL.

If they were taking cocaine, I know them well enough to know that they didn't do it often. I was shocked, because it wasn't in their characters at all. I know that it's not a great look, I get that. Any time a football club is linked to drugs, recreational or performance-enhancing, it's less than ideal, but I thought Collingwood handled it well, leaving a spot open for them on the playing list once their suspensions were complete. They will learn from this, and you will probably see the two hardest working footballers on the list in Josh and Keefy from 2017.

Gary Pert said on the day in August when their suspensions were announced that Collingwood would stand by the players:

> It will ultimately cost them hundreds of thousands of dollars and damage their reputations. They are good people who have made a bad decision that we believe is not part of a pattern of behaviour for these individuals. Our commitment to redraft them says much about our regard for them.

That was the environment we were in during 2015. In May that year, the Fremantle midfielder Ryan Crowley was suspended for a year after he tested positive for a banned substance contained in a painkiller. Crowley said that he took the substance to help him overcome chronic back pain.

Jake Carlisle of Essendon was a slightly different case. He allowed himself to be filmed snorting a white powder while in Las Vegas on an end-of-season trip, around the same time he had been picked up by St Kilda in a trade. Then the video went up on Snapchat, and of course within minutes somebody took a screenshot of it with their phone, passed it on to the media, and it went everywhere.

What got me about this was that a mate's mate had done him in, somebody who thought that they could make a dollar out of passing that on to the media, just because they could. Yes, he has probably done the wrong thing, and it was silly to send the video like he did, but he was betrayed, and I felt some sympathy for him.

The St Kilda player Ahmed Saad had been banned for 18 months at the end of 2013 for a positive test to the stimulant methylsynephrine, which was contained in a Viking brand sports drink called 'Before Battle' that he drank prior to a game, not knowing that it contained a substance banned under the World Anti-Doping Agency code.

No way known is Ahmed Saad a drug cheat, but his situation probably enlightened a lot of players. The lesson is: If you want to try a new sports drink, take it straight to the footy club to be checked. A few years earlier in that situation, a player would not have thought twice. I would guarantee you that now, even if a mate threw you a sports drink in the dressing rooms and it was a brand you'd never heard of, you would have it checked out.

Morally, these guys were not in the wrong, I reckon. I would even say the same for the Essendon players, because as much as people have said about that case, most players I know say that they would have done the same as those boys. I would be staggered if they were trying to deliberately cheat the system; I think they just did what their medical staff told them to do.

All of these cases have had massive publicity, because that's how it works, but how many cases of actual drug cheating have we seen in the AFL? Not too many, I would say, if we look at real drug-cheating, with people injecting themselves with human growth hormone or testosterone or whatever it might be.

If you look at NFL, basketball, cycling, track and field and other sports, there have been so many more people caught. We are the most tested athletes in the world, and if they tested that much in other sports, I would bet their results would be even higher. I have been tested by ASADA half a dozen times a year for my whole career, and even more in the latter years, and I have never returned a positive, so they must think that I have a great metabolism (and looking at my body shape, I surely doubt that), or I'm very lucky!

But it is right that the AFL does the testing for performance-enhancing drugs because you don't want athletes cheating or getting an advantage. I don't have a problem with the code itself, except that a lot of people lump it in with recreational drugs, and that's a broader society issue.

It is the performance-enhancing drugs that they should be focused on, and in my opinion if people in footy clubs are going to leak information about illicit drugs to the media and the journalists are going to make a big deal out of the illicit drugs code, then the AFL Players' Association should tell the league that it will not happen anymore. No policy at all, no problem.

Remember that the illicit drugs code, with the three strikes policy and the educational focus, was agreed to in 2005 by the players. It was the players who allowed the testers to turn up at any date or time, while they were overseas on holidays or with their friends and family.

As for Essendon, I understand 100 per cent what happened to the players. Because as a player, if a doctor or a medical person from the club gives you something that he or she says will make you feel better, then you take it. I felt for the players in that scenario, because all AFL clubs have supplements programs.

Personally, I don't take caffeine tablets, although they are commonly in use (and I don't even drink coffee). The footy club has always had protein supplements, but I don't bother with those, either, and there is a nice new bottle down in the protein bar at the Holden Centre, our headquarters, with my name on it. I never touch it. I will not even take painkillers during the week at training, because I don't want to build up a tolerance. Save those for match day, I say.

With the drug issue, the AFL clubs are hellbent on driving a culture now, and they don't want it wrecked by players misbehaving. It's not just drugs, of course, it's alcohol as well, and I always say that the booze is a gateway. The issues happen late at night; nobody gets in a fight at 7.30 pm over dinner, which is pretty well documented. That's why I can understand footy clubs are hesitant about people going out and having big nights, because it is a billion-dollar industry and the clubs and the competition have to protect their interests. It's the world we live in, and there are thousands of journalists out there hearing all the whispers that happen and the rumours that are fanned by social media, and a lot of them want to catch a footballer who is doing the wrong thing. It creates a market, and people are happy to service that market.

I am sure that the clubs tell every player when he goes off for a break during a bye weekend, or at the end of the year: 'Be careful, there are a lot of people out there trying to take a photo, and all they need is one photo of you doing the wrong thing, and your career could be gone.'

When I first started playing, there was none of that. I mean, today people ask me to pose with them for photos all the time, and that's fine, but you never know if someone is across the room with their phone taking another shot. You do notice people talking about you, looking at you, putting their phones up to take photos, and sometimes they might pretend that they are taking a photo of someone near you.

As a result, I am way more aware of my surroundings than I was as a young player. I have become smarter and better at handling the public attention, which is natural when you get older. I will think, things might get willing, that people are getting pretty drunk, that I should go somewhere else. I'll think, *It's getting late, I'm in a bar, probably shouldn't be here.*

But in the modern world you can get into trouble even if you go back to party at a private home. Mitchell Pearce (the NRL player who was filmed drunk in a Bondi flat, groping a woman and pretending to have sex with a dog) was not out in public, and neither was Harley Bennell, the former Gold Coast player who had footage of himself doing a line of cocaine put out to the media, nor was Jake Carlisle.

In that scenario it is about someone picking up $10,000 bucks or so from a scummy media outlet. The person with the film gets say $10,000; the young kid's career could be over, but they don't even care.

Privacy is pretty much dead, and not only that, the clubs want to know everything and they are paranoid about their image. At the end of 2015 my friend Dustin Martin and my teammate Marley Williams and I were among a group who had planned a trip to the United States in the off-season, but Marley, who had just enjoyed his best year at Collingwood, was more or less stopped from going on that trip by Collingwood and I think I know why.

Apparently Caroline Wilson rang the football club, told them that Marley was planning to travel with me and Dustin, and asked them if it was a good idea. I couldn't believe that Wilson could have a role in deciding where a player would go on holidays and who with. It was none of her business; she has no affiliation with our club and I can't believe she thinks that she has that power or influence.

And while Collingwood never told Marley that he couldn't go to the States, they made their opinion pretty clear, spinning it a little, like 'it's not in your best interests' or something along those lines. So Marley cancelled the trip, flights and accommodation, at a cost of about $10,000 to him. He chose not to come, and while I was not angry with him, I was really annoyed by that situation. The guy was 22 years of age, a grown man, a good player and quite capable of making his own decisions without a journo telling him what to do and what not to do.

He and I are good mates, almost a mini Rat Pack, because Marley has had his brush with the law, an assault case in 2014. I guess what it says is that the club doesn't trust me and Dustin, which makes me angry too, when you look at the great football Dustin is playing at Richmond. In my case, the only time my footy suffered was in 2014 when I was injured.

Ultimately what gets to me is the idea that a club can control you on your eight weeks of annual leave. In my eyes, the club has no rights in this instance. Would any employer exercise that kind of control? So as players, we have lost the annual footy trips, or at least the formal ones where nearly everyone came. And now, even your informal fun kind of holiday is under scrutiny. That's where it has got to.

Talk about Big Brother.

• • •

I was embarrassed about my 2014 season, and it drove me forward into 2015 at Collingwood. It was about proving something to myself, more than anything, although I had one or two of the barbs from certain media commentators in the back of my head.

For me, it's the same every year when I start. I am in the team room half an hour before the bounce of the first game, and I should be ready, but certain thoughts go through my head: *Have I still got it? Have I lost it? Am I still going to get better?* Because there is no doubt that age catches up; your game falls away unless you're Brent 'Boomer' Harvey, the little North Melbourne champion who was still playing as he approached 40.

In 2015 especially I was thinking like that, because I was 31, I was coming off a season in 2014 when my body let me down time after time, and I was confronting the end of my career. I had two years of contract remaining for 2015 and 2016, but the first thing I needed to do was get a hip operation.

I had been tight in the hip, and I had tweaked my hamstring twice in the previous 12 months, and the medicos thought that the operation might free up the hamstring. I needed to have constant work on my back and I also had epidurals, and by the time I came back from the usual overseas trip, I had barely done any training for ten weeks or so from the end of the previous season. At one point, I even broke down at home.

But Bill Davoren, the Collingwood conditioning man, had a plan for me. It was a plan that reflected the fact that I was past 30 and beaten up, it was a slow build-up from walking to jogging, and I didn't really join the rest of the players in the main training groups until February. This worked well for me mentally and physically.

I would go out on the track, run for 40 minutes, go inside to do some weights and that was it. I didn't train the bash and crash that the younger guys did, and I was allowed my own space where I could work hard, but not worry about getting hit or being worn down. I might do some boxing, have a swim. I put my music on and to some extent did as I pleased to get ready. If I did go on the track on cold nights the session would be just finishing as I warmed up to it. I was useless.

Cold weather is not my thing, but for the most part of my career we had to endure the freezing mid-winter beach recovery sessions that were popular for a while. They are the absolute worst. I can remember Ben Johnson wearing a wetsuit down at St Kilda one day, it was so cold. He just said, 'Fuck you, I'm wearing this!' It was a great idea.

I found those sessions horrendous, and I could never work out why they had to be at 7 am when it was even colder. Why not 10 am? The fitness staff would say, 'Ok, everyone under!' And there would be half a dozen of us saying, 'No way, there's E. coli in there, there are sharks around!' Thankfully we stopped hitting the beach ages ago, and it might only happen once a year now, because we have our own pool and ice baths at the club.

Mind you, I've barely had an ice bath in about seven years. They are far too cold; I would go into the room, hang around, and then move on unless one of the staff came into the room, in which case I would jump kicking and screaming into the tub. If they were not looking, then I was not doing it.

It would be fair to say that I did not look after my body as well as most professional athletes over my 15 seasons, not doing proper rehab, being on the booze, not eating properly and not getting into the water after a game. But it takes all types, I say.

As for my self-preservation, it had to happen. At 25, I could play, go out all weekend, train all week and then play again without an issue, but at 31 I would go to the altitude room, get on the treadmill, do some 400-metre sprints, and have a good sweat. I've been lucky that my touch has always been okay, so unlike a lot of players I have never needed a lot of ball-handling work to retain that. The 'train tracks' drills that we do, working in lines, are of no use to me. I felt refreshed, plus I was not getting the bumping and bruising that you get from contested training.

At my age, there were already enough aches and pains without adding to the problem, and I spent as much time in the physiotherapist's rooms as I did on the track, probably five times a week having something or other tweaked. Early in my career I never bothered much with physio or massage, but later it became a necessity.

Even the coaches laid off me a little, because I had come to hate watching my tapes with the line coach. I used to say to them, 'Look, if you really need to show me something then do it, but I don't want to see video of me marking on the wing and kicking to someone.' So if I had been out of position, or there was a learning tool for me in the vision, I would watch it. But if it was a missed tackle or a kicking error, please don't show me! Because I already know!

So while a lot of people seemed to think that I was finished after 2014, only I knew the extent of my injuries in the previous year, and before that I had gone All Australian five years in a row, so I had some faith that I could play good footy again. There was no reason why I would slow down altogether, and that is how it turned out for me.

I had one of my best years in 2015, playing a bit more as a forward, but still finding plenty of the ball. I didn't mind playing further forward; you cannot be a one trick pony in the AFL nowadays if you are medium-sized or small. You need to go and play half-back, to a wing or the forward pocket, not that we even use those names any more. At Collingwood, we had numbers for our forwards designating which player you were. The old terms, like half-forward, have gone. I kicked 21 goals that year, a goal a game, and I've got no doubt that if I had been able to keep playing longer, I could have sneaked 40-plus goals, because I was always a bit of a goalkicker as a midfielder. If you ask the coaches, that would be because I liked to run ahead of the ball but I was not so good with my defensive running!

I always copped it about that, but I naturally chased the footy all my playing life; it's what I learned as a kid. So to run defensively, tackle and chase? It was not really me. If I thought that I could get the ball, there is no one in the world who would be faster than me – I would outrun Usain Bolt. But trust me, if I had to chase someone back the other way, there are 800 people in the AFL and I might be 750th in that lot.

From 2008 to around 2012 when I was flying, I would get tagged so I didn't need to worry so much, because those guys were more worried about finding me. I had to make a decision about which way I leaned, and offence always won for me.

We made another strong start in 2015, getting to 8–3 at halfway, and sadly, followed the same pattern of falling away badly again. I really wish that I could explain why that happened two years in a row, but I have no clue why. The medical staff and the coaches wanted me to have a break, but we were playing so badly in the second half of the year that I couldn't afford to stand out of the team. We ended up losing six in a row after the bye, eight of the last 11 games, and missed the finals for the second year in a row. The slide was well and truly on now.

I'd started the year with 31 touches against Brisbane Lions at the Gabba, and I had 39 against St Kilda in round 3. Later in the year I had a patch of big numbers, including 41 disposals and three goals against Carlton.

My body wasn't perfect but I felt much better than I had in 2014, and my form reflected that. As much as you don't want to hear the negatives, they do resonate a bit, and I've always played for the pride of my family. And for the last six or seven years of my career I had confidence that I could impact a game no matter how I was feeling.

The coaching staff looked after me through the winter, they let me stay inside more. I told Bucks and Bill Davoren, 'I can't keep going outside. I'm too sore, by the time I warm up, we're finished.' So I might do a bunch of 400-metre sprints on the treadmill at the club in intervals. I tried to mimic the way I played footy; I'd go hard, then have a quick rest, then go again. That was how I played the game. I was not like Pendles, running consistently the whole way. On the treadmill I would sweat more than I would outside, and mentally, I felt like I was doing the work that I needed whereas I didn't enjoy being out on the track. After a few sessions on the treadmill, my head would tell me: 'I'm ready for this week's game.'

I reckon the fact I took it easy through the middle part of the season helped me at the end, and my form held up okay even though the team was struggling. I was nominated for the All Australian squad (although I didn't make the final team), I averaged close to 30 touches a game and had 17 Brownlow Medal votes.

My season ended sourly, in a win against Geelong in round 22, the second-last game. I hurt my knee. Joel Selwood tackled me and my medial ligament gave way, so I was out of there with the substitute's jacket. Ben Sinclair hurt his hand but there was no way he was getting the red vest from me: 'I'm taking this.' I had said to my mates Kade and Aaron that I would try to come and watch them in their EDFL grand final the next week, and when I did my knee I texted them: 'See I've torn my medial just to come and watch you!'

I finished second behind Scott Pendlebury in the Copeland Trophy voting, the sixth time I had been in the top two of the club best and fairest and the seventh occasion that I had been in the top three, which is something I am proud of. Coming off the back of my worst year, it was a good result for me, and with a contract for 2016, I was moving on.

Nobody was saying that I was finished now.

DEIRDRE SWAN

Mother

We're a very close-knit family. He's close with his aunties and uncles. We've always been there for him, supporting him 100 percent, and 'family' is ingrained in him. It's just natural for him. He probably knows no other way; we don't think it's extraordinary because that's the way it is.

He was a great child growing up, had a fantastic sense of humour, was well liked by his teachers and he's a smart boy as well.

Of course we get upset when things are said about him, it's heartbreaking. No one wants to hear that about their child. I mean, I hurt because I think that he's hurting as well, and it's just very, very unfair. I did actually reply to that Caroline Wilson article and I said to her, 'You don't see the boys when they go out to see dying children.' Sometimes I think the media are just waiting for bad things to happen.

We've had people who met Dane, particularly footballers' parents who come into the football club, and I suppose they are thinking he's a larrikin, or even words worse than that, and then over time they've seen him kiss his dad hello after the games and it surprised them. They've said that any man who'll kiss his father in public has got a place in their hearts. That's the way he is.

He's done some things that we're not proud of and he's not proud of them either, but you get the good with the bad.

The tattoos? Honestly, I really don't want the head and the neck covered, but they just make up the being that Dane is. Do I particularly like them? No! I remember his little baby body and his lovely clean skin, but it is what it is. Nothing's going to change if I like them or not. Everyone's got them now, so it's not so bad.

I try to take him to church once a year on Christmas Eve, although last year he wasn't here for Christmas, but I do try to get him to mass. He comes without screaming and kicking but I don't think he's thoroughly immersed in the whole thing. That's all I can ask.

It's been an amazing journey and a great social thing for our family and friends but you don't relax because it can change. I look back now and enjoy it. At the time it was lovely but there's always next week.

The last time we caught up with him I said to Bill, 'It's the happiest and the most engaging I've seen him.' Finishing up has made a huge difference. I'm sad of course, I know there will be tears, because it's the end of an era, but football's been amazing to him, it's afforded him a fantastic lifestyle, he's made wonderful friends and basically now he can go and cut any career he wants out of this.

A new journey begins. We'll support him and Taylor whatever he chooses to do and we might get to spend some more time with our little man!

17

SWANSONG

'They say "I'd rather die a hero than live long enough to become the villain". I'd rather go out before my form dropped off. In the end, I knew it was time.'

—Dane Swan

Here is the ironic bit about the way 2016 started for Collingwood, and for me as well: it was all so positive. We won everything in the NAB Cup, even beating Geelong down at Kardinia Park where they never lose, kicking 11 goals in a quarter, we had a good bunch of kids coming through and a lot of the so-called experts had predicted that we would come back into the finals.

I have never been a fan of pre-season games; I viewed them as a necessary evil, but I had myself ready. The kids were flying, especially guys like Adam Treloar, who we'd picked up from Greater Western Sydney. I hadn't seen that much of him at GWS but I could see pretty quickly that he was a jet. We had Jeremy Howe come in from Melbourne, and James Aish from Brisbane Lions, and we had plenty of youth from previous drafts, guys like Darcy Moore, who had shown a bit in 2015.

Practice games to me are about not getting hurt. You run up and down the ground, get some strides in, if the ball comes your way then okay, but if it doesn't, then I don't care. I always remember pulling out of a contest blatantly in a pre-season game in about 2009 against St Kilda, where Nick Riewoldt came storming out to take a chest mark, and I just stopped running.

Brendon Goddard, his teammate at the time, came over and screamed at me, 'Weak dog!' It would have been very obvious but there was no way I was putting my body on the line in a pre-season game! I said to Goddard, 'Absolutely I pulled out. I'm not busting my scone here today. And if it happens again, I'll pull out again!'

NAB Cup games are for the young kids to make their mark and they are for the coaches to practise ball movement, stuff like that. For instance at Geelong that day, the American recruit Mason Cox stepped up, kicked a couple of goals and showed that he had something to offer. I kicked three goals in that game down at Geelong, enough to suggest to me that I was right and ready to go in 2016.

Then in the week before the first game up in Sydney, the proverbial hit the fan, and again the topic was drugs. The *Herald Sun* published a front page story that speculated that 'one-quarter of Collingwood's playing list' had returned positive results to illicit drugs in off-season hair testing done by the AFL. The headline screamed: 'Collingwood drugs scandal: Up to 11 players test positive for illicit substances.'

The league and the AFL Players' Association had agreed to have some hair testing done as part of the new illicit drugs policy, which was to reduce the number of strikes from three down to two after all the heated debate of the previous couple of years where the public, and some of the clubs, seemed to believe that the game was soft on drugs.

The results from the hair testing in the off-season were meant to be confidential, and not to be used against players as a strike. They were supposed to be for the AFL's information, to see what they were dealing with, but of course, there was a leak, a sliver of information that was not even necessarily correct.

The *Herald Sun* didn't know the actual number of positive tests at Collingwood. The journo who wrote the story, Mark Robinson, admitted on television a few days later that the figure of 11 came from a rumour, he had put to Collingwood that the figure was 23, and when he suggested this to the club, someone told him, 'It's less than half that.' Which was fairly sketchy, and Paul Marsh from the AFLPA summed up the feeling of the players, who were annoyed to say the least. Speaking on 3AW, he said:

> It would be good if there was some respect for what we're trying to achieve here. It's predictable that some people are going to be taking a stab at how many players may be testing positive.
>
> This new policy was agreed to late last year, it hasn't even taken effect yet. Give it a chance. This is an issue across society first and foremost, and within the AFL. So you can assume this isn't just limited to one club.

Whatever Collingwood's figure of 'positives' was – and I don't know – my thought was that they should go out to a suburban footy club, do some hair testing, and they might be surprised at how many positives they get. I am not saying it's good or bad, it is just the reality.

Of course this was a distraction in the lead-up to the game in Sydney, which had already attracted a few headlines because the Swans decided at the last minute to transfer it from Homebush, where we usually played them, to the SCG, their usual home ground. Eddie McGuire and the Swans had already had a stoush over that.

I'd trained under Steve Grace, the club's forward coach, all pre-season. The plan was that I'd start on the bench with the intention of going forward when I came on to the ground. I understood where the footy club was coming from with this. We had Scott Pendlebury, Adam Treloar, Steele Sidebottom and others to start in midfield, and for Collingwood to get to where it needed to, it needed to move away from the situation where Pendles and I were the two best players. Between us we'd won all but one of the last seven Copeland trophies, three each.

So in a sense for me to play full-time midfield would have been holding back young kids like Taylor Adams and Jordan De Goey from their full development as midfielders. I was looking forward to the challenge of playing as a forward who would come through the midfield rather than the other way around. If you looked at our mix, I was probably the best forward out of the group, and I reckon that I would have played about 50–50 in 2016.

So in round 1, I came off the bench and a few minutes into the game Zak Jones crashed down on me and my world changed. Collingwood lost the game by a catastrophic 80 points, a dreadful start to the season all round. When I came back to Melbourne, I talked to the medical people about it, and I wanted to get the surgery over and done with. I said, 'What are the chances this year?' They said, 'All going well, with a few risks, you *might* have a chance in August.' That was more than four months away, and even if the best-case scenario applied, I also knew that after so long out of the game, I would have to find my way back to the seniors via the VFL.

So it was going to be a long wait with no guarantee at the end. It was a little disturbing to hear Matthew Richardson, the former Richmond player who had the same Lisfranc injury, say on television that his own recovery from the problem a few years earlier had been more difficult than his rehab from a full knee reconstruction.

Our surgeon, Andrew Oppy, performed the operation at the Epworth, filling my foot with wires and metal plates and screws; like any footballer I'm used to operations, having had both wrists and both hips under the scalpel through my career. I self-injected blood thinner into my stomach at home so that I didn't get a blood clot, and after a month or so, I had more surgery to take the wires out.

After that, the club let me have my own space, let me do what I wanted to do, and to be honest, I've never sat down and cried about it. It is what it is, kind of thing, because I am a pragmatic person and a realist. There was no point worrying or fretting and really, I'd been extremely lucky with injuries, and lucky to have had the career that I had.

Everyone in footy gets hurt sometimes; in my case, the big one came right at the end. It's possible that if it happened when I was 24 I might have been finished then, so to punch out 15 years of footy, I have to be happy.

Obviously you do wonder at the time whether you have reached the end of the road, and I was no different. A Lisfranc rupture generally takes six months or so to recover from, so I knew straight away that to even attempt to play in 2016 was going to be risky. If I was 22 years old, I would have just taken the year off, I reckon, but in my case, I knew that I probably had only one year left beyond 2016, and even that was questionable.

I had come into 2016 unsure whether it would be my last year of footy. In the past I'd said I'd probably retire by 30 yet here I was at 32 about to play my fifteenth season. It was certainly my last year of contract, but it is normal for older players to be contracted a year at a time late in their careers, and I've never looked past a current contract. You'd be stupid to get ahead of yourself in this game. It was all about just getting it done: 'I'm playing good footy, let's roll again.'

I hadn't given 2017 much thought. Liam Pickering, my manager, had spoken to the list management people at Collingwood, but I hadn't given myself a definite finishing point. If I'd done that, I would have let the footy club know so that they could do their planning, and I would've said it publicly: 'This is my last year, I'm going 100 per cent and let's see what happens.' The fact is, I wasn't sure, it really depended how I played in 2016.

After the injury hit me in round one, I was confined to quarters for a few months, unable to drive for a lot of it, and struggling to walk. Having had no idea about the gravity of a Lisfranc rupture, I occasionally ran into people who had experienced the pain and the long period of rehabilitation that follows, and at the footy one night in July, a random guy stopped me to say that he had the same injury. 'It took me four years,' he said.

The Pies missed the finals again, and I was far from the only injury issue that we had. We badly missed Jamie Elliott, for instance, who I planned to spend some time with up forward. There's 70 or 80 goals we lost … and I'm not sure how many Jamie was going to produce!

I had a lot of thinking time over those months, and I gradually came to the conclusion that there was no coming back for me, not just for 2016 but forever. My foot was too sore for too long; when I tried to run on the treadmill at the footy club in August, it ached on me. At the peak of my career I used to smash half a dozen consecutive 500-metre runs on my favourite AlterG treadmill at the club; this time I was just turning it over at 14 km/h and still my foot did not feel right.

There was no way known that I could play football with that pain and when I even thought about kicking a ball, I felt like my foot would smash into a thousand pieces. The surgeon said this was not the case, but that was a real mental blockage for me to break through.

On cold days, it still ached. I was to have the screws taken out of my foot just before going overseas in October and the reality was that it could be 18 months from the time of the injury to when I could run normally again.

I just could not trust my foot to play anymore at the highest level, but for a while, I fought the decision. In my head I knew that I was done but then watching the boys play, I started to think, *I'd like to get back out there.* I spoke to Bucks a couple of times, and he said, 'Deep down, when you make a decision, you'll know.' So ultimately, the head ruled over the heart. In my gut, I was sure.

Early in August, I took my parents to lunch and told them that I would soon announce my retirement from AFL footy; I wanted to do it in a public place to try and stop Mum from turning on a few tears. Dad said, 'Dane if you're happy, we're happy, mate.' They would have loved me to keep playing, but they understood that I had a decision to make about my future health, and that there were no guarantees that I actually could come back anyway, even if I had tried.

Around the same time I ventured into Nathan Buckley's office at Collingwood's headquarters and told him straight out, 'Mate, I'm retiring.' It was a difficult conversation to have, but Bucks was good about it. He had been there before; he told me he knew how hard it was to let go. We talked for a while, and I told him, 'I just can't give you the commitment that you need.'

I used to joke that I was like a cockroach, an indestructible pest. But in the end, my body jacked up and told me what to do. Plus, by the middle of the year, with Collingwood struggling to make finals and with my foot still not long out of a moon boot, something happened to me. I actually enjoyed *not* playing AFL footy.

It was Taylor who made me think about this. One day, after I had been through more than a month of rehab, she just said to me, 'This is the best six weeks we've had.' Because in those few weeks we had been out for dinner on a Friday night a few times, had a bottle of wine together, spent some time as a couple, even if it was just sitting on the couch, and we had enjoyed that time.

When I thought about the change, I realised that I was no longer struggling with the pressures of being a professional footballer. I couldn't train, and I had no games to play, nowhere to go, nothing to do other than catch up with friends for lunch or see a movie or find a nice restaurant. And I loved it.

I like to think I'm good at putting footy out of my head, but quite clearly I wasn't perfect in that area. Taylor would say that I used to go very quiet before a game, just settling into a little zone, my own space, doing things like making sure I was properly hydrated. When I injured my foot in 2016, it was completely different. We would actually engage as a couple, talk to each other.

Over time I've realised how selfish an AFL player is, how selfish you *need* to be and *have* to be. It was all about me and all about footy; Taylor put up with a lot. Players make great money and that gives us a huge head start for the rest of our lives if we play our cards right, so of course it's worth making the effort and compromising on a few things. But it's hard on the partners.

Taylor never had much of a clue about what being a footballer actually meant, and that's the best thing of all. She might even say that she wished I was *not* a footballer; what I do know is that her intentions were pure. She certainly didn't partner up with me because I was a footballer, because at the start, she didn't even know.

Taylor is extremely loyal, she is beautiful, and she has been the best thing for me since she came into my life. After we got together, I was All Australian five years in a row, won three Copelands, won the Brownlow and a premiership, and these were not just coincidences. It came from being in a happy, comfortable place in life.

I was a lousy cook, and before she started working, she cooked for us and went far beyond what she needed to do. I had to change a little, there is no doubt, and I guess she settled me down a fraction because in any relationship, you can't afford to think about only yourself. But Taylor has been amazing for me. Her work ethic is remarkable, she can't sit still for five minutes because she always has something she wants to do, and she is far more motivated than me. Basically, she's the glue that holds everything together in our household. God knows where I would be without her.

Hopefully this is the start of many years together. We might even go and live in New York, who knows? I have no doubt she'd love to go back and live there, although my job opportunities, initially at least, will be in Melbourne because it is the heartland of footy. Having said that, I can't see myself as a coach; in fact, there is no way that I would work full-time at a footy club. I want to reclaim my weekends, for a start, so maybe I can do some ambassadorial work in footy, or host some events for Collingwood, something like that.

I look forward to the past players' functions, and I might even go along to the president's lunch with Dad, or with Tazza, drink a few beers and tell everyone how much better I was than the guys playing now. In ten years, I could be a real superstar! I have no doubt I will be around Collingwood, because I have a lot of friends there.

I played with and against some really great players. I can remember so vividly playing against Chris Judd and Gary Ablett, two of the greatest midfielders of my era and in fact any era. Good luck trying to tackle those two! Judd would just run away from stoppages and Ablett had that evasive ability and strength through the core.

Sam Mitchell is another player I admired, with his refusal to waste a kick, wheeling around in those little mini-circles, and the same for Adam Goodes, a guy who could do anything and someone who became a friend late in my career. Buddy Franklin is a superstar; I remember playing on him directly at a couple of stoppages once when he was at Hawthorn, and the ball came flying out the side and we were together, then by the time a few strides were taken he was 3 metres in front of me and running away with the footy. I put my hand up to go forward at that point, saying, 'I'm not playing on him!'

Retiring from the game means the stats appear. I averaged 26.85 disposals a game across my career, which is a decent number. Prior to my final game in Sydney that figure was actually a fraction higher, the highest recorded since the AFL started taking stats, but sadly my donut game when I broke down still counts as a full game, even though I only ran on, got hurt, and ran off! So the figure dropped a tad below Greg Williams' number of 26.88 disposals per match. Still, being number two to the Diesel is not bad!

I hit 30 disposals in a match 108 times, third in history behind the former St Kilda star Robert Harvey (118 times) and Sam Mitchell (113 times). On average, I had at least 30 touches in 41.86 per cent of games that I played in, which is the highest figure recorded since the numbers have been calculated. I'm pretty happy with those numbers – not bad for an overweight, unfit bloke anyway.

I might miss playing the game, but I doubt it. I was never obsessed with footy; I loved playing, but only match day and the adrenaline rush that comes with it. If it was about the money for me, I would sign a contract for next year and keep going, because Collingwood certainly indicated to me – even when I was recovering from the injury in 2016 – that they would like me to keep playing.

But it is not the money. It's important, of course, but I couldn't even tell you half the time what my exact contract is. One time I was up for resigning and we were talking to Geoff Walsh, the director of football at Collingwood, and I ended up saying, 'You know I'm going nowhere, just get it done. Give me what I'm worth.'

It is just that I have other things that I want to do; things that I could never do while I was playing footy. Yes, the money is great and the lifestyle's amazing, but the travel is limited to off-season. I want to get away from footy for a couple of years, get it out of my system and then think about whether I settle down, maybe have a family.

Without footy, we can travel away for six months, come back again, then travel some more. Europe is on the radar, and so is the Super Bowl. In an ideal world, I will have a trip with my mates and a trip with Taylor every year.

• • •

I have spent half my life at Collingwood, more time than I spent at home with my parents, so no wonder I feel like I'm part of the furniture. I have loved it, no matter how much I have whinged and complained about the training and the restrictions and the cold and about people telling me what to do.

I love Collingwood, I love the club and how big it is, I love the fans and I love the staff and the volunteers who make the place tick, people who work around the club without asking for any money or recognition, great folk like Neil Price, the bootstudder, Ann Martin, our longtime team 'mother', Desi Knight, one of the key matchday staff, and Roger Sturtevant, who handles the VFL team stuff, and many more, too. Really, it's those bonds that you forge that are the best thing that I took from the game.

I pretty much get along with everyone and at some point, it will hit me that I'm not going back, at least not as a player. Collingwood is struggling on-field at the moment, but that doesn't change the fact that it's an amazing football club to be part of, a club that is so big that it still amazes the guys who first walk into that place. I'm lucky to have ended up being a one-club player at a great institution. I owe the club a lot more than they owe me, there is no doubt about that.

My plum job would be to get paid as much as I have at Collingwood and not have to work! But of course, that won't happen. I was earning around $800,000 at my peak as a player, and by the time you throw in bonuses and promotional work outside the game, it would be close to $1 million, so that is a big hole to fill. But I have been preparing for the after-life in my head since I was about 29, and you'd be mad not to do that. A player has to get ready because you can't play footy forever. And I am ready.

I have talked to a lot of my footy friends about this, the ones who are no longer playing, and they tend to say, 'You don't understand the freedom you have, the ability to go where you want, do what you want.' Right now, I will have a chance to reconnect with people who I haven't seen as much as I'd like to, go to the snow in July, have a winery tour. Of course I will still see my old teammates, but in the long run these are the friends who I will be with for the rest of my life.

I am about to find out who my true friends are, and they tend to be the people I have grown up with, the same people. I'm looking forward to having a tight-knit group of friends, Wednesday night beers, going to the pub on Saturday and having a bet and telling everyone how good I was! I'll take my lead from the retired Rats – that's pretty much what they've been doing since they hung up their boots.

I know that I will be more anonymous, and I am not complaining. As a higher profile person in Melbourne you are invited to nice events, and you draw a few benefits, but the downside is that you get criticised if you mess up, so there is a fine balance, and I had to take the good with the bad.

The profile helps my business interests. It has given me an amazing head start with the money I have made, the network I have created, the business opportunities it launched. So for all the moaning I might have done about playing in the AFL, I am under no illusion about what it has done for me.

No matter whether I make $10,000 a year or $10 million a year when I'm finished, I know that I will be happy because I can do things that I've never been able to do before. I really believe that. I am actually looking forward to the next phase of my life, not pining for what I've lost now that my footy career is done.

In this day and age, there are not many careers that go for 15 years, and it is all I have known since I was 17. Already, the relationships with my family and friends are better just because not everything revolves around me anymore. Previously it would be: 'Tomorrow I'm playing footy so we've got to have pasta for dinner' or 'Sunday I'll be sore so we can't go out.' Taylor might say, 'Can we go out for lunch?'

And I would be too shitty because we'd lost a game and I'd played badly. Now, it has changed. I will say, 'Let's go see Tazza and Lauren', or 'Let's go and get a pizza and a bottle of wine.'

The whole Swan family went to Bali for a week to celebrate my father Bill's sixtieth birthday, and I realised how much I had missed out on. I always thought I had put friends and family first, but the fact is as an AFL player, you don't. You can't. I see my family more than ever now and in Bali, they said to me, 'You seem better. You're spending more time with us.'

I've never had a normal life, I guess, and what I've found as I went through my recovery in 2016 is that I have no stress any more, that I was under more pressure than I'd actually acknowledged. The newspapers have the Pies in them every day, and my profile was high, so the cameras would be on me: 'What's wrong with Swanny?'

Of course, that builds up, and the world can close in on you, but in 2016 and beyond, there is no ceiling for me. I come home and I am the happiest that I have been. Yes, I would love to win five premierships, play a few more years, get to 300 games, win another Copeland, but it's not going to happen. So when I reflect, I know that I am content with my career, and everything that I have done – right or wrong – has made me the person I am today. Whether people like me or dislike me, I really couldn't give a toss.

• • •

The club certainly sent me out in style. On 23 August 2016, about a week after I'd told Bucks of my decision, I announced my retirement from AFL footy at the Holden Centre. Collingwood always draws a crowd, and there were more than 100 people there including my family, all the players and staff, as well as dozens of media people and a bunch of cameras.

The invitation to media had a different ring about it: 'I've got one headline left in me, let's write it together. Swanny'.

Of course, the news had already leaked out to most of the media around the country, so on the morning of my official retirement, I posted a photo of my boots hanging on my locker at the club: 'That's a wrap.'

The announcement was a production in itself, hosted by Anthony Hudson, live streamed on the club's website and broadcast live on SEN sports radio in Melbourne. Only at Collingwood, I guess! They even had a hashtag for the day: #swansong. My whole family was there in the front row, and we managed to get Eddie McGuire, Mick Malthouse and Nathan Buckley up on a stage together, after everything that had happened at the footy club in the last five years. Dad was up there too.

Many nice things were said about me, so much so that I made the point that I was becoming a better footballer by the minute now that I had retired. Eddie McGuire reeled off the TV grabs:

> He personified everything that we hold true to the
> Collingwood ethos. He's a bit of a lad, he worked harder
> than anyone, he made the most of his abilities, when the big
> games were there he stood up, he stood side by side with his
> teammates, he looked with the supporters, never down on
> them. He went to the hospitals looking after the kids. Anyone

who was on a hard day, Swanny was always in your corner. He's everything you could hope for. He might be leaving the club as a player, but he'll never leave Collingwood. He's Collingwood DNA and his family's DNA is intertwined in that.

I reminded Mick Malthouse that when he told me in 2003 that I was on my last chance, I actually proved him wrong. Because there were several more 'last chances' for me! Plus I managed to slip in a little barb for Mick about why the club had allowed me to slip as far as No. 58 in the national draft of 2001, to which my longtime coach replied, 'We knew we'd get you. His feet were pointing east and west at the same time so we were on pretty good grounds to get this bloke.'

Mick made the point that I rarely argued with umpires on the field, and I threw in, 'That's how you win Brownlows, Mick.'

Dad was part of the presentation and he had a few tears, but we also had some laughs:

B. Swan: 'I didn't think he'd reach the heights that he did.'
D. Swan: 'Thanks, mate!'

Afterwards, we went off as a family and celebrated the end of that story. My plans? I will go on holiday and think about it, I'd say. Europe is first on the list. Coaching is not on the menu; I am not the kind to spend eight hours a day at a footy club. I have dabbled in media, and I like my work with *The Footy Show*, so we will see where that takes me.

Collingwood will thrive, I'm sure, although I can see the pressure building in 2017, it's what happens when you miss finals three years in a row. That's the reality of the business we're in, and it will not only be Bucks who is under the heat; the board and the players will feel it too, if they don't perform.

The players will be fighting for their lives because they play at the highest-pressure club in Australia. They just need to show some more improvement, at the very least, when the season starts, and hopefully they get some luck with injuries that has been sadly missing in the past few years.

As for me, I'll be watching, well and truly ready for the next chapter. How do I want to be remembered? I'd rather that I was not, so that I can slip away quietly, quite frankly. But I don't fear the future. The rest of my life starts now.

DANE SWAN

Born: 25 February 1984
Debut: 19 years
Last game 32 years
Height: 185 cm
Weight: 93 kg

WESTMEADOWS FOOTBALL CLUB

Dane Swan's first award was U10 Best and Fairest.

CALDER CANNONS

2001 TAC Cup Premiership Team

The U18 Victorian TAC Cup premiership is a primary source of recruitment to Victorian AFL clubs.

2015 Calder Cannons Hall of Fame

2015 Calder Cannon's Hall of Fame inductees:

Jude Bolton (Sydney), Paul Chapman (Geelong & Essendon), Phil Dunk (Cannon's Trainer), Robert Hyde (Collingwood & Essendon VFL teams), Jason Johnson (Essendon), James Kelly (Geelong & Essendon), Darren Milburn (Geelong), Ross Monaghan (Cannon's regional manager), Ryan O'Keefe (Sydney) and Dane Swan (Collingwood).

2015 Calder Cannons Team of the First 20 Years

The 22 stars include a Brownlow medallist, two Norm Smith medallists, an NAB Rising Star winner, nine premiership players and numerous best and fairest winners. All have played at least 50 games in the AFL.

Backs: Mark Johnson (Sunbury) Tom Lonergan (Assumption College)
Daniel Talia (Greenvale)

Half-backs: Andrew Welsh (Westmeadows)
Jackson Trengove (Strathmore) Darren Milburn (Kilmore)

Centres: James Kelly (Sunbury) Jude Bolton (Aberfeldie)
Ryan Crowley (Gisborne)

Half-forwards: Paul Chapman (North Coburg)
Ryan O'Keefe (Strathmore) Jason Johnson (Kilmore)

Forwards: Eddie Betts (Templestowe) Jake Carlisle (Craigieburn)
Richard Douglas (Kilmore)

Rucks: Ivan Maric (Keilor) Dane Swan (Westmeadows)
Tom Liberatore (St Bernard's)

Interchange: Zac Dawson (Doutta Stars) Dion Prestia (Greenvale)
Brent Reilly (Gisborne) David Rodan (Oak Park)

2001 AFL DRAFT

Pick 58 Dane Swan (Collingwood Football Club)

The draft of 2001 included many star players including Luke Hodge (Pick 1 Hawthorn), Luke Ball (Pick 2 St Kilda), Chris Judd (Pick 3 West Coast), David Hale (Pick 7 North Melbourne), Jimmy Bartel (Pick 8 Geelong), Nick Dal Santo (Pick 13 St Kilda), James Kelly (Pick 17 Geelong), Steve Johnson (Pick 24 Geelong), Lewis Roberts-Thomson (Pick 29 Sydney), Sam Mitchell (Pick 36 Hawthorn), Leigh Montagna (Pick 37 St Kilda), Gary Ablett Jr (Pick 40 Father/Son), Brian Lake (Pick 71 Western Bulldogs), and Dane Swan (Pick 58 Collingwood).

All of the above players have played in at least one grand final. All but Dal Santo and Montagna have played in a premiership team. Judd, Mitchell and Hodge have captained their respective teams to victories in the 2006, 2008, 2013, 2014 & 2015 grand finals. Judd (2004, 2010), Bartel (2007), Ablett (2009, 2013), and Swan (2011) have won the Brownlow Medal.

WILLIAMSTOWN FOOTBALL CLUB

2003 Williamstown Premiership Team

VFL: 42 games, 38 goals

Williamstown Football Club aligned with Collingwood reserves for 7 years from 2001–2007. Dane Swan made his debut for Collingwood in June 2003 at the age of 19, though he only played three games (against Western Bulldogs, Richmond and Essendon). He played the rest of that year with Williamstown and was a member of its 2003 premiership team.

COLLINGWOOD FOOTBALL CLUB (2003–2016)

AFL Debut

Western Bulldogs v Collingwood, Round 13, 2003 at the Docklands

250th AFL Game

Port Adelaide v Collingwood, Round 15, 2015 at the Adelaide Oval

50th AFL Game

Collingwood v North Melbourne, Round 22, 2006 at the MCG

Total Games: 258 games
Total Goals: 211 goals

100th AFL Game

St Kilda v Collingwood, Semi-Final, 2008 at the MCG

Pre-Season Competition

23 games, 13 goals, 2 supergoals

150th AFL Game

Collingwood v St Kilda, Grand Final, 2010 at the MCG

2010

Collingwood Premiership Team

200th AFL Game

Richmond v Collingwood, Round 4, 2013 at the MCG

2011

Collingwood Pre-Season Premiership Team

AWARDS

2007
J.F. McHale Trophy

(4th Best and Fairest)

2008, 2009, 2010
E.W. Copeland Trophy

(Best and Fairest)

2008, 2010, 2013
Bob Rose Award

(Best Player in Finals)

2009
Bob Rose-Charlie Sutton Medal

(awarded for a Western Bulldogs/
Collingwood match)

2009, 2010
Herald Sun Player of the Year

2009, 2010
**Australian Football Media
Association Most Valuable Player**

2009, 2010, 2011, 2012, 2013
All Australian

2010
Lou Richards Medal

(awarded for a Richmond/
Collingwood match)

2010
International Rules Series Team

2010
Jim Stynes Medal

Best Player for Australia in
International Rules competition

2010
Leigh Matthews Trophy

AFL Players' Association Most
Valuable Player

2010
**AFL Coaches Association Champion
Player of the Year**

2011, 2013, 2015
R.T. Rush Trophy

(2nd Best and Fairest)

2011
Brownlow Medal (votes 34)

Third: 2010, 2013

2012, 2014
ANZAC Day Medal

2012
J.J. Joyce Trophy

(3rd Best and Fairest)

2013, 2015
**Magpie Army Player of the Year
Award**

(Fan-voted award)

DANE SWAN

307

STATISTICS

Dane Swan Statistics

Year	Games	W-D-L	Kicks	Marks	Handballs	Disposals	Goals	Behinds	Tackles
2003	3	3–0–0	14	4	13	27			3
2004	13	4–0–9	105	49	66	171	2	5	18
2005	14	4–0–10	143	67	91	234	3	2	22
2006	21	13–0–8	311	168	176	487	19	12	44
2007	25	15–0–10	422	187	173	595	13	14	85
2008	24	13–0–11	368	163	222	590	22	23	75
2009	25	16–0–9	444	161	325	769	18	25	77
2010	26	20–2–4	505	146	315	820	24	23	123
2011	24	21–0–3	472	129	288	760	32	23	77
2012	21	14–0–7	442	138	283	725	25	22	71
2013	23	14–0–9	436	131	281	717	21	21	79
2014	17	9–0–8	244	79	180	424	11	12	49
2015	21	10–0–11	336	104	273	609	21	14	81
2016	1	0–0–1							
Totals	**258**	**156–2–100**	**4242**	**1526**	**2686**	**6928**	**211**	**196**	**804**
Averages	**18.43**	**60.85%**	**16.44**	**5.91**	**10.41**	**26.85**	**0.82**	**0.76**	**3.12**

Year	Inside 50s	Clearances	Brownlow votes	Contested Possessions	Uncontested possessions	Contested marks	Marks inside 50	Goal assists
2003	2	2		7	19	1		1
2004	10	14		70	95	5	8	2
2005	20	22		72	158	2	3	3
2006	71	46	11	149	328	10	18	17
2007	74	76	20	214	368	12	15	11
2008	100	83	12	215	369	19	25	12
2009	122	101	12	270	487	16	19	22
2010	130	141	24	311	485	12	13	16
2011	124	147	34	307	425	9	19	23
2012	95	140	25	283	429	13	24	17
2013	119	115	26	265	437	12	29	18
2014	59	54	5	150	258	6	11	6
2015	97	118	17	241	347	9	13	16
2016								
Totals	**1023**	**1059**	**186**	**2554**	**4205**	**126**	**197**	**164**
Averages	**3.97**	**4.10**	**0.78**	**9.90**	**16.3**	**0.49**	**0.76**	**0.64**

PICTURE CREDITS

All the following AFL images are used with permission of AFL Media and the photographer credit is included where the information was available. Unless otherwise stated, photos that are not AFL images are from private collections.

Page 4: First game, round 13 against the Western Bulldogs at Telstra Dome, 28 June 2003; In action during the round 5 Anzac Day match against Essendon at the MCG, 25 April 2004.

Page 5: With Mick Malthouse during the round 10 match against Hawthorn at the MCG, 28 May 2005; Reaching for the mark during the round 19 match against Essendon at the MCG, 11 August 2006.

Page 6: With Chris Tarrant, Dale Thomas, Shane Wakelin and Harry O'Brien after beating the Kangaroos in round 3 at Telstra Dome, 17 April 2006; Celebrating a goal during the drawn semi-final against West Coast at Subiaco, 14 September 2007.

Page 7: New leadership group (back row, L-R) Josh Fraser, Scott Pendlebury, Dane Swan and Shane O'Bree; (front row, L-R) Mick Malthouse, Eddie McGuire and Nick Maxwell, 17 December 2008 (Michael Willson); In action during the semi-final against Adelaide at the MCG, 12 September 2009 (Andrew White).

Page 8: Tackled by Cameron Ling during the preliminary final against Geelong at the MCG, 19 September 2009 (Andrew White); Marking in front of Alan Didak during the preliminary final match against at the MCG, 17 September 2010 (David Callow).

Page 9: With Heath Shaw, Ben Johnson and Alan Didak after the 2010 Grand Final (Michael Willson); Collingwood returns to the ground after the 2010 Grand Final, 2 October 2010. (David Callow).

Page 10: With partner, Taylor Wilson, during the Brownlow Medal blue carpet arrivals at Crown Palladium, 26 September 2011 (Lachlan Cunningham); During Collingwood press conference at St Kilda Sea Baths, 27 September 2011 (Michael Willson); Tackled by Heath Hocking during the round 5 Anzac Day match against the Bombers at the MCG, 25 April 2011 (Lachlan Cunningham).

Page 11: During round 5 Anzac Day match against Essendon at the MCG, 25 April 2012 (Michael Willson); During a training session at St Kilda Sea Baths, 29 November 2012; During the round 12 match against he Western Bulldogs at Etihad Stadium, 16 June 2013 (Michael Willson).

Page 12: Chris Tarrant is chaired off by teammates Ben Johnson and Dane Swan after the round 20 match against Port Adelaide at AAMI Stadium, 6 August 2011; With Heath Shaw and Scott Pendlebury after the round 12 match against the Bulldogs at Etihad Stadium, 16 June 2013. (Michael Willson)

Page 13: Celebrating a goal during the round 6 Anzac Day match against the Bombers at the MCG, 25 April 2014 (Lachlan Cunningham); With coach Nathan Buckley during a training session at Olympic Park Oval, 19 August 2014 (Michael Willson).

Page 14: Swan's 250th game against Port Adelaide at the Adelaide Oval, 9 July 2015 (James Elsby); Masks in the cheer squad during the round 16 match against the Eagles at Etihad Stadium, 18 July 2015 (Justine Walker)

Page 15: Leaving the field injured during the round 1 match against the Swans, SCG, 26 March 2016 in Sydney (Cameron Spencer).

Page 16: With grandmothers Betty (left) and Moira (right) during the retirement press conference at The Holden Centre, 23 August 2016 (Michael Willson).